Juvenile Justice
The Progressive Legacy and
Current Reforms

*Contributors*

LaMar T. Empey

David J. Rothman

Jackson Toby

Paul Lerman

Travis Hirschi

Justine Wise Polier

Herman Schwendinger

Julia Schwendinger

# Juvenile Justice

## *The Progressive Legacy and Current Reforms*

Edited by LaMar T. Empey

University Press of Virginia

Charlottesville

THE UNIVERSITY PRESS OF VIRGINIA
Copyright © 1979 by the Kenyon Public Affairs Forum

*First published 1979*

Prepared under Grant #76JS–99–0005 from the Office of Juvenile Justice and Delinquency Prevention, Law Enforcement Assistance Administration, U.S. Department of Justice.

Points of view or opinions in this document are those of the authors and do not necessarily represent the official position or policies of the U.S. Department of Justice.

Parts of LaMar T. Empey's essay "The Progressive Legacy and the Concept of Childhood" are drawn from an earlier version entitled "The Social Construction of Childhood, Delinquency and Social Reform," published in *The Juvenile Justice System,* ed. Malcolm W. Klein (Beverly Hills: Sage Publications, 1976), pp. 27–54. Appreciation is gratefully expressed to Sage Publications for permission to reprint sections of the original.

Library of Congress Cataloging in Publication Data
Main entry under title:

Juvenile justice.

   Essays presented at a Kenyon Public Affairs Forum conference held Sept. 16–19, 1976.
   1. Juvenile delinquency—United States—Congresses.   2. Juvenile Justice, Administration of—United States—Congresses.   I. Empey, LaMar Taylor, 1923–   II. Kenyon Public Affairs Forum.
HV9104.J873   364.4′0973   78–17536   ISBN   0–8139–0799–3   ISBN   0–8139–0800–0 pbk.

Printed in the United States of America

# Contents

# Foreword

The original subject of the conference which resulted in this volume was "The Sources of Juvenile Delinquency and the Problems of Juvenile Justice." I was invited to participate in my then capacity as Staff Director and Chief Counsel of the U.S. Senate Subcommittee to Investigate Juvenile Delinquency.

It is a significant aspect of the methodology of the Kenyon Public Affairs conferences that the deliberations lead to a thorough rethinking of the thematic framework. Consequently, the focus in this volume was narrowed to the reevaluation of current reform of the juvenile justice system. This was made possible both by the high caliber of the participants, academicians and practitioners, and by the basic procedures of the conference. Papers are critically reviewed by the conferees and additional papers commissioned to meet the broad concensus reached during the deliberations.

The participants reacted very favorably to the conference. Among the comments which were received by the Forum, the assessment of Mr. Wilmer S. Cody, Superintendent, Birmingham, Alabama Board of Education, was representative:

I don't know of any activity or publication that has so thoroughly explored the many aspects of the problem. I do hope there is a next step, under Kenyon's or LEAA's or someone's auspices, in which a limited number of policy-relevant issues are selected and pursued in depth by persons with the diversity in points of view that were present last week. Such an occurrence can readily lead to not only knowledge-building for the participants but, also, to an increase in the general state of contemporary understanding of the problem.

I hope that this volume will do just that and I know that it will be very useful for the work of the Office of Juvenile Justice and Delinquency Prevention.

JOHN M. RECTOR
*Administrator*
*Office of Juvenile Justice*
*and Delinquency Prevention*

# Preface

The juvenile court was invented in 1899. From that time until the 1960s, it operated in relative quietude with only occasional outcries from a few concerned judges, national associations, and scholars. Now, however, the juvenile court is being radically altered.

Because it was concerned with these changes, the Kenyon Public Affairs Forum brought together a group of theoreticians, historians, and practitioners representing a wide spectrum of opinions. They met in conference September 16–19, 1976. The conference itself was made possible by a grant from the Office of Juvenile Justice and Delinquency Prevention of the Law Enforcement Assistance Administration, U.S. Department of Justice.

The original theme for the Conference was developed by Dr. Samuel M. Kelman, and the Forum then commissioned a series of essays to deal with that theme. The intensive discussions stimulated by these essays brought into sharper focus the complex historical, social, and cultural problems associated with the topic. They also highlighted vast differences in perspective among scholars, government officials, social scientists, and practitioners.

When the Conference adjourned, both a general consensus and a problem remained. The consensus was that although the juvenile justice system is being irrevocably altered, that alteration is taking place without much greater awareness of the complexities involved than when the juvenile court was invented almost a century ago, or when prisons and reformatories were first built a century before that. Though today's reformers are as fervent in their prescriptions for change as were reformers from earlier epochs, their attention to the place of the juvenile justice system in the larger context of American society is often limited. It is one thing to advocate change and quite another to have that change congruent with the vast alterations that are also occurring elsewhere in American society—changes in the general status of children, in society's economic and political structures, and in current beliefs about the roots of crime and delinquency.

It was this consensus which helped to highlight the problem the conference had produced: How could its essays and deliberations be refocused and reorganized in such a way that they would shed greater light on the complex issues that the conference had highlighted?

In order to address this problem, Professor LaMar T. Empey, of the University of Southern California, was asked to refocus the conference theme, to commission additional essays, and to act as the editor of this volume. As a result, a collection of essays, divided into three parts, has been prepared.

### Part I: The Historical Roots of Progressivism

The juvenile court grew and flowered during the Progressive era in American history. In order to understand its contribution to the development of that court, two essays were written.

The first, entitled "The Progressive Legacy and the Concept of Childhood," was written by Professor Empey. It traces the development of the modern concept of childhood in Western civilization and the contribution of this concept to the invention of the juvenile court. It explains why it was that, until the dawn of the twentieth century, relatively little thought was given to the idea that a unique justice system for juveniles was needed or why that system was charged with redressing almost every conceivable youth problem.

The second essay was written by Professor David J. Rothman of Columbia University and is entitled "The Progressive Legacy: Development of American Attitudes toward Juvenile Delinquency." This essay provides a much needed history of the elaboration of the juvenile court during this century, its rapid spread throughout the country, and the optimism with which it was hailed.

### Part II: The Current Construction of Delinquency

"Delinquency" is not a social phenomenon that is unchanging and immutable. In order to highlight its present character, therefore, three essays were written.

The first was again prepared by Professor Empey and is entitled "Juvenile Lawbreaking: Its Character and Social Location." Since there is great debate over the extent, nature, and trends of juvenile lawbreaking, this essay provides a much needed account derived from three sources: *official* accounts by police and courts, *unofficial, self-reported* accounts from juveniles themselves, and accounts from the *victims* of crimes. When looked at from three perspectives, some surprising disparities and agreements occur.

The second essay in this section was written by Professor Jackson Toby of Rutgers University. Entitled "Delinquency in Cross-cultural Perspective," Professor Toby's essay places delinquency in a wider context by examining its incidence and causes in cultures other than our own. Noting the increase in concern over delinquency that attends the development of urbanism in every society, he attempts to account for, and to explain, that concern.

The third essay in Part II is by Professor Paul Lerman, also of Rutgers University. It deals with the preoccupation of Americans with the "status" offenses of children—truancy, running away, incorrigibility, and sexual behavior—offenses that would not be illegal if committed by adults. The title of this essay reflects this preoccupation: "American Concerns: Keeping Order versus Fighting Crime." Despite their concerns over criminal acts, Americans still devote remarkable attention and resources to the presumed immoralities of children.

### Part III. Prescriptions for Reform

Having set the historical context for the emergence of the juvenile court and the nature of the problems it is supposed to address, Part III deals with current prescriptions for reform.

In the first essay, Professor Travis Hirschi of the State University of New York at Albany, traces the evolution of scientific theories of delinquency during the twentieth century and their changing implications for social policy. His analysis, entitled "Reconstructing Delinquency: Evolution and Implications of Twentieth-Century Theory," is an incisive account of just how markedly different our theoretical views of delinquency are today as contrasted with the views that prevailed when the juvenile court was invented. By no means is it clear that widely hailed explanations today come any closer to providing final solutions than did those of an earlier era.

In the second essay of this section, the Honorable Justice Wise Polier, former Judge of the Family Court in New York, notes the extent to which American society has failed to support its system of justice for juveniles. Though that system is now being blamed for failing to redress a host of childhood ills—child abuse, dependency, and neglect, as well as delinquency—it has never enjoyed the resources its optimistic founders anticipated that it should have. Her essay is entitled: "Prescriptions for Reform: Doing What We Set Out to Do?"

In the last essay of the volume, Professors Herman Schwendinger and Julia Schwendinger, of the State University of New York at New Paltz, have written a critical review of current reforms from a radical perspective. Entitled "Delinquency and Social Reform: A Radical Perspective," their work is noteworthy for two reasons. While they argue that the worst features of delinquency, dependency, and neglect can never be eliminated until radical transformations are made in the whole of American society, they are much concerned with the effects of "reform" in the short run. Much like Judge Polier, they also express great concerns over the possibility that current efforts to decriminalize status offenses and to divert juveniles from the juvenile justice system will result in nothing more than benign neglect. Rather than helping those who need it most, we will merely ignore them.

Finally, Professor Empey provides a short epilogue devoted to the many and perplexing issues which these essays raise and which may remain unresolved by the revolution in juvenile justice that is taking place. He suggests many reasons for pause, reflection, and reconsideration.

In much the same vein, the Honorable Howard A. Metzenbaum, member of the United States Senate Judiciary Committee, wrote a letter to the Law Enforcement Assistance Administration in which he expressed appreciation for the valuable exchange which had occurred in the Kenyon Forum. The senator also stated that neither Congress nor the Administration is in exclusive possession of solutions for current problems in juvenile justice. Thoughtful and critical reviews are needed and welcome from all segments of society.

It is in this spirit that this volume is presented to the public. The hope is that it will contribute to the cultivation of further debate on a most complicated issue—the future of justice for American children.

ROBERT A. BAUER
*Director*
*Kenyon Public*
*Affairs Forum*

# Part I
# The Historical Roots of Progressivism

# The Progressive Legacy and the Concept of Childhood

## Lamar T. Empey

THE reputation of the juvenile court today has become badly tarnished: its rehabilitative philosophy is under attack; its basic procedures have been challenged; and its effectiveness is being questioned. Indeed, the court is like an overpainted old beauty in whose company only a few former friends want to be seen. Everyone else has joined a reform group, seeking either to find some foster parents or perhaps a sterner legal body to replace her. In light of the fanfare that she enjoyed when she made her debut, therefore, the sudden sullying of her glamorous reputation is all the more remarkable.

Although it has now become customary to cite Roscoe Pound's famous warning, made in 1913, that "the powers of the court of star chamber were a bagatelle compared with those of the American juvenile courts," his remarks to the National Council of Juvenile Court Judges in 1959 are noted less often. The juvenile court, he said on that occasion, is "the greatest step forward in Anglo-American jurisprudence since the Magna Charta!" [1] Though there were dangers, Pound's contradictory remarks seemed to indicate, the potential advantages far outweighed the disadvantages.

Certainly that was the feeling of Judge Julian W. Mack, one of the first judges of the juvenile court in Chicago, when he spoke before the American Bar Association in 1909. The purpose of the juvenile court, he made clear, was to decriminalize the misconduct of children.

---

[1] President's Commission on Law Enforcement and Administration, *Juvenile Delinquency and Youth Crime* (Washington, D.C.: U.S. Government Printing Office, 1967), p. 60; National Probation and Parole Association, *Guides for Juvenile Court Judges* (New York: National Probation and Parole Association, 1957), p. 127.

Why isn't it just and proper to treat these juvenile offenders as we deal with the neglected children, as a wise and merciful father handles his own child whose errors are not discovered by the authorities? Why isn't it the duty of the State instead of asking merely whether a boy or a girl has committed the specific offense, to find out what he is, physically, mentally, morally, and then, if it learns that he is treading the path that leads to criminality, to take him in charge, not so much to punish as to reform, not to degrade but to uplift, not to crush but to develop, not to make him a criminal but a worthy citizen.[2]

Judge Harvey H. Baker of Boston expressed a similar view. "The fundamental function of the juvenile court," he said, "is to put each child who comes before it in a normal relation to society as promptly and permanently as possible, and while punishment is not to be dispensed with, it is to be made subsidiary and subordinate to that function."[3]

According to these advocates, then, the juvenile court would intervene, not as a harsh and punitive monitor of evil conduct, but as a thoughtful parent. Further, there was little need to draw sharp distinctions between seven-year-olds and sixteen-year-olds or between criminal children and those who were poor, neglected, or failing in school. All were to be saved. The enforcement of rules would be characterized by help, not punishment.

### Today's Disillusionment

Today, of course, we have become cynical about the intent of these early proponents and the optimism expressed in their objectives. This cynicism stems from almost every conceivable source.

*Revisionist historians.* The Progressive era out of which the juvenile court grew has been described by revisionist historians

[2] Julian W. Mack, "The Juvenile Court as a Legal Institution," in *Preventive Treatment of Neglected Children,* ed. Hastings H. Hart (New York: Russell Sage, 1910), pp. 296–97.

[3] Ibid., p. 318.

as a period "garnished with various myths."[4] The primary goal of nineteenth-century child saving was not the welfare of children but the maintenance of control by a group of rural and paternalistically oriented child savers who were the captives of major corporations and financial institutions, people who had been co-opted into securing the existing political and economic order.[5] The juvenile court was nothing more than a device for protecting the capitalist class from the unruly children of the working class.

*Scientific explanations and ideologies.* Each new body of scientific theory, since the days of Shaw and McKay, has tended increasingly to discredit the premise of the juvenile court that delinquent behavior can be prevented and controlled by tinkering with the mind and morality of the individual delinquent.[6] To do so is to treat symptoms, not causes. It is society that segregates people by age, class, and race, that produces delinquent subcultures among children, that defines rules favoring the powerful and then labels and stigmatizes the powerless who break them. It is society that is criminogenic, not individual children and their families. Hence, prevention strategies, far more sweeping in character, are required, perhaps even the elimination of the oppressive class structure of capitalism and the installation of a socialist society.[7]

[4] Anthony M. Platt, "The Triumph of Benevolence: The Origins of the Juvenile Justice System in the United States," in *Criminal Justice in America,* ed. Richard Quinney (Boston: Little, Brown, 1974), p. 364.

[5] Anthony M. Platt, "Introduction to the Reprint Edition," *History of Child Saving in the United States* (1893; reprint ed., Montclair, N.J.: Patterson Smith, 1971), p. ix.

[6] Clifford R. Shaw and Henry D. McKay, *Delinquency Areas* (Chicago: University of Chicago Press, 1929).

[7] Howard S. Becker, *Outsiders: Studies of the Sociology of Deviance* (New York: Free Press, 1963); Richard A. Cloward and Lloyd E. Ohlin, *Delinquency and Opportunity* (New York: Free Press, 1960); Albert K. Cohen, *Delinquent Boys: The Culture of the Gang* (New York: Free Press, 1955); Richard Quinney, ed., *Criminal Justice in America* (Boston: Little, Brown, 1974); Edwin H. Sutherland and Donald R. Cressey, *Principles of Criminology,* 5th ed. (New York: Lippincott, 1955).

*Ordinary citizens.* Since the turbulent years of the 1960s, many ordinary Americans have grown disenchanted with the benevolent goals of the juvenile court and with its capacity to protect society. Its Progressive ideology, like Progressivism in general, has contributed not to order but to anarchy. Reflecting these concerns, Richard Nixon promised, in 1968, that, if elected president, he would wage a "war on crime," even if the nation's young were numbered among the enemy. And the National Commission on the Causes and Prevention of Violence asked rhetorically whether we were about to "witness widespread crime, perhaps out of police control." [8] The feeling was that the country no longer faced losses of one kind or another from young people; it was in danger of losing everything! The only solution, therefore, was to return to a more retributive form of justice, favoring punishment rather than rehabilitation.

*Liberal ideology.* People and organizations of liberal persuasion, along with labeling theorists, have protested the idea that the juvenile court has been empowered to catch and to stigmatize youngsters for violating the moral rules of childhood. "Serious consideration," said the President's Crime Commission, "should be given to complete elimination of the court's power over children for noncriminal conduct." [9] Such things as truancy, insubordination, drinking, or running away should no longer be grounds for the use of coercive court power.

*The Supreme Court.* In 1966 for the first time in its history, the juvenile court was censured by the United States Supreme Court for its failure to insure constitutional safeguards and due process for children. "Juvenile court history," said the Supreme Court, "has again demonstrated that unbridled discretion, however

[8] National Commission on the Causes and Prevention of Violence, *Crimes of Violence* Vol. 2 (Washington, D.C.: U.S. Government Printing Office, 1969), p. xxv.

[9] President's Commission on Law Enforcement and Administration of Justice, *The Challenge of Crime in a Free Society* (Washington, D.C.: U.S. Government Printing Office, 1967), p. 27.

benevolently motivated, is frequently a poor substitute for principle and procedure." [10]

*Sexism and assembly line justice.* The juvenile court has been attacked for sexual discrimination and the paternalistic treatment of females; for the excessive use of detention pending court action; for failing to discriminate in its treatment of status and criminal offenders; and for the dispensation of assembly line justice.[11]

The juvenile court, in short, has been attacked for almost every conceivable reason from almost every conceivable ideological position—retributive, liberal, and radical. But a question that is seldom asked is why it was that attacks on the juvenile court did not become widespread until the late 1960s. As late as 1962 Judge Orman Ketcham of the Juvenile Court in Washington, D.C., still felt that the juvenile court deserved the highest of praise: "The first two decades of the juvenile court movement," he said, "produced a wealth of philosophical comment so sound in conception and so modern in tone that it has scarcely been modified or improved upon since that time." [12] Why, after this late date, did so many Americans have second thoughts?

The most obvious answer lies in the criticisms already mentioned. But those criticisms often overlook an important fact,

[10] *Kent v. U.S.*, 383 U.S. 541, 16L. Ed.2d 84, 86 S. Ct. 1045 (1966).

[11] Meda Chesney-Lind, "Judicial Paternalism and the Female Status Offender," *Crime and Delinquency* 23 (April 1977):121–30, Rosemary C. Sarri, *Under Lock and Key: Juveniles in Jails and Detention* (Ann Arbor: University of Michigan Press, National Assessment of Juvenile Corrections, 1974); Mark Creekmore, "Case Processing: Intake, Adjudication, and Disposition," in *Brought to Justice? Juveniles, the Courts, and the Law*, ed. Rosemary Sarri and Yeheskel Hasenfeld (Ann Arbor: University of Michigan Press, National Assessment of Juvenile Corrections, 1976); Lawrence Cohen, *Juvenile Dispositions: Social and Legal Factors Related to Processing of Denver Delinquency Cases* (Washington, D.C.: U.S. Government Printing Office, LEAA, 1975).

[12] Orman W. Ketcham, "The Unfulfilled Promise of the American Juvenile Court," in *Justice for the Child*, ed. Margaret K. Rosenheim (New York: Free Press, 1962), p. 26.

namely, that the juvenile court, a nineteenth-century invention, has been evaluated not only from the perspective of late twentieth-century intellectual and scientific thought but from the perspective of a nation that has been torn by civil rights protests, rising crime rates, urban riots, and challenges to an exceedingly unpopular war in Vietnam. What with a changing set of values, therefore, and concern about crime and social unrest, it has been easy for the nation to overlook the possibility that the juvenile court was designed less as a device for suppressing crime than as a device for enforcing an ideal concept of childhood which did not reach full flower until after the turn of the twentieth century and which, even today, retains considerable vigor. While modern critics may wish to assert a different purpose for the juvenile court today, it is useful to be clear about the nature of the institution that is being attacked and the reasons it has persisted. Indeed, many people, even now, remain ambivalent about making radical alterations in it.

The laws of most states, although revised in the past ten years, have not eliminated status offenses—truancy, running away, incorrigibility, or drinking—as grounds for court action. Though these are not criminal offenses, they continue to reflect traditional concerns over appropriate behavior for children and efforts to use the court as an institution for backing up the authority of parents, schools, and other community agencies.

In its review of various cases the Supreme Court reflected some of the same ambivalence. While on the one hand it did say that procedures which insure fairness for children cannot be discarded merely because the juvenile court purports to be benevolent and rehabilitative, it made clear, on the other, that guarantees of due process need not interfere with the traditional goals of the juvenile court.[13] Ironically, therefore, it left anything but a clear mandate for judges. "The observance of due process standards" it said, "will not compel the states to abandon or displace any of the substantive benefits of the juvenile court."[14]

[13] Monrad G. Paulsen, and Charles H. Whitebread, *Juvenile Law and Procedure* (Reno, Nev.: National Council of Juvenile Court Judges, 1974), p. 20.

[14] *In re Gault*, 387 U.S. 1, 18L. Ed.2d 527, 87 S.Ct. 1428 (1967).

Prosecutors and defense attorneys still play a reluctant role in adjudicatory proceedings: "Lawyers generally tend to share the view that misbehaving children ought not to be permitted to believe that they can get away with breaking society's rules. To the extent that a vigorous demand for legal rights would produce an acquittal on delinquency charges, there develops a conflict between this shared belief and the professional role as children's advocate."[15]

Status offenders are as likely to be detained, to be tried, and to be sentenced by the juvenile courts as criminal property offenders. Only juveniles charged with serious personal crimes are more likely to be handled formally. But since the latter are far less numerous, they constitute a minority of the juveniles processed by the court.[16]

Influential judges continue to plead that the limitations of the juvenile court stem less from inherent weaknesses in its fundamental premises than from community intolerance and a lack of adequate resources. It is their contention that, without the juvenile court, communities would possess even fewer legal and social services for those juveniles who are most in need of help.[17]

The persistence of this kind of ambivalence notwithstanding, the tides of change are strong. It would appear that eventually the juvenile court will be irrevocably altered. It may even be discarded entirely, particularly for adolescents. But if that is the case, what new images of childhood and justice for juveniles are being projected? What will be the social and legal standing of children in the years to come? Because of our concern with symptomatic issues, it is these kinds of questions to which almost no attention has been paid.

While the various criticisms of the juvenile court imply significant alterations in our late twentieth-century construction of childhood, we have paid little heed to the possible implications of

[15] Sanford Fox, "Juvenile Justice Reform: An Historical Perspective," *Stanford Law Review* 22 (1970):1187–1239.

[16] Lawrence E. Cohen, *Juvenile Dispositions;* Sarri, *Under Lock and Key;* Sarri and Hasenfeld, *Brought to Justice?*

[17] Justine W. Polier, *A View from the Bench: The Juvenile Court* (New York: National Council of Crime and Delinquency, 1964).

that construction. Indeed, historians, like social scientists and policymakers, confess to an almost total neglect of the history of childhood, to say nothing of attempting to project its future. It is for these reasons that the remainder of this chapter will be devoted to the history of childhood in Western civilization and to the cultural context out of which the juvenile court grew. Historical studies of childhood, which are as recent as criticisms of the juvenile court, paint a somewhat different picture of the court's invention and purpose than the one we conjure up when we attack it. By paying closer attention to it, therefore, we may be able to put our current constructions of childhood and delinquency into better perspective and to approach our own "reforms" somewhat more knowledgeably.

## History of Indifference to Children

The juvenile court was created because of widespread beliefs that children are different from adults, more innocent, less capable of criminal intent, and therefore in greater need of both protection and disciplined guidance. Hence, it may come as some surprise to find that children, in Western civilization at least, have not always been viewed in this way. If historians are correct, our concept of childhood, like delinquency, is a relatively new invention. Childhood has not always been a time in the life cycle to which much importance was attached.[18] Indeed, the opposite was often true. Mause, for example, says that "the history of childhood [in Western civilization] is a nightmare from which we only recently began to awaken." And while Stone is

[18] Philippe Ariès, *Centuries of Childhood*, trans. Robert Baldick (New York: Knopf, 1962); Peter Laslett, *Household and Family in Past Time* (Cambridge: Cambridge University Press, 1972); Robert H. Bremner et al. ed., *Children and Youth in America: A Documentary History*, 2 vols. (Cambridge; Harvard University Press, 1970); David Hunt, *Parents and Children in History: The Psychology of Family Life in Early Modern History* (New York: Basic Books, 1970); Lloyd Mause, ed., *The History of Childhood* (New York: Psychohistory Press, 1974); Lawrence Stone, "The Massacre of the Innocents," *New York Review of Books*, Nov. 14, 1974, pp. 25–31.

somewhat more cautious, he still concludes that the historical treatment of children is a "catalogue of atrocities." [19]

Infanticide and the abandonment of newborn infants were regular practices in ancient civilizations and were not uncommon in Europe as late as the seventeenth and eighteenth centuries. Newborn infants were thrown into rivers, flung into dung heaps, left to be eaten by animals of prey, or sacrificed to gods in religious rites. The bones of child sacrifices are still being discovered in the walls of buildings constructed all the way from 7000 B.C. to A.D. 1843.[20] Apparently the killing of legitimate children was only slowly reduced during the Middle Ages, and the practice of killing illegitimate ones persisted even into the nineteenth century. In seventeenth-century England, for example, midwives had to take the following oath because of the apparent persistence of infanticide: "I will not destroy the child born of any woman, nor cut, nor pull off the head thereof, or otherwise dismember or hurt the same, or suffer it to be so hurt or dismembered." [21]

Cultural beliefs tended to define which children should and should not survive. Any child who was not perfect or seemed to cry too much was generally killed; boys were considered to be of much greater value than girls; and infanticide, rather than contraception or abortion, were methods of controlling family size. Two sons might be raised, possibly three, but seldom more than one girl.[22]

Even for those infants allowed to live at birth, survival was tenuous. Up to about the eighteenth century, most children of well-to-do or even middle-class parents spent their earliest years in the care of a wet nurse. The police chief of Paris estimated in 1780 that of approximately 21,000 *recorded* births, 17,000 were

[19] Mause, *History of Childhood*, p. 1; Stone, "Massacre of the Innocents," p. 29.

[20] Mause, *History of Childhood*, p. 25.

[21] Joseph E. Illick, "Child-rearing in Seventeenth-Century England and America," in *History of Childhood*, ed. Mause, p. 306.

[22] Mause, *History of Childhood*, p. 26, and Elizabeth Marvick, "Nature vs. Nurture: Patterns and Trends in Seventeenth Century French Child Rearing," in *History of Childhood*, ed. Mause, pp. 283–86.

sent to the country to be wet-nursed; only 700 by their own mothers.[23] The practice of wet-nursing was apparently denounced by moralists from the time of the ancient Greeks onward because of its apparent harm to infants. Many did not survive because commercial wet nurses were often cruel and malnourished themselves, and even killed their own infants in order to extend their money-making milk supply.[24]

Other infant-raising practices such as swaddling, burning with a hot iron in order to prevent "falling sickness," dipping them in ice water or rolling them in the snow to harden or to baptize them, as well as disease and filth, took a high toll. Indeed, a high death rate among babies and young children may have been a major reason that childhood as a place in the life cycle received so little attention. As late as the seventeenth century approximately two-thirds of all children died before the age of four, "Before they are old enough to bother you," said one Frenchman, "you will have lost half of them, or perhaps all of them." [25] Under such conditions, says Stone, "no parent could retain his or her sanity if he or she became too emotionally involved with such ephemeral creatures as young children. Aloofness, or the acceptance of God's will, or sending one's children away from home were three natural solutions to this problem of how to deal with their deaths." [26] Thus, Ariès maintains that various languages of the Middle Ages and later did not possess words to distinguish babies from bigger children, and people had no conception of adolescence. And Skolnick says that people believed that infants existed "in a sort of limbo, hanging between life and death, more as a kind of animal than a human being, without mental activities or recognizable bodily shape." [27]

[23] Mause, *History of Childhood,* p. 35.

[24] Stone, "Massacre of the Innocents," p. 29.

[25] Priscilla Robertson, "Home as a Nest: Middle-class Childhood in Nineteenth-Century Europe," in *History of Childhood,* ed. Mause, pp. 410–12; M. J. Tucker, "The Child as Beginning and End: Fifteenth and Sixteenth Century Childhood," in *History of Childhood,* ed. Mause, p. 242; Mause, *History of Childhood,* pp. 31–37. Bremner et al., *Children and Youth,* I:3–4. Ariès, *Centuries of Childhood,* p. 38.

[26] Stone, "Massacre of the Innocents," pp. 28–29.

[27] Arlene Skolnick, *The Intimate Environment: Exploring Marriage and the Family* (New York: Little, Brown, 1973), p. 333.

Child-raising practices beyond the years of infancy revealed the continuance of relative indifference, at least in our terms. Upon reaching the age of seven, children of the poor and aristocracy alike became apprentices in the homes of others.[28] This was the way they were prepared for adulthood. The social life in which they participated was highly communal. The equivalent of our middle class lived in large households holding as many as twenty-five people—parents, apprentices, relatives, servants, and visitors—while the large floating lower-class population, whose life, if not less communal, was spent in smaller dwellings, on the streets, and in the fields.

Prevailing conditions meant that the behavioral rules of the time were vastly different from our own. Measured by contemporary standards, says Ariès, "it is easy to imagine the promiscuity which reigned in those rooms [of the communal household] where nobody could be alone, . . . where several couples and several groups of boys or girls slept together (not to speak of the servants of whom at least some must have slept beside their masters . . .), in which people foregathered to have their meals, to receive friends or clients." [29]

Ariès's comment points to the apparent fact that children were not spared a full and participatory role in all aspects of existence —sex, work, life, and death. He concludes, as a result, that because children were not segregated by age as they are today, this led to a happy and sociable life for them. They were the natural companions of adults.

Other historians are far less sanguine.[30] While children were not segregated from adults, historians contend that their status was at the bottom of the social scale. In antiquity, both boys and girls were sometimes placed in brothels, suffered castration and clitoridectomy, and then become the sexual playthings of adults. The literature of the Renaissance is likewise full of moralist com-

[28] Ariès, *Centuries of Childhood*, p. 35.

[29] Ibid., p. 394.

[30] Mause, *History of Childhood;* Richard B. Lyman, Jr., "Barbarism and Religion: Late Roman and Early Medieval Childhood," in *History of Childhood,* Mause; Tucker, "The Child as Beginning and End"; Illick, "Childrearing"; Bremner et al., *Children and Youth;* Stone, "Massacre of the Innocents."

plaints about the sexual abuse of children. The apprenticeship
system, which persisted well into the nineteenth century, even
in this country, led to the exploitation of child labor. Finally,
methods of social control were often brutal and countenanced
severe beatings with whips, rods, and cudgels. In short, even if
one took a temperate view, he might conclude as Stone did that
children in Western civilization, until very recently, have not
counted for much.[31] Legal institutions designed to protect them
from neglect, as we define it, or to punish them for lewd conduct,
drinking, or staying out late would have been ludicrous and
totally anachronistic.

### Discovery of Childhood

The forces that eventually led to a more modern view of childhood apparently had their origins in the early Renaissance and
for a long time existed coterminously with the conditions just
described. Christian beliefs had long stressed the innocence and
frailty of children, though in practice people had not paid much
attention to them. During the fifteenth and sixteenth centuries
signs of ambivalence and change began to appear. People were
warned to do a better job of selecting wet nurses, the color white
came to symbolize children, children became a source of amusement for adults, like little dogs or puppies, and children in paint-
ings began to look like children rather than mature dwarfs.[32]

By the late sixteenth and seventeenth centuries, criticisms of
prior child-raising practices grew pronounced. Although the
Renaissance, the Reformation, the commercial revolution, and
the discovery of the New World were undoubtedly influential,
most historians suggest that the real innovators, insofar as children are concerned, were a relatively small band of moralists,

[31] Stone, "Massacre of the Innocents," p. 29.

[32] James Bruce Ross, "The Middle-class Child in Urban Italy, Fourteenth
to early Sixteenth-Century," in *History of Childhood*, ed. Mause, p. 185;
Tucker, "The Child as Beginning and End," p. 232; Ariès, *Centuries of
Childhood*, pp. 129, 33.

churchmen, and schoolmen, both Catholic and Protestant.[33] A moralization of society was taking place in which the ethical aspects of religion were gradually taking precedence over the ritualistic. Efforts were being made to reshape the world and to do so, in part, through children.

Children were seen by the moralists as rather odd creatures—fragile, innocent, and sacred, on the one hand, but corruptible, trying, and arrogant, on the other. What children most need, they felt, is discipline and training. Their premature induction into the adult world not only injures them but affronts adults. The remarks of two Puritan reformers in 1621 capture this moralist theme very well. "The young child which lieth in the cradle is both wayward and full of affections; and though his body is small, yet he hath a *reat* (wrong-doing) heart, and is altogether inclined to evil. . . . If this sparkle be suffered to increase, it will rage and burn down the whole house. For we are changed and become good not by birth but by education. . . . Therefore, parents must be wary and circumspect." [34]

What was emerging, of course, was the modern concept of childhood, namely, the idea that until a child has been given distinctive preparation, he is not ready for life. Until he has been subjected to a sort of moral and educational quarantine, he cannot be allowed to join the adults.[35] In support of this idea the moralists stressed the importance of two societal institutions, in addition to that of the church—the family and the school. During the Middle Ages children were a common property and, except for a few years, were not raised by their own parents. The moralists, however, placed direct responsibility on parents—a responsibility that, among other things, probably contributed to the emergence of the nuclear family. With respect to that issue, Peter Laslett has shown rather conclusively that the English family became increasingly nuclear during the seventeenth century.[36]

---

[33] Ariès, *Centuries of Childhood,* p. 330; Illick, "Child-rearing," pp. 316–17; Marvick, "Nature vs. Nurture," p. 261; Bremner et al., *Children and Youth,* 1.

[34] Illick, "Child-rearing," pp. 316–17.

[35] Ariès, *Centuries of Childhood,* pp. 411–12.

[36] Laslett, *Household and Family,* pp. 1–89.

Not entirely trusting corrupt parents, however, the moralists also sought to use the school as a place for moral as well as intellectual training. Unlike the humanists of the Renaissance, who stressed the idea that learning should be pursued by people of all ages, the moralists were particularly concerned with schooling for the young. Hence, they were responsible for opening many of the first schools whose purpose was general education rather than technical training for the clergy. While space precludes a detailed discussion of the evolution of these schools, a recognition of their importance as a social innovation designed to reorganize the lives of the young is what is most important.[37]

The Ideal Child

By the late seventeenth and eighteenth centuries a vision of the ideal child had been developed and widely projected. The vision is easily deduced by allusion to the child-raising principles set forth in a multiplicity of tracts, sermons, and pamphlets common both in Europe and in the American colonies.[38] Briefly, the principles were these:

1. Never permit children to be alone, since they are not fit to govern themselves.

2. Discipline, do not pamper, children. They must learn submission and self-control.

3. Teach modesty. Children should not undress in the presence of others; should not lie in an immodest position, especially girls; should not sleep together if of the opposite sex; should not hear songs, read books, or observe performances that express dissolute passions.

4. Train children to work. Teach them diligence in some lawful trade.

5. Above all, teach respect for, and obedience to, authority.

[37] See Ariès.

[38] Ibid., pp. 114–19; David J. Rothman, *The Discovery of the Asylum* (Boston: Little, Brown, 1971), pp. 15–17; Bremner et al., *Children and Youth*, 1.

Disobedience leads inevitably to dishonor, disease and death.

In short, the ideal child should be submissive to authority, hard-working, self-controlled, obedient, modest, and chaste. Parents who do not produce such children, and schools that fail to mold them, are suspect. What these principles meant, in effect, was that over the space of several centuries indifference to children had been replaced by an increasing preoccupation with them. The significance of this change is difficult to overstate. Before turning exclusively to its impact on the organization of child raising in American society, a few corollary matters should be observed.

First, historical analyses generally suggest that both the ideal concept and organization of childhood were possessions largely of the middle class.[39] The nuclear family, for example, seemed to have greater appeal for a growing number of entrepreneurs, merchants, and professionals than it did either for the peasant class or the nobility. Middle-class families were inclined increasingly to shrink from the indiscriminate mixing of the generations and the classes in large households and to stress the benefits of family privacy. Formal schooling was likewise seen as particularly useful by the middle class. For a long time schools were privately run, both in Europe and America, and though they sometimes made provision for poorer children, many of these either could not, or did not, attend schools, and those who did rarely went beyond the first few grades. Virtually no effort, moreover, was made to educate black and Indian children in the colonies.[40]

Second, sexual stratification continued. Nineteenth-century French peasants were known to declare, "I have no children, monsieur. I have only girls." And in Naples it was customary to hang out a black flag if a girl were born so that neighbors might be spared the embarrassment of coming to congratulate the parents. Hence, European schools were off limits to girls and remained so for some time. In the American colonies, particularly

[39] Ariès, *Centuries of Childhood*, pp. 414–15; Bremner et al., *Children and Youth*, 1:343; Anthony M. Platt, *The Child Savers* (Chicago: University of Chicago Press, 1969).

[40] Bremner et al., *Children and Youth*, 1:72–79.

the Northeast, girls were taught to read and write but beyond that were still relegated to domestic roles.[41]

Third, changes in the concept of childhood did not mean that all older child-raising practices were eliminated. Child labor, for example, was highly important. Hence, apprenticeship practices continued, although with some class differentials. The American colonies used large numbers of indentured children who were swept off the streets of London and shipped over in wholesale lots.[42] Native-born children, meanwhile, began work at about age six, but for their parents, not for another family. Boys were not apprenticed until about age fourteen, and girls might not be apprenticed at all.

Finally, methods of discipline remained harsh. The debate was not whether children should be whipped but at which age whipping should begin, how and where it should be administered, and until what age. However, the conflicting character of child-raising principles—stressing parental love, on one hand, but stern, unyielding punishment for disobedience, on the other —did seem to foster ambivalence.[43]

### Childhood in Eighteenth-Century America

Throughout the Middle Ages, and as late as the eighteenth century, children participated in acts which, if committed today, could not only result in their being defined as delinquent but could require that their parents be charged with contributing to their delinquency. As soon as they could talk, most children learned and used (by our standards) obscene language and gestures; many engaged in sex at an early age, willingly or otherwise; they drank freely in taverns, if not at home; few of them went to school, and when they did, they wore sidearms, fomented

[41] Robertson, "Home as a Nest," p. 409; Ariès, *Centuries of Childhood,* pp. 269–85.

[42] Bremner et al., *Children and Youth,* 1:5–9.

[43] Robertson, "Home as a Nest," pp. 414–20; Illick, "Child-rearing," p. 326.

brawls, and fought duels.[44] In modern society these same acts occur, but they are legally defined as undesirable and authorities are charged with curbing them. We are interested, of course, in how this came about.

It was during the nineteenth century that most laws applicable to children were actually written and the juvenile court created. But only by clarifying their eighteenth-century precedents is it possible to illustrate the remarkable societal changes that led to their development.[45] First, let it be said that the influential Puritan reformers justified coming to this country as a method of carrying the gospel to the New World and of permitting the young to escape the corruption of the Old. The fountains of learning and religion had been destroyed, said John Winthrop, such that "most children, even the best wits and of fairest hopes, are perverted, corrupted and utterly overthrown." [46]

Although Puritan child-raising practices were by no means universal throughout the colonies, the principles they espoused obviously had great impact upon subsequent generations of nineteenth-century reformers—the principles stressing obedience, hard work, modesty, and chastity. Furthermore, the small towns in which the colonists lived were admirably suited to an implementation of these principles. Life was dominated by a network of three major institutions: family, church, and community. "Families were to raise their children to respect law and authority; the church was to oversee not only family discipline but adult behavior; and the members of the community were to detect and correct the first signs of deviancy." [47]

The moralist emphasis upon education was carried to the New World, particularly by the Puritans. So committed were they to

[44] Wiley B. Sanders, ed., *Juvenile Offenders for a Thousand Years* (Chapel Hill: University of North Carolina Press, 1970) and Ariès, *Centuries of Childhood.*

[45] The framework for this analysis relies heavily upon David J. Rothman's provocative work *The Discovery of the Asylum*. Attention is invited to this work for greater detail and extended documentation of many of the points made here.

[46] Bremner et al., *Children and Youth,* 1:18–19.

[47] Rothman, *Discovery of the Asylum,* p. 16.

schooling, in fact, that in 1642 the Massachusetts Bay Colony passed the first law of its kind, designed to broaden and enforce the educational as well as the socialization functions of the family. The new law required that each family teach its children a trade and how to read. Parents who failed could be brought before the authorities, while children who disobeyed could be dealt with severely. But since parents were often ill-equipped to teach their children, the General Court of Massachusetts took the first step in 1647 toward a public educational system. Connecticut and New Hampshire followed suit: towns of fifty households were supposed to provide a schoolmaster for elementary training while towns of one hundred were expected to have a grammar (secondary) school. But since school attendance at the grammar school level was not required and was dependent upon private support, it tended to favor the well-to-do. Such distinctions were even more apparent in southern and middle Atlantic colonies, where education, particularly for the poor, depended upon churches and their pastors. And for black and Indian children, formal education was simply unavailable. Slaveowners had almost total control over black parents and children. Hence, while some whites sought to convert blacks to Christianity, they shied away from educating them. To do so, they believed, would be politically and socially dangerous.[48]

Deviant Behavior

The colonists were concerned about deviant behavior and adopted harsh methods for dealing with it. But they did not see it as a critical social problem in the sense that they blamed themselves for it, nor did they expect to eliminate it.[49] The reason lay in their religious explanation of deviance. They equated crime with sin and assumed that the seeds for both are inherent in everyone. By nature, people are forever inclined to the temptations of the flesh. While careful training and submission to

[48] Bremner et al., *Children and Youth*, 1:28–29, 72–73, 317–18.
[49] Rothman, *Discovery of the Asylum*, p. 15.

authority might help to control evil impulses, such impulses can never be eliminated. Hence, the colonists were not bothered by any strong inclinations to rehabilitate offenders. Rather, sin demanded retribution.

Colonial criminal codes defined a wide range of behaviors as criminal, from parental disobedience to murder, and drew few distinctions between adults and children or between major and minor offenses. Any offense was a sure sign "that the offender was destined to be a public menace and a damned sinner." [50] If offenders were allowed to escape, everyone would be implicated in his crime and God would be displeased.

Punishments served protective as well as retributive functions. Since police departments as we know them did not exist, the wide use of public whipping, placement in the stocks or pillory, branding, or public hangings all helped to reinforce public morality through mechanisms of shame as well as mechanisms of pain and fear. By sending an offender to the gallows, moreover, a community could be rid of his dangerous presence forever. And since the colonists did not believe in reform, they built no prisons. That invention was still to come.[51]

There was at this time no distinct legal category called juvenile delinquency. Americans still relied on the English common law, which specified that children under the age of seven could not be held guilty of serious crime. Between the ages of eight and fourteen, their legal status was ambiguous. Juries were expected to pay close attention to the child, and if it was felt that he or she could discern right from wrong, he or she could be convicted and even sentenced to death. Anyone over the age of fourteen was presumably judged as an adult, although some colonies made exceptions. The inclination to put children to death, however, or to whip them in public, may have been less common than originally thought.[52]

---

[50] Ibid., pp. 15–17.

[51] Harry E. Barnes, *The Story of Punishment*, 2d ed. rev. (East Orange, N.J.: Patterson Smith, 1972).

[52] Bremner et al., *Children and Youth*, 1:307–8, and Platt, *The Child Savers*, pp. 183 ff.

Poverty

Of crucial significance to our understanding of nineteenth-
century views of childhood and delinquency was the colonial
conception of poverty. Unlike nineteenth- or twentieth-century
Americans, the colonists accepted the long-standing Christian belief that the poor would always be with us. But, again, they did
not lament its presence as evidence of a tragic breakdown in
social organization. Rather, they "serenely asserted that the
presence of the poor was a God given opportunity for men to do
good." [53] Because of the presence of poor widows, orphaned children, or unfortunate families, persons at all levels of society
could be benefited. The poor could be given charity, and in-
dustrious stewards could do God's work by providing it. The
one exception was the idle ne'er-do-well, who might be told to
move on to some other town. Otherwise, poor adults did not
live in constant dread of the poor house, and children, simply
because they were destitute, did not face the prospect of placement in an orphan asylum. Indeed, neither type of institution
existed.

There is perhaps no better way to sum up the ambivalent feelings that must have been associated with the stern yet caring
character of dominant eighteenth-century child-raising practices
than the following lines penned by Anne Bradstreet, an eighteenth-century New England poet. Lamenting the death of her
eight-year-old granddaughter, she wrote:

> Farewell dear babe, my heart's too much content,
> Farewell sweet babe, the pleasure of mine eye,
> Farewell fair flower that for a space was lent,
> Then ta'en away unto Eternity.

But, in writing about the birth of a new grandson, she expressed
prevailing sentiments about the inherent depravity of children:
"Here sits our grandame in retired place/And in her lap, her
bloody Cain newborn." [54] Responsibilities for raising the right
kinds of children were not without tensions.

[53] Rothman, *Discovery of the Asylum*, p. 7.
[54] Quoted in *Illick*, "Child-rearing," p. 326.

### Nineteenth-Century Enlightenment

Colonial social organization did not survive long into the nineteenth century. After the War of Independence, Americans were subjected to a series of changes which, on the one hand, were intoxicating but which, on the other, altered irrevocably the tight-knit communities to which they were accustomed.

### Changes in Belief

The first of these changes was ideological. Whereas the religious doctrines of the past two centuries had suggested that people are inherently depraved and foreordained to a particular destiny, the American Constitution and the Declaration of Independence were based upon the philosophy of the Enlightenment—a philosophy that was individualistic and stressed universal and unlimited human progress. Through the use of reason, and by applying the principles of democracy, humankind could reach unlimited heights. The consequences of such thinking were often dramatic.

Just as they began to cast off the strictures of some of their theological beliefs, Americans began to feel that their eighteenth-century methods of social control were obsolete.[55] Feeling that the legal codes of the mother country had stifled their better inclinations and seizing upon the writings of people like Cesare Beccaria, they revised both their criminal codes and vastly reduced the severity of their punishments. Americans had a grand mission to fulfill, and one way to do it was to uplift a formerly helpless segment of mankind, the criminal class.[56]

Ways by which this mission could be accomplished were suggested by new explanations for deviant behavior that began to emerge at the turn of the century. More and more there was a tendency to reject the assumption that crime and sin were

[55] Rothman, *Discovery of the Asylum*, pp. 57–59.

[56] Cesare Beccaria, *Essay on Crime and Punishment*, Am. ed., trans. Stephen Gould (New York, 1809); Barnes, *Story of Punishment*, pp. 106–7; Rothman, *Discovery of the Asylum*, pp. 60–61.

synonymous. In its stead grew the belief that deviancy could be traced back to family corruption and an absence of discipline. Orphaned children or the children of drunken and licentious parents were those most likely to fall prey to temptation and vice. What was lacking in the lives of deviant children and adults was an adequate preparation for life.

Another social evil—community corruption—was soon added to that of family disorganization.[57] So familiar are the profound demographic changes of the nineteenth century that there is no need to repeat them here. Suffice it to say that in 1750 there were only about one and a quarter million people in the country. By 1850 the figure had reached over twenty-three million—only the beginning of an incredible growth.[58] Simultaneously, as manufacturing and commerce increased, as the movement westward began in earnest, and as the size and density of major cities grew markedly, the simple social organization of colonial towns was no longer adequate. But, while this was true, the memories of small, tight-knit towns remained fresh in the minds of many influential people. Hence, when they looked about them and saw growth, instability, and change, they concluded that these factors also promoted deviant behavior. Community disorder went hand in hand with the disorder of unstable families.

Such thinking demanded a major intellectual turnabout. Rather than being preoccupied with the sinner, reformers now had to be concerned with the forces that shaped him—a significant turnabout indeed, and it had paradoxical consequences: If, on one hand, crime and misconduct were endemic to societal life, and not to the human soul, then they could be rooted out or at least greatly reduced! If the offender was no longer innately depraved, he could be redeemed! If there were young children in danger of becoming criminal, their misconduct could be prevented! The grounds for optimism were considerable.

On the other hand, the impact of such thinking could do little

[57] Rothman, *Discovery of the Asylum*, pp. 57–59.

[58] U.S. Bureau of the Census, "Revised Projections of the Population of the United States, by Age and Sex: 1960, 1975," *Current Population Reports*, series P-25, no. 123 (Washington, D.C.: U.S. Government Printing Office, 1955).

to alter the child-raising principles derived from the eighteenth century. Indeed, if families and communities, and not the devil, were at fault, then greater stringency, if anything, was required. Parents were warned of the awful consequences of an absence of discipline and admonished to take stern measures against any loss of family control. Likewise, the attention of community leaders was directed toward the sources of societal corruption — the taverns, the houses of prostitution, the gambling houses, and other sources of vice that abounded in growing and transient cities. So sensitive to these matters were nineteenth-century reformers, says Rothman, that "they stripped away the years from adults and made everyone a child." While societal ills could be eliminated, unyielding measures would be required.[59] But how? If the powers of community cohesion were being stripped away and if the use of corporal and capital punishment were to be reduced, what new mechanisms of social control and socialization could be found?

## The Institution as Panacea

Out of many possible alternatives leading reformers chose institutional confinement — prisons for adults and houses of refuge and orphan asylums for children. Asylums for abandoned children had been used in Europe for some time, but the idea that places of confinement could be used effectively to reform criminals or to substitute for family and community as the best method to raise children was entirely new.[60] It was no accident either that the first houses of refuge and asylums appeared around 1825 in the most populous cities and states. The progressive destruction of colonial social organization led to the belief that child-saving institutions could become society's new superparents.

Houses of refuge were to become family substitutes, not only for the less serious juvenile criminal, but for runaways, dis-

[59] Rothman, *Discovery of the Asylum*, p. 76.
[60] Barnes, *Story of Punishment*, p. 122; Blake McKelvey, *American Prisons* (East Orange, N.J.: Patterson Smith, 1968), pp. 6–11; Rothman, *Discovery of the Asylum*, pp. 208–9.

obedient children, or vagrants. Well-run institutions that incorporated both parental affection and stern discipline could only work to the child's benefit. Orphan asylums would likewise serve the same purposes for abandoned or orphaned children, for the children of women without husbands, or for those children whose parents were unfit. These children should not be penalized merely because they were the offspring of degenerates or paupers.[61] Older colonial practices, of course, continued to operate in many rural areas, but the communities or states which had asylums or refuges were considered to be the progressive ones. The construction of such facilities signified not a disregard for children but an overwhelming preoccupation with them. The concept of *parens patriae* was embodied in obvious physical structures.

By 1850 criticisms of the new superparents had begun to mount; by 1870 there were overwhelming demands for change. Rural-oriented and paternalistic middle-class reformers, however, were on the horns of a dilemma. On the one hand, rather than becoming model superparents, child-saving institutions had become prisonlike warehouses for ever larger numbers of children from the margins of society. Rather than turning out ideal children, they were producing young things who marched, thought, and acted like automatons.[62]

On the other hand, the need for child saving seemed to be greater than ever. By the early 1850s immigrant children constituted almost three-quarters of the New York Refuge, over half of the Cincinnati Refuge, and two-thirds of the Philadelphia Refuge.[63] The parents of these children were often penniless when they arrived in the United States and ended up crowding into the ghettos of eastern cities and swelling the ranks of the unemployed. All the things that reformers feared most were coming to pass. Furthermore, their Janus-like reactions to children and their old fears about lax families and corrupt communities could only have been exacerbated by the development of

[61] Rothman, *Discovery of the Asylum*, p. 207.
[62] Ibid., pp. 258–60; Bremner et al., *Children and Youth*, 1:696–97.
[63] Rothman, *Discovery of the Asylum*, pp. 261–62.

new social theories and scientific study. In the last half of the nineteenth century, Americans were subjected to the thinking of social Darwinists and to the results of biological studies like those of Cesare Lombroso.[64] If they were correct, there was need to worry about the impact of physical depravity, as well as bad environment on the young. These new emphases upon processes of natural selection and biological depravity could only have helped native-born Americans to take the new and strange customs of immigrant groups as evidence of inherent inferiority.

Such ideas certainly appeared in the thinking of leading reformers. Enoch Wines, the most prominent reformer of the 1870s, described the criminal as being the consequence of three great "hindrances": "depravity," "physical degeneracy," and "bad environment."[65] Peter Caldwell, a reformatory superintendent, said that a typical delinquent is "cradled in infamy, imbibing with its earliest natural nourishment the germs of depraved appetite, and reared in the midst of people whose lives are an atrocious crime against natural and divine law and the rights of society." And the Illinois Board of Public Charities warned that "every child allowed to grow up in ignorance and vice, and so to become a pauper or a criminal, is liable to become the progenitor of criminals." Poverty, and now perhaps depravity, had become the inevitable precursor of the worst nightmare of all, the delinquent child.[66]

It was likely for reasons such as these that, despite the initial failure of the institution as a superparent, a new generation of reformers after the Civil War merely reaffirmed its utility. The task of saving children, if anything, had taken on more monumental proportions. Hence, reformers reasoned that the fault with surrogate places of child raising lay in poor execution, not in concept; the methods, not the goals, had been bad. Furthermore, the literature of the period reveals the persistent ambiv-

[64] Richard Hofstadter, *Social Darwinism in American Thought*, rev. ed. (New York: Braziller, 1959); George B. Vold, *Theoretical Criminology* (New York: Oxford University Press, 1958), pp. 50–51.

[65] Charles R. Henderson, ed., *Prison Reform and Criminal Law* (New York: Sage Foundation, 1910), pp. 12, 19.

[66] Platt, *The Child Savers*, pp. 52, 130.

alence of people toward potential or actual offenders, young or old. On one hand, the Cincinnati Prison Congress of 1870 stressed the importance of reward rather than punishment, of cultivating self-respect rather than self-denigration. Yet when these principles were translated into action by Z. R. Brockway at the country's model reformatory, the stress was upon a "monarchical" type of control marked by a stringent regulation of the young person's life.[67]

At any rate, some new names for places of confinement were found—"reformatories" for young criminals and "industrial schools" for children who need "to be kept safe for a year or two." Guidelines stressed the importance of locating both institutions in the country; reaffirmed the idea that they should emulate the character of a well-disciplined family and community; and, for the law violator, added the indeterminate sentence, a "marking" system, and parole supervision.[68] The institution was dressed up in a new ideology and sent out again to rescue children. Reformers were prepared to help children no matter how long it took. There were a few dissenters, of course, and most southern states did not bother with special institutions for juveniles.[69] Otherwise, the new reformatory movement swept the country. By 1900, however, it had come full circle, just like the refuge movement before it. It was not a panacea.

## Invention of the Juvenile Court

From our privileged vantage point, it does not seem surprising that places of confinement should fail as superparents. Even if reformatories had been built on every street corner, it is unlikely that they could have done much to stabilize the effects of

---

[67] Henderson, *Prison Reform*, pp. 39–63; Z. R. Brockway, "The American Reformatory Prison System," in Henderson, *Prison Reform*, pp. 88–107.

[68] *Preventive Treatment of Neglected Children*, ed. Hart, p. 72; Henderson, *Prison Reform*, pp. 39–63; Brockway, "American Reformatory System"; Platt, *The Child Savers*, p. 54.

[69] Bremner et al., *Children and Youth*, 1:672; Platt, *The Child Savers*, pp. 61–62.

immigration, urban growth, ideological change, industrialization, and social mobility, or to have served as a parent surrogate capable of producing the same kind of person as a nuclear family located in a rural community. The means were totally inappropriate for the goals. Indeed, it was a whole constellation of educational, economic, legal, and social problems which, in addition to the failure of institutions, led to the eventual creation of the juvenile court. By the end of the nineteenth century, that creation seems to have been a part of a larger effort to invest the problems of childhood with an even greater rank and to give them an even more dramatic place in the whole of society.

When the juvenile court was actually created, it strengthened the traditional concept of *parens patriae*, gave legal sanction to the stratification of society by age, and, for the first time, located responsibility for official action in a unique legal body for children. Much broader in concept than the reformatory, it was to become an even more powerful superparent. The law was to be "liberally construed to the end . . . that the care, custody, and discipline of a child shall approximate . . . that which should be given by its parents." [70] Because the court was empowered to take a child from an unfit home, it need not wait until he was in jails, bridewells, and reformatories after he has become criminal in habits and tastes, but [can] seize upon the first indications of the propensity as they may be evinced in his conditions of neglect or delinquency.[71]

## The Child-saving Rules

The legal rules that were written to insure these child-saving objectives tended to follow the same general blueprint. Consider the South Dakota statute, which was not revised until 1968. It defined a delinquent as

any child who, while under the age of 18 years violates any law of this state or any ordinance of any city or town of this state; who is

[70] Reviewed Statutes of Illinois, 1899, Sec. 21.
[71] Report of the Chicago Bar Association Committee, October 28, 1899. Platt, *The Child Savers*, pp. 138–39.

incorrigible, or intractable by parents, guardian or custodian; who knowingly associates with thieves, vicious, or immoral persons; who, without cause and without the consent of its parents, guardian, or custodian, absents itself from its home or place of abode; who is growing up in idleness or crime; who fails to attend school regularly without proper reason therefor, if of compulsory school age; who repeatedly plays truant from school; who does not regularly attend school and is not otherwise engaged in any regular occupation or employment but loiters and idles away its time; who knowingly frequents or visits any policy shop or place where any gaming device is operated; who patronizes, visits or frequents any saloon or dram shop where intoxicating liquors are sold; who patronizes or visits any public poolroom where the game of billiards or pool is being carried on for pay or hire; who frequents or patronizes any wineroom or dance hall run in connection with or adjacent to any house of ill-fame or saloon; who visits, frequents, or patronizes, with one of the opposite sex, any restaurant or other place where liquors may be purchased at night after the hours of nine o'clock; who is found along with one of the opposite sex in a private apartment or room of any restaurant, lodging house, hotel or other place at nighttime or who goes to any secluded place or is found alone in such place, with one of the opposite sex, at nighttime with the evident purpose of concealing their acts; who wanders about the streets in the nighttime without being on any lawful business or lawful occupation, or habitually wanders about any railroad yards or tracks, or jumps or attempts to jump onto any moving train, or enters any car or engine without lawful authority; who writes or uses vile, obscene, vulgar, or indecent language, or smokes cigarettes or uses tobacco in any form; who drinks intoxicating liquors on any street, in any public place, or about any school house, or at any place other than its own home; or who is guilty of indecent, immoral or lascivious conduct.[72]

Clearly, such laws were intended not merely to prohibit criminal conduct among children. Only one or two lines in the South Dakota law even allude to it: a child should not violate "any law of this state or any ordinance of any city or town of this state." Otherwise, the long list of prohibitions is simply the

[72] Ted Rubin, "Transferring Responsibility for Juvenile Noncriminal Misconduct from Juvenile Courts to Nonauthoritarian Community Agencies" (Phoenix: Arizona Conference on Delinquency Intervention, 1974), Mimeo, pp. 1–2.

obverse of what the ideal child was expected to be, as expressed in the child-raising manuals of the eighteenth century, namely, that he or she should be submissive to authority, obedient, hard working, a good student, sober, chaste, circumspect in habit, language, and associates and should avoid even the appearance of evil. The child who remained faithfully quarantined within these rules was playing the game of childhood appropriately while the one who violated them was delinquent.

In his valuable historical analyses, Platt along with other radical criminologists prefers to interpret the child-saving objectives of the juvenile court in Marxian terms. "The child savers were concerned not with championing the rights of the poor against exploitation by the ruling class but rather integrating the poor into the established social order and protecting 'respectable' citizens from the 'dangerous classes.' " [73] The juvenile court, therefore, would simultaneously protect capitalist rulers and insure the availability of an adequate labor supply by disciplining unruly lower-class youth and seeing that they were properly trained for industrial work.

There is much in late nineteenth-century history to support such a view. Before the Civil War several states passed laws requiring that children attend school, that those under twelve be prohibited from employment, and that the workday of a child over twelve be limited to ten hours. Such laws, however, proved unworkable. Employers ignored them; many children worked rather than attending school; and parents, particularly in hardpressed immigrant groups, joined in circumventing the law. Thus, as the country industrialized, child employment went up, not down. According to the census of 1870, one out of every eight children was employed (to say nothing of children who worked for parents), but by 1900 the figure had risen to one out of six. Many child laborers, particularly in southern mills, were between the ages of ten and thirteen.[74] It was the poorer classes who found the employment of children, to the exclusion of school, an economic necessity. And just as poorer children were the ones

[73] Platt, *History of Child Saving*, p. ix.
[74] Bremner et al., *Children and Youth*, 1:559.

most likely to be found in child-saving institutions, so they were the ones most commonly found in sweat shops.

Such evidence notwithstanding, a Marxist interpretation probably does not do justice to the events of history. If there is anything to the notion that American behavior toward children was a reflection of cultural changes that had been going on in Western civilization for centuries, then some heed has to be paid to the total context of those changes, not just to the economic and political. Consider the example just cited.

For centuries children of all classes had been expected to work, and their labor was viewed both as socially productive and personally beneficial. Given the vestiges of the long-standing practice of apprenticing children to others and the undeniable stress that American colonists had placed upon the virtue of hard work, the fact that children were employed should not be surprising. Nonetheless, values favoring child labor were running into increasing opposition by those who took a developmental view of childhood and who emphasized the importance of education.

Hence, the employment of children generated efforts at reform led by social workers, lawyers, women's groups, and even some industrialists. Like the moralist reformers of the sixteenth and seventeenth centuries, they used such terms as "cannibalism," "child slavery," and "slaughter of the innocents" to describe the treatment of working children. Nor should it be forgotten that in middle-class American homes children were not exactly indulged.[75] Perhaps it was no coincidence that by 1899, the year the juvenile court was invented, twenty-eight states had passed more stringent laws to control child labor. Again, enforcement lagged behind concept, but there is no gainsaying the fact that the educational value gradually gained ascendancy.


## Conclusions


The key question is whether we are to view the nineteenth-century treatment of children through late twentieth-century

[75] Ibid., 2:601–4; Robertson, "Home as a Nest."

spectacles or through the spectacles provided by earlier history. Though we now find ourselves intellectually at odds with, if not morally repulsed by, the beneficent presumptuousness of nine-teenth-century child savers, we must also ask whether that presumptuousness was somehow worse than the practices of in-fanticide, abandonment, sexual exploitation, and indifference to children in the Middle Ages. As recently as a century or two ago American colonists were inclined to blame the innate de-pravity of the child for sins and to punish him severely. Later, reformers tended to externalize blame and to seek "treatment" rather than punishment. Indeed, given the whole history of punishment, one of the most significant elements of the first juvenile court act may be its justification of a special children's court on the grounds that its principal purpose was child care, not retribution. Such changes in perspective were considerable.

# The Progressive Legacy: Development of American Attitudes toward Juvenile Delinquency

David J. Rothman

ONE vital function that a historian concerned with social policy performs is to remind his contemporaries that their particular concerns are not especially novel. When the media proclaim the breakdown of the family, the historian in no time at all can uncover numerous quotes beginning in the seventeenth century and continuing through the 1930s that announce the same demise. Puritan clergymen in the 1670s were convinced that the authority of the family was crumbling. Social observers in the Jacksonian period lamented the decline in parental power; critics in the 1920s were convinced that the family could never survive in a period when women were smoking in public and doing the Charleston. And this reminder is important, for it helps to clear away the smokescreen and focus attention on the continuities as well as discontinuities in our social history.

But there is a second, and no less important task for the historian, and that is to highlight just what is novel about our own circumstances. And it is this role that I would like to pursue in this essay. For as a historian familiar with earlier American attitudes and policies toward juvenile delinquency, I am convinced that this issue has never before sparked as much confusion and uncertainty as it does today. Our predecessors were remarkably confident that they understood both the causes of delinquency and its cure. We, for our part, can no longer accept their premises or programs, but we share little agreement on what ought to be substituted. Indeed, to make matters worse, this ambivalence characterizes all social policy toward deviancy and dependency. There is just as little consensus on what should define mental illness and poverty and adult criminality and on what should characterize the state's response. We may well envy earlier Americans their spirit of optimism and boldness, but we are, for better or for worse, far more skeptical and cautious about our abilities to comprehend or to solve these problems.

The inherited approaches and procedures that we now find inadequate date from the first two decades of this century, from the Progressive era. Between 1900 and 1920 there emerged an interpretation of the etiology of delinquency and novel procedures to combat it that would dominate the field for the next fifty years. It was the Progressives who offered an environmental and a psychological interpretation of the causes of delinquency that with minor changes and shifts in emphases would characterize social thinking for the next several decades. Even more important, it was the Progressives who dramatically expanded the discretionary authority of the state. These well-meaning reformers insisted on breaking away from ostensibly formal, rigid, and unbending procedures in treating the delinquent, and their innovations would persist down until yesterday. Progressives were certain that their programs would satisfy everyone. No trade-offs were necessary, no judgments on balancing rights important. Rather, the best interests of the child coincided with the best interests of the state; what was good for the individual offender was good for the community. Not until the late 1960s did this Progressive synthesis come under attack. Thus if we are to understand what is unique about our own dilemmas and positions, we must first understand the nature of this Progressive tradition.

At the core of the Progressives' program for the delinquent was the juvenile court. It represented to them a new and powerful combination of benevolence and efficiency, of individual uplift and social good. The court, as reformers enthusiastically promoted it, was to represent a wholly new way to treat juvenile delinquency and dependency. Heretofore, they claimed, the state had been forced to follow one of two equally pernicious routes, to choose between evils. It could intervene against the

young offender with the full rigor of the adult criminal law:
detain him in a jail, prosecute and try him with all the strictness
appropriate to criminal procedure, and sentence him to a prisonlike institution. In short, it could adopt a tactic that almost certainly would transform a juvenile delinquent into an adult
criminal. Or, shying away from so disastrous an intervention, the
state could refrain from acting, keep its hands off, turn the delinquent loose again, and in so doing know that it had encouraged
him to resume his criminal behavior. Now, with the invention of
the juvenile court, for the first time the state could intervene in
constructive fashion. Reformers believed that they had created a
middle course between the poles of harshness and neglect.[1]

This middle course was to alter every aspect of the state's
action. The delinquent, upon being apprehended, would go to a
juvenile detention center, not a jail; the court hearing would be
an informal investigation focusing on the needs of the child, not
on his guilt or innocence. The disposition of the child looked to
his welfare, not his punishment. Judges, rather than simply dismiss a case or send the offender to a reformatory, could now
substitute probation, keeping the child in his family and in his
community under court supervision; or, in exceptional circumstances, the court could send the youngster to a training school,
a more controlling environment than the home but a less punitive
place than the reformatory. Convinced that these procedures
were all in the best interests of the child as well as the society,
reformers did not hesitate to endow the state with the necessary
discretion to pursue these goals. As one advocate, Bernard Flex-
ner, declared, the great discovery of the juvenile court was that
"individual welfare coincided with the well-being of the state.

---

[1] For general surveys of the juvenile court, see Herbert Lou, *Juvenile
Courts in the United States* (Chapel Hill, 1927); Anthony Platt, *The Child
Savers* (Chicago, 1969); Robert Mennel, *Thorns and Thistles: Juvenile
Delinquents in the United States* (Hanover, N.H., 1973); Sanford J. Fox,
"Juvenile Justice Reform: An Historical Perspective," *Stanford Law Review*
22 (1970):1187–1239. On nineteenth-century practices, David Rothman,
*The Discovery of the Asylum* (Boston, 1971). For a contemporary survey
of court practices, see Evelina Belden, *Courts in the United States Hearing
Children's Cases*, U.S. Children's Bureau, no. 65 (Washington, D.C., 1920).

Humanitarian and social considerations thus recommended one and the same procedure. . . . Sympathy, justice and even the self-interest of society were all factors in bringing about the changed attitude."[2] The juvenile court testified to a harmony of interests among all sectors of the society, the state's ability to solve problems without sacrifice.

Reformers believed this program to be so humane and so useful that they could not anticipate or understand sources of opposition. "Only ignorance of what it really is could make anyone oppose the juvenile court," one proponent insisted. What well-meaning citizen or organization would want to find flaws in so noble an enterprise? And the very speed with which states rushed to enact such legislation confirmed this outlook. The first formally constituted juvenile court opened in Chicago in 1899. Within five years, ten states had implemented similar procedures, and by 1920 every state except three provided for a juvenile court system. As one official of the New York juvenile court aptly concluded: "Considering the slowness which changes in judicial procedure are brought about, the rapid extension of the children's court is extraordinary and bears witness to its social need and constructive worth."[3]

To appreciate both the origins and the appeal of the juvenile court, it is appropriate to look first at the ideological under-pinnings of the movement, specifically, at the promise of benevolence that pervaded it. As we shall see soon enough, the program made friends for the best of reasons and for the worst of reasons. It satisfied the most humanitarian of impulses and the most crudely self-interested considerations. Nevertheless, the best beginning point for understanding the court's rise and rapid success is with its optimistic and doing-good quality. These impulses were central to the court's creation. Further, the rhetoric of benevolence, more than any other single element, legitimated the movement, giving it public standing as a reform deserving enactment.

The groups that campaigned most diligently and enthusias-

---

[2] *Survey* 22 (1910):607.
[3] *Juvenile Court Record* (*JCR*), Feb. 1903, p. 5.

tically on behalf of the juvenile court carried unchallenged credentials as philanthropists. None were more active than the club women. Whether organized in congresses of mothers or in federations of clubs, it was the women who most fervently presented the mission of the court as uplift and rescue. Chicago's first juvenile court judge, Richard Tuthill, understood their goals and their political role accurately: "The women's clubs are the parents of all children. They have taught the state how to be a parent. . . . The women got the juvenile law passed." And it was women's clubs who carried the court idea to other states. In Ohio, for example, the Mothers' Congress was so active that one supporter pleaded with his friends "that the men would not leave all the work of securing passage of the bill to the women." [4]

Other prestigious organizations and leaders testified to the essential benevolence of the court. The first founders of schools of social work, like Henry Thurston, and their counterparts in the settlement house movement, like Jane Addams and Julia Lathrop, gave the measure their stamp of approval. Moreover, those who first administered the new system were among its most articulate advocates. It is difficult to exaggerate the significance of the founding of the juvenile court in Chicago to the movement as a whole precisely because its judge, Richard Tuthill, and its chief administrator, T. D. Hurley, were indefatigable in popularizing the court ideals. Hurley, in fact, from 1900 to 1910, published a monthly, the *Juvenile Court Record*, which not only reported every step in the progress of the movement but issued countless editorials and columns promoting it as well. And Tuthill and Hurley were not the exceptions. Denver's juvenile court judge, Ben Lindsey, was a one-man traveling road show; and if most of his speeches were variations on the theme of the brilliance of Lindsey as a savior of children, time did remain to praise the idea of the court as well. Further, by 1910 the court also received the support of psychologists and psychiatrists, with Chicago's Dr. William Healy probably the most active among them. In sum, not only the rhetoric of the movement but the

[4] Ibid., Jan. 1903, p. 7; Summer issue, 1903, p. 14; All on East, *A History of Community Interest in a Juvenile Court* (1943), pp. 9–17.

character of its advocates made the court seem a clear victory for progress and humanity.

The starting premise of the reform that gave it both energy and irresistible public appeal was its self-definition as a *child-saving* mission, a rescue operation for the *very young*. In juvenile courts "children were treated as children." Delinquents were of "tender years," or "little ones" whom the court should take "in hand as you would take your own children in hand who had done something wrong." [5] Indeed, the first laudatory accounts of juvenile court proceedings were filled with accounts of dissolving children into tears and sobs.

But there was nothing self-evident about such descriptions. In fact, the overwhelming majority of cases of delinquency, whether coming before the old police courts or the new juvenile courts, involved, in our terms, teenagers; in their terms, adolescents or young adults. The fourteen-, fifteen-, sixteen-year-olds typically ran afoul of the law, not children per se. Such statistical age distributions did not distract reformers, and not because they were naive or simplistic in their ability to characterize stages of youth. By the opening of the twentieth century, they knew well to differentiate between infancy, childhood, adolescence, and young adulthood. But reformers quite deliberately disregarded such classifications, preferring, for their own good reasons, to extend the period of childhood right up to the onset of adulthood, to present the sixteen-year-old as a seven-year-old. In this way they could give full play to the powerful notions of sentimentality that many of them shared about the young. At the same time this perspective made their promise of effective intervention appear both all the more realistic and all the more appropriate.

Undoubtedly the sentimental rhetoric did have strategic value to reformers. How better persuade a legislature of the desirability of their program than by presenting the objects of benevolence as little ones, not tough and dangerous young adults? But more than political opportunism was at work here. The language and

[5] *JCR*, June 1901, p. 7; no. 8, 1901, p. 18, summer issue, 1903, p. 7; Mar. 1904, p. 4.

impulse also testified to the critical influence of the women's clubs and congresses of mothers. Having been taught by a pervasive social ethos to make themselves into the special guardians of children, the women were determined to transform all child-related social institutions into their own image. The sixteen-year-old belonged to them, offender or not.

Second, the aggressiveness and self-confidence with which reformers moved in the area of delinquency reflected a consistently environmental interpretation of the roots of deviancy, a shared sense of its origins as external to the child. Surroundings and circumstances, not innate characteristics, bred delinquents. "Their faults," insisted Richard Tuthill, "are due not to hereditary taint but to bad environment. . . . Children are creatures of habit. Bad habits, like weeds, will grow in any soil," that is, unless proper care is taken. "The trouble with the delinquent is that he has had no such care." [6]

Seemingly there was nothing novel about an environmental interpretation of delinquency. Jacksonian reformers, in the 1830s and 1840s, had shared such a view. But Progressives gave an entirely different cast to the argument. The Jacksonians had offered a far more general and sweeping analysis, locating the roots of delinquency in the very structure and organization of their society, in its fluidity and mobility, its lack of stability and cohesion. For them, delinquency testified to the failings of the system, and their analysis, quite logically, inspired a movement to create alternatives to the community, institutions which would exemplify the virtues of a well-ordered setting.[7] The Progressives, however, traced delinquency to much more specific and limited causes. The problem was endemic only to one particular segment of the society, the slum. The juvenile offender was not prototypical of the citizenry, but of only part of it, the immigrant population.

The classic statement of this view came from Sophonisba Breckinridge and Edith Abbott in *The Delinquent Child and the Home*. The roots of delinquency, as they explored them, related

[6] *Report* of the Illinois Board of Public Charities, 1900, p. 338.
[7] Rothman, *Discovery of the Asylum*, ch. 9.

to immigrant life-styles, their tenement houses, and their street life. Breckinridge and Abbott, not without sympathy, explored first how the very process of immigration played a critical role in producing delinquents. Immigrant parents did not know that the law said that children had to be in school; they could not immediately understand that picking up coal from railroad yards was not the same thing as going over a field to glean what harvesters had left behind. Again, not without sympathy, Breckinridge and Abbott described how the conditions of poverty themselves produced delinquency. Desperate need could cause children to steal; the very difficulties of factory work could lead a girl to search for easier ways to earn money. Mothers were all too frequently busy earning a living; and even those who remained at home often could not cope adequately with their children's needs.

The problem went still deeper, however, and here the tone of *The Delinquent Child* grew harsher. Some immigrant parents were guilty not just of "undue frugality" but "avarice." So intent were they on owning a home or satisfying their "land-hunger" that they readily sacrificed the welfare of their children to realize their own economic ambitions. Worse yet, immigrant children often ended up as orphans or homeless. Sometimes the death of the parent was due to industrial accidents; but at other times vices, especially intemperance, brought about a speedy end and left children without care or protection. Finally, and most despicably, when immigrant family life was degraded and vicious, delinquency was the unfortunate result. What else but delinquency, concluded Breckinridge and Abbot, could occur when children were raised in homes "in which they have been accustomed from their earliest infancy to drunkedness [*sic*], immorality, obscene and vulgar language, filthy and degraded conditions of living."[8]

Other Progressive reformers offered this same diagnosis of the roots of delinquency, consistently turning an analysis of the evil effects of a poor environment into a checklist of the inade-

[8] *The Delinquent Child and the Home* (New York, 1912), pp. 15, 105; chs. 5–7; cf. Thomas Travis, *The Young Malefactor* (New York, 1908).

quacies of immigrant ghettos and habits. To all of them, delinquency was symptomatic not of any inherent failings in the organization of American society, but in the ghetto; not in the corruptions of an American life-style, but in the immigrant life-style.

Yet despite the grimness of the descriptions, the Progressives had a marvelous and enviable optimism about their ability to respond effectively to the problem, precisely because it was local and specific and not endemic to the system. The direction that reform should take was evident and indisputable. Broadly put, immigrants had to become Americans, middle-class Americans. They were to abandon not only their ethnic but their class characteristics. They had to learn to respect private property, to send their children to school, to give up whatever vices they brought with them from the old country. They were also to become child centered in their homes. Immigrant mothers were to emulate American mothers, devoting themselves to the particular needs of the individual child, insulating him within the protective shell of the family. To be sure, they could not do this alone. Progressives did not doubt the necessity of their own intervention, the role they would have to play in uplifting the slum environment and educating the immigrant. But confident of the preeminence of their social and economic system, of their own values, reformers brought to this task a missionary's vigor and dedication.

There was another and seemingly quite different approach to the origins of delinquency that gained credence in the Progressive period (and even more popularity in the next several decades), an interpretation that was based upon psychological as opposed to environmental considerations. This explanation looked to the mental state as opposed to the social circumstances of the delinquent; and this interpretation too, for different reasons, defined the juvenile court as the proper antidote to delinquency.

The outstanding exponent of this new view was William Healy, a doctor who began his psychiatric training in Chicago, went on to direct the Psychopathic Institute of the Chicago juvenile court, and eventually headed up the Judge Baker Child Guidance Clinic in Boston. In 1915 he published *The Individual Delinquent*, as its subtitle put it, *A Text-Book of Diagnosis and Prognosis for All*

*Concerned in Understanding Offenders.* Healy was certain that a detailed analysis of the individual offender alone, a close examination of the personal dynamics of each case, would allow him to locate the critical determinants of delinquency. He was not an environmentalist, specifically noting that "poverty, and crowded housing, and so on, by themselves alone are not productive of criminalism. It is only when these conditions in turn produce suggestions, and bad habits of mind, and mental imagery of low order, that the trouble in conduct ensues." In sum, "all problems connected with bad environmental conditions should be carefully viewed in the light of the mental life."

It was the roots of the "bad habits of mind" and "mental imagery" that Healy set out to explore. His very terminology, like so much else of the psychological work in this field, suggests how eclectic his approach was. The "habit" orientation he owed to his predecessor G. Stanley Hall. His notion of mental imagery carried a debt to Freud. (Healy was an early reader of Freud, but his grasp of Freudian principles was woefully weak.) But what was most notable about Healy's approach was its very lack of consistency. He was trying to offer psychological explanations without accepting or promulgating psychological theories. He had, in other words, no organizing principles to mind. Instead, he substituted a devotion to the "individual case," to examining each boy or girl as closely as possible in order to discover just what was the causative psychological mechanism at work.

Just how bankrupt intellectually such a method was is evident throughout Healy's book. In his summary of "causative factors" of criminality, Healy presented a list that went from mental abnormalities and defective home conditions, to mental conflict, improper sex experiences, bad companions, and defective interests. The list was strikingly similar to the charts on the origins on insanity that mid-nineteenth-century medical superintendents liked to include in their annual reports. And Healy's efforts to refine the categories did not go very far. He attempted to differentiate between "major causes" and "minor causes," but beyond his own personal judgment he offered no criteria for making such distinctions. His statistics were self-confirming. Since he told the reader that mental abnormalities were more significant factors than the environment, it was only to be expected that the one scored higher than the other on the scale of significance. Healy did finally acknowledge that causation was intricate; still he believed that he could plot the various links in a diagram. The result was lines crossing each other in bewildering fashion.[9]

Despite the intellectual weaknesses of his constructs, Healy quickly won acceptance among reformers. His work too became another prop for the juvenile court. For one, he was no less optimistic than the others that psychological maladies could be successfully treated. The case study approach would not only uncover the causes of delinquency but bring with it immediately effective prescriptions for improvement. The mental set of the juvenile offender was as easily corrected as the noxious environment of the slum or the bad example of parents. For another, Healy's practical suggestions were quite traditional. For all the novelty of his language, his remedies sounded very much like what the old-fashioned, friendly visitor or her more modern counterpart, the trained social worker, was to do. Put another way, Healy's enemies, those who damaged the mental health of the young, were the Progressive's enemies. He gave them new labels, but he intended to combat them with very many of the old weapons.

As a case in point, take his approach to Mary Doe, age eighteen, a shopgirl who repeatedly stole from department stores. Healy traced her problem to the fact that she had "poor educational advantages"; she had been kept away from school so much as to have "a dirth of healthy mental interests." Moreover, Mary Doe suffered from "mental conflicts over sex affairs," the result of "no guiding hand" instructing and protecting her. Bad companionship was another contributory cause, since the other shopgirls at the department store corrupted her. No Progressive would feel uncomfortable with such an analysis—terms like "mental conflict" might be new, but the noxious role of department stores, the corruptions of bad companions, and school truancy were very familiar lines of thought to them. Further, Healy's recommendations for cure fit

[9] *The Individual Delinquent* (Boston, 1915); for quotations in the paragraphs below, see pp. 124–25, 130–32, 165, 284.

well with Progressive programs. Mary Doe would improve, he declared, "if some good woman would give her a helping hand. . . . Change of occupation, friendship with some woman competent to become her confidante, advisor and helper, and development of healthy mental interests we feel sure will do what is needed." Just the task for the friendly visitor, the well-meaning settlement house resident, or the young social worker.

Moreover, Healy's insistence on a case-by-case approach, his unwillingness, or his inability, to offer a general theory made him, just like other reformers, a devout exponent of treating individuals as individuals, or responding to each incident on a one-to-one basis. "Whatever it involves," insisted Healy, "the depths and structure of causation must, for the sake of efficiency, be unearthed in the individual case." Unable to offer general classifications, "we have let facts gradually do this for us, and it develops that, for the ends of diagnosis and prognosis, no classification along systematic lines is adequate." Once again, therefore, the Progressive focus on the uniqueness of the child, on the need to individualize treatment, received support.

In the end Healy's psychological interpretation of delinquency fit well with reformers' ultimate confidence in the soundness of the American social system. The fault for delinquency rested with the individual, not with the community at large. *If mental conflict was at the root of the problem, then social conflict was not.* How confirming Healy's line of interpretation then was, indeed, how seductive. Small wonder that such a doctrine ganied more and more strength over the years, that in the 1920s and even in the 1930s it remained the most attractive and least disturbing interpretation of the origins of delinquency.

Juvenile court proponents shared a third and final assumption: all of them trusted to the beneficence of state action, all of them were eager to expand the scope of state intervention. The fact that criminal behavior was at stake here, that a well-established civil libertarian tradition insisted upon the propriety of limiting the state, or maintaining procedural safeguards, did not give reformers pause. To their minds, the state was the friend and not the enemy of the child, and its powers, appropriately, had to be broadly extended, not scrupulously limited.

In part, this consensus reflected the fact that the object of state action was children. "No child," T. D. Hurley declared, "has liberty in the sense we understand the term." And reformers had little difficulty in citing a history even older than the Bill of Rights in defense of enlarging the state's powers over the child. Citing English courts of chancery and seventeenth-century colonial education statutes, juvenile court advocates presented their program as part of a long and well-established tradition of *parens patriae,* the state as parent to the child.[10]

In part, too, Progressives' impatience with restricting state action reflected their own sense of themselves as doing good. Few proponents of self-styled benevolent programs ever demonstrate much patience for restricting the scope of their actions. In the 1830s medical superintendents, convinced that their well-ordered insane asylums could cure insanity, wanted legislators to place no barriers between the patient and his commitment to the institution. And Progressive child savers were no different. Why should the state be restrained from trying to help the youthful offender by procedures that were appropriate only to the punishment of adults?

Even more important, however, the juvenile court was only one of many instances in which Progressives were eager to enhance state powers. The most distinguishing characteristic of the entire reform movement was precisely its view of *the state not as the enemy of liberty but as the friend of equality.* The state was not the embodiment of special interests but of the commonweal. It was the conservative opposition that was attempting, for example, to restrain the state from regulating child labor. To Progressives, on the contrary, the only way to fulfill the promise of American life was to expand state action. No longer could Americans assume, as Herbert Croly so brilliantly argued, that the sum of individual self-interested actions would promote the common good. The nineteenth-century dream of such a balance evaporated with the rise of cities, factories, and corporations. "No pre-established harmony can then exist between the free and abundant satisfactions of private needs and the accomplishment of a

---

[10] *JCR,* Dec. 1900, pp. 6–7.

morally and socially desirable result." Rather, Croly insisted, "the American problem is a social problem"; the nation now stood in need of an active state, "a more highly socialized democracy." Succinctly put, the major dogma of Progressivism was that only the state could make the individual free. Without the slightest sense of paradox, it contended that only the enlarged authority of government could satisfy the individual needs of the citizenry.[11]

It was just this belief that juvenile court reformers carried with them. In the context of their special concerns, the problem was not how to protect the juvenile offender from the arbitrariness of the state but how to bring the state more effectively to the aid of the juvenile offender. The state was not a behemoth that had to be chained and fettered but a wise, all-knowing, and all-caring parent who alone could settle disputes amicably and justly. Thus a court for the young should not be constrained by procedural niceties but be given free rein to act in the best interests of the child. In Croly's very sense of the term the new court was to be a "social court."

On these premises the juvenile court built its program. As was appropriate to a system that defined the delinquent as a child who was the victim of peculiar environmental or psychological circumstances and had now come under the protective wing of the state, the court took as its first charge the reformation, not the punishment, of the offender. This was a totally novel orientation, insisted proponents, but only half accurately. As is so typical of reform enthusiasts, they minimized the benevolent intentions of their predecessors—those, for example, who had established the first reformatories in the antebellum period—and thereby both celebrated their own special humanitarianism and maximized their own prospects for success. The first juvenile court judges in Chicago, like Richard Tuthill and Julian Mack, imagined that heretofore "the main duty of the legislature was to devise punishments to fit almost every crime on or off the calendar. . . . The fundamental thought in our criminal jurisprudence was not, and in most jurisdictions is not, reformation of the criminal but punishment."

---

[11] Herbert Croly, *The Promise of American Life* (1909; Capricorn ed., 1964), pp. 5, 22–25.

But our goal, as Tuthill phrased it, is "to banish entirely all thought of crime and punishment," to go far beyond a "mere attempt at punishment." [12]

To achieve this noble end, the court had to be concerned not with the specific crime or charge facing the delinquent but with his state of being, his moral character and life-style. Now it was not the actions but the mind of the child that determined the court's response. We intend, Mack proudly announced, to discover "what he is, physically, mentally, morally, and then if he is treading the path that leads to criminality," we will take him in charge, "not so much to punish as to reform, not to degrade but to uplift, not to crush but to develop, to make him not a criminal but a worthy citizen." To Boston's juvenile judge Harvey Baker, "of course the court does not confine its attention to just the particular offense which brought the child to its notice." If a boy came to the court "for some trifle," like failing to wear the badge entitling him to sell newspapers, but it turned out upon investigation that he was a chronic truant, then the court would respond to the larger problem, not simply to the charge at hand. The boy who came in guilty of playing ball in the street but turned out to be a loafer, a gambler, and a petty thief would be treated by the court not for the stated offense but for the vicious habits he was practicing. [13]

Clearly a court that was determined to explore the "state" and not the act of the delinquent was unwilling to be bound by formal rules of procedure. Since the aim of the court was to effect reform and not punishment and since the state could be trusted not to abuse its expanded prerogatives, proponents everywhere moved to relax the style of juvenile court proceedings. While they could not banish lawyers from the courtroom, they certainly did not think their presence appropriate. In a similar spirit, juvenile court judges would not keep to accepted rules of testimony designed for adult proceedings. Not that the codes establishing juvenile courts

[12] *JCR*, Nov. 1900, p. 11; 9th *Annual Report*, New York State Probation Commission, pp. 440–41.

[13] *Survey* 22 (1910):649. See also *Harvey Humphrey Baker, Upbuilder of the Juvenile Court* (Boston, 1920); Homer Folks, "The Probation System," *Proceedings* of the Child Conference for Research and Welfare (New York, 1910), pp. 224–31.

invariably and explicitly gave them the authority to disregard these rules. Rather, as juvenile court judge Orr of Minnesota accurately put it, "the laws of evidence are sometimes forgotten or overlooked." [14] In almost every anecdote that judges or other observers recounted about the workings of the court, a gentle and clever judge persuaded a stubborn or recalcitrant offender to "fess up," to tell the truth. Obviously this was not a violation of the rights against self-incrimination but the first step of the delinquent on his way to rehabilitation.

Trial by jury seemed no less out of place in a juvenile court. The judge who was competent to act as lawyer and district attorney was just as equipped to find the facts as well. Juries were useful when the court wanted to know precisely what the offender had done. But the "facts" in these cases were not traditional facts, not involving the commission of an act, but involving the condition, circumstances, levels of growth, and morality of the child. And these were determinations that a judge and not a jury could make best.

Similarly, the design of the courtroom was to mirror these goals. The judges were to sit alongside the participants in the case, not look down upon them from an elevated and isolated bench. Reform tracts frequently included photographs of the newly established courtrooms, on the assumption that physical intimacy testified to sympathetic treatment. Thus, a photograph of the new Columbus, Ohio, juvenile court depicted a simple chair set upon a low platform and carried this caption: "The conventional bench has given way to a desk or table so arranged as to permit the judge to come into a close personal touch with the children." A photograph of the Boston court revealed a larger desk, with an X inserted alongside it to mark the spot where the child stood. Here "the judge can see him from top to toe and can reassure him if necessary by a friendly hand on the shoulder." [15]

The most vital new service that the juvenile court would provide, indeed, the very heart of its program, was probation. As T. D. Hurley put it, probation represented "the keystone which supports the arch of this law." In the more grandiloquent phrases

[14] *JCR*, May 1906, pp. 21–24.    [15] *Survey* 22 (1910):608, 648.

of Judge Tuthill, it was "the cord upon which all the pearls of the juvenile court are strung. . . . Without it, the juvenile court could not exist." [16] Probation had for these reformers two very distinct aspects: the presentence investigation and the postsentence supervision. The probation officer's initial task was to provide the juvenile court judge with all the information necessary for him to understand the "state" of the child, to enable him to look beyond the offense to his condition. Thus the Illinois legislature charged probation officers "to make a personal inquiry into the facts of the case with the view to assist the court in what ought to be done. To this end it will be necessary to record the history and the circumstances of the child as fully as possible. . . . The court will desire to ascertain the character, disposition and tendencies and school record of the child; also the character of the parents and their capability for governing and supporting the child, together with the character of the home, as to comforts, surroundings, inmates, etc." To satisfy so far-reaching a mandate, the law gave the probation officer full latitude in making his investigation. "This information will be obtained in your own way, from the child, from the parents, neighbors, teachers, clergymen, police officials, and from the records of the poor department, the police department, and the various charitable agencies." [17] Just as no restrictions fettered the judge in his effort to do good, no restrictions should bind the probation officer in his search for information.

Probation fulfilled a second and even more critical function: the postsentence supervision of the delinquent. The judge might well decide to send the juvenile offender back to his family and community, but such a step would be foolhardy since the child would then be reentering the very environment or psychological conditions that were responsible for his troubles in the first place. Probation represented the way out of this dilemma. Probation officers had the tasks, as incredible as they were, of correcting the child's difficulties and at the same time correcting faults in the family and in the community. They were to counsel and guide the child, responding to his specific needs in firm but friendly fashion. Proponents assumed that the very one-to-one quality of this relation-

---

[16] *JCR*, Dec. 1900, p. 4; June 1902, p. 5.          [17] Ibid., Dec. 1900, p. 4.

ship would guarantee its success. More, they magnified the probation officer's potential to effect change within the family. "With the great right arm and force of the law," declared Judge Tuthill, "the probation officer can go into the home and demand to know the cause of the dependency or the delinquency of a child. . . . He becomes practically a member of the family and teaches them lessons of cleanliness and decency, of truth and integrity." [18] The task might not be easily accomplished: "Threats may be necessary in some instances to enforce the learning of the lessons he teaches, but whether by threats or cajolery, by appealing to their fear of the law or by rousing the ambition that lies latent in each human soul, he teaches the lesson and transforms the entire family into individuals which the state need never again hesitate to own as citizens." So, once again, proponents confidently enlarged the scope of the program. The same latitude and discretion that characterized courtroom procedure and presentence investigations belonged to the probation officer in his remedial efforts with the family.

Reformers also expected that the probation officer would simultaneously upgrade community conditions. One of the first of Chicago's probation officers, not by accident a woman, Minnie Low, found nothing implausible in this definition of purpose. "The efforts of the probation officer by no means end with the children placed in her care by the court. She soon becomes a neighborhood factor, being looked upon as a 'general utility man'. . . . She must be prepared to respond to calls; enter into consultations and give advice to children, parents, relatives, principals, teachers, societies, clubs, institutions, and police departments." In effect, Low concluded, probation "stands not only for the solution and treatment of crime but most valuable of all is its preventive force." [19]

For all their faith in probation, reformers were fully prepared to empower the courts to exercise still another option: to incarcerate the juvenile offender. In some cases of delinquency, and estimates of their frequency varied widely, institutionalization was a fully legitimate response, an integral part of a rehabilitative program. Probation was a proper first resort. Progressive reformers

[18] Ibid, June 1902, p. 5.     [19] Ibid., no. 8, 1901, p. 9.

did insist that an institution offered too mechanical a routine to produce very much good. Nevertheless, it still had its uses. It was, in the first instance, an appropriate backup sanction for those who did not take probation seriously. Moreover, as Richmond, Virginia, juvenile court judge James Ricks noted, "if the child's parents are hopelessly weak or morally bad, or if he has no home, he should then be given a chance in a good institution or foster home." Finally, a confirmed delinquent, the hard-core case, did belong in an institution. In Judge Tuthill's terms: "Far better that he should be incarcerated in a setting 'where he can be taught even against his own will the primary duty of obedience to authority,' than to be left alone with his vicious habits and demoralizing associates." [20]

In fact, juvenile court proponents were, at time, determined to expand the numbers and kinds of institutions available for training and correcting the delinquent. This impulse was present from the very start of the movement. No sooner did Richard Tuthill take his seat as Chicago's juvenile judge than he was busily agitating for the construction of an Illinois state school for delinquents. The only existing facility for the care of delinquents, he complained in 1901, was the John Worthy School, and it was, quite simply put, "a prison." Moreover, the Worthy school was so overcrowded that the boys typically remained there for a few months, hardly enough time to allow for much reformation. Tuthill proposed that the state erect an institution in the countryside, one that would be a modern substitute for the traditional rural home. It would teach not only basic classroom skills but give the boys vocational, particularly agricultural, training. "To enact a juvenile court law and not to provide for such an institution," concluded Tuthill, "is as illogical as if the state should . . . provide that insane persons should be sent to a state asylum, but do nothing toward the erection of one." Tuthill quickly had his way. In December 1904 the Illinois State School at Saint Charles opened and the juvenile courts now had a new institution to which its charges might be committed. The institution-building role of the juvenile court proponents was apparent in other cities as well.

[20] Ibid., Dec. 1900, p. 5.

The child savers saw nothing inconsistent, or to put it more positively and appropriately, saw it entirely fitting to make the construction of institutions an integral part of their movement.[21]

Reformers' willingness to incarcerate at least some among the delinquent was but one example of a more general readiness to expand the power of the juvenile court over the family, to elevate the authority of the state over the home. Indeed, to many proponents, the most notable feature of the new law was its clear enactment of this principle. The codes gave the state the unequivocal right to intervene over and against the wishes of the family. And supporters eagerly justified this entitlement. The first case histories that T. D. Hurley reprinted in the *Juvenile Court Record* were designed to legitimate the extended reach of the state. Hurley recounted how he once "stood outside the door of a shanty and watched 'Mother Shevlin' teach a beautiful young boy to steal a handkerchief out of a coat pocket without being detected." (Hurley was a master at propaganda—the story was about "shanty" Irish, and the victim was a "beautiful boy," as though good looks ought to have precluded delinquency.) To be sure, Hurley continued, existing statutes would have permitted court intervention, but under the older system the boy could have been sent to an institution only for a brief time and "the rest of the family of degenerate children, was, perforce, left to pursue its infamously criminal way, because there was no law on the statute books of the state of Illinois whereby they could be brought into court and cared for as they should have been." It was such cases as the Shevlin family, concluded Hurley, that convinced his organization, the Chicago Visitation and Aid Society, as well as the women's clubs and the Chicago Bar Association, to advocate a new law that would "provide a more comprehensive way . . . to bring about desired results than any that had been so far devised."[22]

Hurley's perspective was widely shared. Martha Falconer, a Chicago probation officer, was quick to tell the 1901 meeting of the National Congress of Mothers that "the women who cannot control their boys of eight or nine years of age should not have the care of them." Fully aware that she was addressing middle-

[21] Ibid., Nov. 1901, pp. 15–16.        [22] Ibid., June 1902, p. 6.

class women on the problems of lower-class children, that it was other mothers, less capable and prepared than they, who had to be controlled, Falconer contended: "I want those boys in a reform school; I feel there is no love there in the home, and that his home is no place for that boy." And her audience ought not to be fooled for a moment by the public protests of these parents. "Those who neglect their children most are the ones who weep and wail loudest about them in court. To those women I say, 'You will keep your children off the streets or the city of Chicago will do it for you.' "[23]

Clearly reformers had fashioned a rationale and a program whose goals seemed to offer something to everyone. It is small wonder that their synthesis lasted for most of this century. The juvenile court rhetoric and procedures were at once soft-hearted and tough-minded, sentimental and rigorous, protective of the child and altogether mindful of the safety of the community. One might debate endlessly, and futilely, whether the child savers used the language of benevolence to cloak a repressive innovation, whether "social control" factors were the motivation, rather than humanitarian concerns. The critical point is that reformers saw no conflict here; they did not believe they were in an either/or position. There was nothing hypocritical in their approach, no covert messages that had to be sorted out, no code language that had to be cracked. Openly and confidently they presented a program that seemed so very right and necessary precisely because it did not require trade-offs. The welfare of the child was synonymous with the welfare of society; there was no need to balance gains against losses. The juvenile court, the entire program for understanding and combating delinquency, was in the best interests of everyone.

Thus the rhetoric of sentimentality and helpfulness that might open a speech or pamphlet on behalf of the juvenile court would effortlessly and painlessly give way to a rhetoric of repression and public safety. As the most important organ of the movement, the *Juvenile Court Record* well demonstrated this capacity. Its col-

[23] National Congress of Mothers, *Fourth Annual Convention,* June 1901, p. 187.

umns would ask society to be "patient and forgiving! Whereas, it is often necessary to bring the little ones to court in order that they may be taught to discriminate between right and wrong, in truth we must hold them guiltless. . . . Would we have done better in their places?" But its motto, prominently displayed in every issue, declared: "Every homeless child is a menace to society and the State." [24] In just this way Judge Franklin Hoyt, of the New York juvenile court, opened his anecdotal account of his service with saccharine phrases addressing the "spirit of justice" to the "spirit of youth." "You are bruised and bewildered . . . but you need not fear. . . . Trust in me, for I am here to help you. . . . In me you will find no fair-weather friend, but a guide and protector who will stand by you through storm and stress." And then Hoyt proceeded to fill his pages with stories of how he combated the various "isms" of the young, how he won, with no embarrassment at using the phrase, "recruits for law and order." To Hoyt the wisdom of the juvenile court arrangements were never better demonstrated than when a boy came before him on a petty charge, but upon discussion it turned out that he was nothing other than a Socialist. Then the judge had the chance to teach someone who thought "that our established institutions are but forms of slavery" the Progressive credo: "Kindliness, common sense, and humane justice can exist side-by-side with the enforcement of law and order." Or, as Hoyt told one offender: "You are already a unit of our society and when one unit becomes diseased it is apt to infect other units, and thus endanger our whole social edifice. If you are to remain in the country, I want you to become a healthy, clean-minded American." [25]

The ease with which proponents moved from one kind of message to another, the aplomb with which they shuttled back and forth between the promise to uplift and the threat to coerce, testified to the very Progressive character of their thinking; that is, to their ultimate confidence in the moral and social superiority of the American system. Reform and correction were one and the same thing because both aimed to integrate the deviant into the society,

[24] *JCR*, no. 8, 1901, p. 8; Apr. 1, 1902, p. 9.
[25] Franklin Hoyt, *Quicksand of Youth* (New York, 1921), pp. 3–4, 54, 65.

or, put another way, to bring to him the opportunities for upward mobility and an improved standard of living that the American way promised. There was no conflict between the helping power and the policing power because both sought to adjust the deviant to his environment, an environment that would provide the optimal conditions under which to pursue his own well-being. Since the delinquent was both young and an immigrant, in both senses a newcomer to the scene, he was doubly blind to the American promise, and in that very way a threat to it. Hence the rights and wrongs of the situation were easily drawn up: intemperance, vulgarity, antiquated customs, loose street life, ignorance, all on one side of the ledger; the careful nurture of the child, education, training to lawfulness, obedience, close supervision, all on the other. The juvenile court was the bridge between the two. Through the skills of the probation officer and the discretionary authority of the presiding judge, this new court would at once reform and correct, uplift and protect, the delinquent and the society.

Moreover, the breath-taking speed with which the juvenile court won legislative approval reflected not only the all-encompassing quality of the goals but the character of its means as well, its determination to expand the prerogatives of the state. This aggrandizement of authority attracted an incredibly variegated block of supporters from members of voluntary and philanthropic associations to more public-minded Progressive reformers. Shifting the balance from private rights to state responsibility fit very neatly and conveniently with their own concerns and agendas. To be sure, some among these proponents, especially those from voluntary agencies, would discover to their dismay that the state's intervention in the affairs of the delinquent and his family could also bring state interference in their own affairs. But that recognition only came later. In their early enthusiasm, a host of organizations assumed that the added reach of the court would extend their own influence. *For functional as well as for ideological reasons, the ranks of proponents of the court spread widely through the society.*

Certainly that was the case with the women's clubs. More intent on educating mothers than on delivering services, more eager to spread knowledge of the principles of child care than to supervise other families, the clubs saw in the juvenile court the ideal mechanism for translating their broad aims into practice. The club ladies, in effect, defined the overall needs and style of approach to children. Then the state took over the day-to-day implementation. Those Progressives living in neighborhood settlement houses or staffing the first schools of social work were no less enthusiastic about a program that broadened state responsibility to publicize and to ameliorate the conditions affecting citizens' health and welfare. Just they urged the public sector to provide relief for needy widows, so they wanted it to investigate and to offer care and training to juvenile dependents and delinquents.

Perhaps somewhat more surprisingly, the private child-caring organizations also supported the juvenile court movement. When the state under Progressive prodding had moved to assume responsibility for giving needy widows outdoor relief, the private sector had protested. Charity should be a voluntary activity, not a state activity. But here, unlike the widow pension reform, the private charities found themselves lined up with the more public-minded Progressives. The difference in the two instances lay in the fact that private charity work in the pre-Progressive era did not require any coercive legal authority over the client. It was the poor who came to the agency soliciting help, and the agency could set whatever conditions it wished upon the clients in return for its aid. The charity society held all the cards and the client had to play the game by its rules, or else go without assistance. But the circumstances confronting private child care agencies were very different. These types of organizations often wanted to intervene on behalf of a child, but the parents, vested with full legal authority, could, and did, refuse to accept their services or suggestions. The private agency could take the parent to court; in gross cases of abuse or neglect, the agency might well win custody. But in more complicated moments—when the agency's judgment as to the best interests of the child did not coincide with the parents' but the child was not in imminent danger—then the agency was helpless. It was just this situation that the private agencies looked to the juvenile court to correct. The extension of the state's authority over the child would provide the agency with the ability

to intervene more frequently and effectively. What the private organizations anticipated was a scenario in which they alerted the
court to the child's unfavorable circumstances, and the court then
delegated to them, through its new authority, the right to take
all necessary corrective action.

The part that the Chicago Visitation and Aid Society played
in the passage of the Illinois juvenile court act exemplified this
process at work. No one person was more diligent in promoting
the movement than T. D. Hurley, and Hurley was in charge of
this Catholic child-caring organization. From Hurley's perspective, his society was too weak in authority. "Before the law," he
frankly explained, his agency "could take only such children as
were voluntarily surrendered to them; if the parents would not
surrender their child, no matter how distressing the case, they
could do nothing. To this class belong the children of drunken
fathers and drunken mothers, the lazy and licentious and those
who lived off the beggings and stealings of their children." Hurley
was probably distorting the facts but for obvious reasons preferred
to exaggerate the helplessness of his organization. It was in the
borderline case, the one where the agency found the parent lazy
or too attached to his favorite pub, that the Society could do nothing. But in all events Hurley welcomed the innovation. As he anticipated, when the court found a child "to have no home or that
for some reason it must be taken from its home, the court assigns
it to that society or institution willing to take it, best furnished to
care for that particular child." And parents could not block the
delegation of authority; no less important, they could not later
cancel it. Under traditional law, noted Hurley, even when parents
had initially given the Society control over the child, they frequently changed their minds and tried to get the child back. "As
the law stood before the Juvenile Court Act, a parent might re-
claim his child, notwithstanding he had surrendered it and it had
been adopted in a proceeding in court in strict accordance with
his agreement. . . . It was held that the right of a parent to the
custody could not, by common law, be contracted away." It was
this common law tradition that the juvenile court overrode. Now
the court made the commitment and the parent would be unable
to abrogate it at some future date. "I have always advocated the

idea that it was the duty of the State to strengthen the hands of the different Child-Saving Societies," declared Hurley. "And now . . . it is but natural that I should be a firm believer and advocate in what might be called the 'new movement.' " [26]

Superintendents of institutions for deviant or dependent children, like the heads of private agencies, also initially looked to the juvenile court to define and to substantiate their own authority. A fair amount of confusion had characterized the type of child that any one institution could hold, and superintendents frequently found themselves caught in the middle of sudden reversals of opinions. Could a state reformatory, for example, admit not only those found guilty of delinquency but those who were in need of supervision or suffering from neglect? Some courts said no, others said yes, and still others changed their minds in midstream. Or, in the opposite case, could institutions incorporated for dependent and neglected children take in those guilty of delinquency? Here again confusion reigned and courts reversed themselves regularly. And all observers recognized that in practice these distinctions were minor; the difference between the dependent and the delinquent child frequently depended not so much upon what the child did but on the credentials of the complaining officer. If he was a policeman, the child came up on delinquency; if he represented a child-caring agency, the youngster came up on neglect. The juvenile court was to eliminate these ambiguities. Freed from the technical need to find anyone guilty in a criminal sense, it could dispatch the child, at its discretion and with its full authority, to the kind of institution it believed appropriate.

A fair number of administrators from within the criminal justice system also joined the reform coalition. One state legislator in Missouri, James Blair, who painstakingly organized committee hearings in support of a pending juvenile court bill, was able to bring together, in an incredible array of officials, the president of the board of police commissioners, the chief of police, the chief of detectives, a police sergeant with twenty years' experience, the

[26] *JCR*, Nov. 1900, p. 11; June 1901, pp. 16–17; Fox, "Juvenile Justice," pp. 1222 ff.

police matron, the city jailer, the superintendents of both the house of refuge and the city workhouse, and a criminal court judge. These speakers articulately put forth the basic principles of the movement, particularly drawn to the argument that to mix juvenile with adult offenders was to educate the young to a life in crime. But one senses too in their testimony an underlying assumption that the extended authority of the juvenile court would simplify their jobs and make their tasks more simply accomplished. For functional as well as ideological reasons they too joined the reform ranks.

To police officials the new judicial authority meant that delinquents would be kept off the street for a longer period of time. As the Saint Louis commissioner noted: "Instead of being committed to the House of Refuge for thirty to sixty days, as under present practice, after which he would return to his old environment, educated in crime and . . . just in line to be rearrested over and over again . . . he will at once be committed to an institution where he will be cared for and educated." If incarceration reformed the offender so much the better; at least he would be out of circulation, and away from the responsibility of the police, for a few years instead of a few weeks. So too, as one would expect, the criminal court judge welcomed the added discretion to treat delinquents. Under the old system, he complained, "I have no power to deal with them. . . . To punish them as criminals is worse than useless." Now, however, he had new options from the use of probation to commitment to a state training school. And the various workhouse keepers seemed no less eager to be rid of nursemaid responsibilities. Even if their roster of inmates went down, they would be spared the very burdensome duty of caring for the young.[27]

At least one district attorney quite frankly supported the juvenile court because it would substantially reduce the number of cases his staff would have to deal with. At a time when court dockets were becoming unusually crowded, this was no minor con-

[27] *JCR*, summer 1903, pp. 9–14; Oct.-Nov. 1904, p. 5; *Survey* 22 (1910): 634–35, cf. Thomas Eliot, *The Juvenile Court and the Community* (New York, 1911), pp. 33–40.

sideration. As this Illinois D.A. calculated, his grand juries were relieved of some two hundred cases a year because of the enlarged jurisdiction of the juvenile court. And further, grand juries had typically thrown out three-quarters of the cases involving young offenders. The juvenile court promised, then, not only to help clear up the D.A.'s own calendar but to do it without sacrifice to the state's supervisory capacity, indeed, to do it while expanding the state's supervisory capacity.[28]

The opposition to the juvenile court was weak and divided. Some police departments objected to it, afraid that probation would return too many offenders to the street. Some of the lower level municipal judges of the police courts, those who had traditionally exercised jurisdiction over the petty crimes involved in the bulk of delinquency cases, were also prone to protest a transfer of their authority to a new court. But neither of these groups could mount effective opposition. All they could claim was that they had been doing a good job, and that was no answer to the grandiose promises that reformers issued.

More important, a handful of lawyers did attack the core principles and assumptions of the juvenile court. For civil libertarian reasons they criticized the vast discretionary authority of the judges. Roscoe Pound in 1913 brilliantly suggested the line of argument. "The powers of the court of star chamber," wrote this ranking legal scholar of the criminal justice system, "were a bagatelle compared with those American juvenile courts. . . . If those courts chose to act arbitrarily and oppressively they could cause a revolution quite as easily as did the former." [29] The next year Edward Lindsey, a Pennsylvania lawyer writing in the prestigious *Annals* of the American Academy of Political and Social Science, presented a cogent explication of this view. The juvenile courts exhibited, Lindsey argued, "the entire disregard, as far as the statutes themselves go, of established legal principles and the absence from them of any limitation on the arbitrary powers of the court, which always involves dangerous possibilities." Lindsey had little trouble in accounting for this phenomenon. The statutes

[28] *JCR*, Feb. 1901, p. 13.
[29] Roscoe Pound, "The Administration of Justice in the Modern City," *Harvard Law Review* 24 (1913):302–28.

"are, of course, the expression of certain theories for social betterment, rather than of social experience or practice." In the name
of social betterment, the courts had abandoned their traditional
doctrinal allegiance to "the right of the minor to his liberty as
against the state except after conviction of crime." [30]

Lindsey described the justifications for abandoning this principle as nothing more than "evasions." Label it what you will, the
intervention of the state remained pernicious. "In the case of commitment to an institution there is often a very basic deprivation of
liberty nor is that fact changed by refusing to call it punishment
or because the good of the child is stated to be the object." As far
as he could see, the result of this intervention "is that the child
is handed over to some organization or institution . . . which in
some cases does its work well and in others badly." Moreover, on
constitutional principles, "everything should not rest with the
personality of the judge. While with the right man in the right
place the very indefiniteness of his powers may be productive of
immediate good, in the long-run it will be just as unsafe as experience proved it to be in the criminal law." Lindsey's conclusion
was simple and to the point: "All criminal questions should be
dealt with by a criminal court. Every child accused of crime
should be tried and subject to neither punishment nor restraint
of liberty unless convicted."

These conceptual objections were also at the root of legal challenges to the constitutionality of the juvenile court. Enough parents were ready to contest court commitments of their children to
institutions to mount test cases in more than a dozen states. Lawyers for these defendants took issue, as one would expect, with
the vast discretion that statutes allowed the juvenile courts; specifically, they challenged the court's right to deprive a child of
liberty without due process, to ignore the right to a trial by jury,
to deny the right to appeal, to impose unequal penalties, and to
disregard provisions for the equal protection of the law. But such
efforts almost without exception were to no avail. In practically

[30] Edward Lindsey, "The Juvenile Court Movement from a Lawyer's Perspective," *Annals* of the American Academy of Political and Social Science
52 (1914):33–40.

every jurisdiction, appellate courts liberally interpreted constitutional provisions so as to uphold juvenile court procedures.

Defendants' briefs typically cited and relied upon the Illinois court decision of 1870, the *People* v. *Turner*.[31] This case, brought when public disillusionment with institutional conditions first emerged, declared unconstitutional Illinois's 1867 statute that allowed a police court judge or a justice of the peace to commit to the Chicago reform school "any boy or girl, within the ages of six or sixteen years, who he has reason to believe is a vagrant, or is destitute of proper parental care, or is growing up in mendicacy, ignorance, idleness or vice." The judge under this provision was allowed to have such a boy or girl brought before him, and "if upon examination such judge shall be of opinion that said boy or girl is a proper subject for commitment to the reform school, and that his or her moral welfare, and the good of society require that he or she should be sent to said school for employment, instruction and reformation, he shall decide . . . and such child shall thereupon be committed." In other words, the statute allowed children who had not been found guilty of a crime, and who had been examined and sentenced without a jury trial, with only "slight evidence required," and under an "informal mode of procedure" to be confined to an institution against their will and their parents' will.

The Turner decision struck down the law, the court unequivocally elevating the rights of minors and their parents over the power of the state. It found such terms as *idleness* and *vice* excessively broad and general. "Vice is a very comprehensive term," wrote the court. "Acts wholly innocent in the estimation of many good men would according to the code of ethics of others show fearful depravity. What is the standard to be? . . . What degree of virtue will save from the threatened imprisonment?" The fact that the object of state action was children did not obviate the need for stricter standards. "The disability of minors does not make slaves or criminals of them. They are entitled to legal rights, and are under legal liabilities." And the fact that the state was trying to act in their best interests did not justify a sentence to a

[31] 55 Ill. 280 (1870).

reformatory. Foreshadowing the modern doctrine of "least restrictive alternative," the court insisted that the state devise alternatives to incarceration. "Other means of a milder character; other
influences of a more kindly nature; other laws less in restraint of
liberty, would better accomplish the reformation of the depraved,
and infringe less upon inalienable rights." In sum, the court concluded, "the principle of the absorption of the child in and its
complete subjection to the despotism of, the State, is wholly in-
admissable in the modern civilized world."

But the courts in the Progressive period overrode the Turner
precedent, taking the reform perceptions and rhetoric at face
value. Justifying the powers of the court by the ends of rescue
and rehabilitation, they upheld the legislatures' grant of vast discretionary authority. Their arguments frequently were tautologi-
cal. Of course if the child were being punished, he had a right to
trial by jury; of course if this was a criminal proceeding, due process protections were vital. The very fact, however, that the proceedings were without a jury and without procedural protections
was evidence that this was not a criminal action but instead an
effort to help, not to injure the child. The most noted and frequently cited decision upholding the juvenile court, *Commonwealth of Pennsylvania* v. *Fisher*, argued in just this manner. The
decision assumed as fact what the defendants were contesting.
The defendants insisted that such juvenile proceedings were in
fact criminal proceedings, and therefore all due process protections were necessary. The court answered that the very absence
of due process protections demonstrated that these were not criminal proceedings and were, therefore, constitutional.

Such lapses of logic reflect not on the inadequate reasoning
powers of the judiciary but, rather, on how deeply and thoroughly the courts accepted the reform rhetoric. The promise had
become the reality. And once this judgment was made, it was a
simple matter to overrule all constitutional objections. The laws
created different punishments for different children? Answered
*Commonwealth* v. *Fisher:* This claim "overlooks the fact . . .
that it is not for the punishment of offenders, but for the salvation
of children," that the court operates; the state was concerned not

with the welfare of a special class of children "but all children under a certain age." The appellant is denied a trial by jury? "Here
again is the fallacy that he was tried by the Court for any offense."
The juvenile court "denies the child not the right of a trial by jury,
for the simple reason that, by the act, it is not to be a trial for anything"; the state was not acting to establish the child's guilt but
to effect "its salvation." To incarcerate the young was to deprive
them of liberty? No, the law does not contemplate "restraint upon
the natural liberty of children"; the state was merely assuming
the privileges that parents enjoy, simply exercising "the whole-
some restraint which a parent exercises over his child. . . . No
constitutional right is violated but one of the most important du-
ties which organized society owes to its helpless members is performed." [32]

Court after court echoed these findings. The Idaho appellate
judges dismissed the claims that juvenile courts abrogated rights
to trial by jury, speedy and public hearing, defense by counsel,
and bail, because "this statute is clearly not a criminal or penal
statute in its nature. . . . Its object is to render a benefit upon
the child and the community in the way of surrounding the child
with better and more elevating influences." The Utah appeals
court would not entertain challenges on procedural inadequacies
of the juvenile court, insisting that "it is the welfare of the child
that moves the state to act, and not to inflict punishment or to
mete out retributive justice." One Illinois judge, who did not find
Turner a binding precedent, opened his opinion with the observation that "there are great numbers of the best men and women of
this state who are working along the lines for the advancement
and interest of the children. I know there is a present sentiment
or disposition to treat children with more consideration than they
have been treated in the past . . . which will prevent them from
becoming charges upon the community in the way of pauperism,
degeneracy and crime." By the time the Kentucky appeals court
passed on the issue in 1911 it could note that supreme courts in
thirteen other states had already upheld the constitutionality of

[32] 213 Pa., 48 (1905).

the juvenile court, all "upon the theory that the proceedings are not criminal, but merely the services of the government called into play for the purpose of protecting, training and correcting a class of children who . . . are unable or unwilling to care for themselves." In sum, the courts had taken the best of the reform claims and made them the bases for their decisions. It was all light; no darkness intruded. It was all an effort to do good; the possibility for mischief was rarely entertained. The Progressive outlook and the Progressive program had recieved full approval.[33]

The contemporary relevance of this historical analysis does not rest in evaluating the actual successes or failures of the program. I will not here describe the implementation of the juvenile court and probation procedures for the period 1900–1945. The record, let it be clear, is grim. Probation staffs were invariably undertrained and overworked; case loads of two hundred to three hundred per officer obviously made it impossible for them to carry out their tasks. Further, the Progressive commitment to changing the environment of the slum never did accomplish very much. And the psychological theories which underlay probation work were woefully inadequate to the task of adjusting the deviant to his society. State training schools never did become places of education as opposed to places of punishment. In all, the net result of the juvenile court through its first decades of operation may have been to supplement incarceration, not to substitute for it. More offenders may have been brought under the surveillance of the state, but even that surveillance, given the case loads, was of little significance.

But the record of failure is not what is of immediate concern to our present consideration of the premises of social policy toward the delinquent. History in no simple sense repeats itself; and just because a policy of massive discretion did not work in the past, there is no reason to assert that it would not work now or in the future. Rather, the critical relevance of this analysis is that *the underlying assumptions of the Progressive program no longer seem*

[33] Lou, *Juvenile Courts*, pp. 10 ff.; In re Sharp, 15 Idaho, 120 (1908); *Mill* v. *Brown*, 31, Utah 473 (1907); *Marlowe* v. *Commonwealth*, 142 Kentucky, 106 (1911).

*valid.* We are in rebellion today against inherited procedures because their premises seem misguided and even wrong headed.

We are no longer confident that we understand the roots of deviant behavior. While some theories of deviancy may be more compelling than others, none of them are likely to muster enough intellectual support or to be sufficiently compelling to become the basis for a program that can be expected to rehabilitate the deviant. Unlike our predecessors, we are ever more skeptical about anyone's ability to reform the delinquent, not only because of sociological findings that rehabilitation has not in fact occurred, but because we lack the conceptual tools that would justify such a confidence. In this sense, then, we are unwilling to see in probation the cure-all for the problem; we are even less willing to trust institutions to transform the delinquent into a law-abiding citizen.

But probably most important, we have come to share a very different attitude toward the proper role of the state. In essence, we are far less willing than the Progressives to trust to its discretionary authority. Part of this distrust emanates from our sense of the failure of rehabilitation. Even more fundamental to it, however, is our belief that a harmony of interests, which Progressives assumed to be possible, can no longer be achieved. I cannot explore here the roots of this attitude. Allow me, however briefly, to note that from all points on the political spectrum we are now witnessing a reaction against discretion, an effort to return to a mandatory system of sentencing, a focus once again on the "act," not the "state," of the offender. To some critics the juvenile court has been too lenient, and hence the pressure to establish mandatory minimum sentences for serious juvenile offenders or to move them into the adult courts. To others, the juvenile court has been too meddlesome, and hence the urge to reduce its authority, to eliminate such categories as PINS, to force the court to respond only to overt acts, not to the moral condition of the child.

These particular points are only symptomatic of a broader judgment, a judgment that the power of the state cannot be exercised in a way that will satisfy all interests. We no longer share a belief in the possibility of the state acting as a parent to decide in the best interests of the child. We no longer even trust to the biological parent to act in the best interests of the child.

In sum, the Progressive ideology has lost hold in all sectors of the society. The historical record does not point us toward solutions, to what ought to be substituted in place of inherited wisdom. But it does make clear just how far we have traveled from the paths of our predecessors. We remain uncertain of how to map the future, but we cannot revive the past.

# Part II
# The Current Construction of Delinquency

# Juvenile Lawbreaking: Its Character and Social Location

## Lamar T. Empey

ANY discussion of the magnitude and character of the delinquency problem requires that we recognize that it is a Janus-like social construction—a creation with two opposing faces. The first is concerned with saving children. The juvenile court was set up under the benevolent assumption that it could save all children in danger of slipping through the institutional and moral cracks of society, not just the serious lawbreakers. Consequently, the legal rules defining delinquency have placed far more attention upon the capacity of the court to act as a surrogate parent than as a criminal court. They have represented an attempt to enforce by legal means a concept of childhood that began developing in the seventeenth and eighteenth centuries and reached full bloom in the nineteenth century namely, that ideal children should be submissive to authority; obedient, hard working, studious, sober, chaste; circumspect in habit, language, and associates; and should otherwise avoid even the appearance of evil, such as staying out late, wandering the streets, or being alone with a person of the opposite sex.[1]

Besides criminal and juvenile status offenses, legal rules have also given the juvenile court the power to deal with neglected, poor, and abused children. The reason lies in the persistence of nineteenth-century traditions that fail to see much difference between poor and neglected children and those who have actually

[1] Phillippe Ariès, *Centuries of Childhood*, trans. Robert Baldick (New York: Knopf, 1962), pp. 114–19; David J. Rothman, *The Discovery of the Asylum* (Boston: Little, Brown, 1971), pp. 15–17; Robert H. Bremner, J. Barnard, T. K. Hareven, and R. M. Mennel, *Children and Youth in America: A Documentary History*, vol. 1 (Cambridge: Harvard University Press, 1970).

violated the law.[2] Since destitute and neglected youngsters are but one short step from becoming lawbreakers, there is little need to treat them differently. Hence, it is still true that in many jurisdictions a "delinquent" may have committed a criminal act, a status offense, simply been neglected, or all three. As a result the so-called delinquent population nationwide is a heterogeneous population indeed.

The ambiguity of the concept led one eminent lawyer-sociologist to suggest, at mid-century, that "delinquency has little specific behavioral content either in law or in fact."[3] About all that can be said is that "the juvenile delinquent is a person who has been adjudicated as such by a court of proper jurisdiction." In general, that definition still holds.[4] We are probably on the threshold of making monumental changes in it, but, for the present, we should not expect to find precision where there has been none. Rather, imprecision was intended. The child-saving face of delinquency has been one of generalized, sometimes smothering, beneficence designed to legislate and enforce a particular concept of childhood.

### The Law-and-Order Face

The opposite Janus-face in our construction of delinquency is a law-and-order face. Ironically, at the very time when the first really serious questions were being raised about the child-saving face of delinquency—during the late 1960s and early 1970s—concern over youth protest, civil rights struggles, and rising crime

[2] Rothman, *Discovery of the Asylum,* chap. 2; Anthony M. Platt, *The Child Savers* (Chicago: University of Chicago Press, 1969), p. 130; Charles R. Henderson, ed., *Prison Reform and Criminal Law* (New York: Russell Sage, 1910).

[3] Paul Tappan, *Juvenile Delinquency* (New York: McGraw-Hill, 1949), p. 30.

[4] Mark M. Levin and Rosemary C. Sarri, *Juvenile Delinquency: A Comparative Analysis of Legal Codes in the United States* (Ann Arbor: University of Michigan; National Assessment of Juvenile Corrections, 1974); Office of Youth Development, *Juvenile Court Statistics, 1973* (Washington, D.C.: Department of Health, Education and Welfare 1974), p. 6.

and delinquency rates reached a peak. As a result, a significant segment of the populace responded positively to a body of rhetoric suggesting that the nation must wage a war on crime. The theme was that the country no longer faced a few temporary losses but that it was in imminent danger of losing everything.[5]

Beliefs in the imminence of peril were reinforced by the FBI's annual account of traditional crime. During the 1960s the seven Index crimes (murder, rape, robbery, aggravated assault, burglary, larceny, and auto theft) increased by 120 percent. Even more striking was the implication that, if a crime war were to be waged, it would have to be waged against the nation's youth.[6] More burglaries, larcenies and auto thefts were being committed by adolescents, ages fifteen to seventeen, than by any other group. Fifteen-year-olds were arrested most often, with sixteen-year-olds a close second. For crimes of violence, those from eighteen to twenty were the most responsible, with the second largest group in the twenty-one to twenty-four age range. In short, serious crime was very much a youthful phenomenon, hardly separable from something called "delinquency."

A recognition of this fact evoked a vision of millions of Americans sitting crouched behind locked doors, fearful that if they ventured forth, they would become victims of their own criminally disposed youth. Will we, asked the National Commission on the Causes and Prevention of Violence, have to "expect the establishment of the 'defensive city,' the modern counterpart of the fortified medieval city?" Will we "witness frequent and widespread crime, perhaps out of police control?"[7] Such questions clearly illustrated the extent to which the law-and-order face of delinquency stood in opposition to the child-saving face. Senti-

[5] Egon Bittner, *The Functions of the Police in Modern Society*, Publication no. 2059 (Washington, D.C.: U.S. Government Printing Office, 1970), p. 48.

[6] President's Commission on Law Enforcement and Administration of Justice (PCLEAJ), *The Challenge of Crime in a Free Society* (Washington, D.C.: U.S. Government Printing Office, 1967), p. 44.

[7] National Commission on the Causes and Prevention of Violence (NCCPV), *Crimes of Violence*, vol. 2 (Washington, D.C.: U.S. Government Printing Office, 1969), p. xxv.

ments favoring a war on crime were contrary to sentiments suggesting that children should occupy a special protected status. Society was on the horns of a dilemma.

More to the point, the dilemma has only grown more pronounced in the intervening years. As never before, we are possessed of different ways for measuring delinquency which, rather than easing concerns, only confound them. These measures are of three types: (1) traditional *official* measures from courts and police; (2) *self-reported,* but secret, accounts from young people themselves; and (3) *victimization* studies which document who it is that is being victimized and in what ways. Such measures permit us to adopt the methods of the navigator who locates a position by triangulating it, by taking bearings upon it from different angles. When the extent and nature of delinquency are located in this way, the picture that emerges fits well neither with the benevolent assumption that children are trying but innocent nor that, from their highly sheltered place in society, they escape from predation while preying upon others.

### Official Delinquency

The Office of Youth and Development estimated that over one million (1,143,700) delinquency cases, excluding traffic offenses, were handled by juvenile courts in 1973.[8] However, because some children appeared in court more than once, the actual number of individuals involved (986,000) was less than the number of court cases. Since the total child population, ages ten through seventeen years, was approximately 33.4 million in that year, the number of children who appeared in court, 986,000, was not proportionally large: only 3 percent of the total. Furthermore, less than half of those who were listed as court cases (46%) were actually tried in court; the remaining 54 percent were handled unofficially. Hence, such figures do not appear particularly alarming, although it must be remembered that official reports only count how many court cases there are in a given year, not how many times children appear in court throughout their entire childhood.

[8] Office of Youth Development, *Juvenile Court Statistics, 1973.*

But in terms of the trends that the country has been so worried about, the latest information indicates that the number of court cases has continued to rise. Between 1960 and 1973 they increased by 124 percent while the number of children in the country increased by only 32 percent. This long-term pattern, which is displayed in Figure 1, does lend some support to the concerns that have been expressed.

The latest evidence also shows that the number of girls involved in delinquency cases is becoming a larger proportion of the

Figure 1. Trends in Juvenile Court Delinquency Cases and Child Population 10–17 Years of Age, 1957–1973

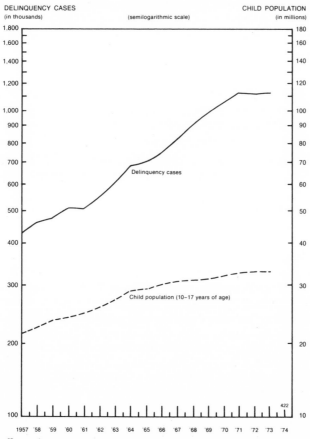

Source: Office of Youth Development, *Juvenile Court Statistics, 1973.* (Washington, D.C.: Department of Health, Education and Welfare, 1974), p. 9.

total. In 1960 only 19 percent of all cases handled by the courts were females. By 1973 the figure had reached 26 percent. Between 1965 and 1973 girls' delinquency cases increased by 110 percent, whereas boys' cases increased by less than half that amount, 52 percent.

This kind of official information is important because it suggests that the juvenile courts are dealing with an increasing number of cases, but it is of limited value as an accurate indicator of the level and trends of youth crime. In the first place, the Office of Youth Development does not provide information on the types of offenses for which delinquents are referred to court; rather, criminal and status offenses are lumped together. Even more fundamental, the number of juvenile court cases reported each year is sometimes a better reflection of the changing practices and policies of the courts and police than it is of the illegal acts of the young. For example, several studies of police practices reveal that there is tremendous variation in the proportion of juveniles actually referred to court after encounters with the police—anywhere from 15 to 98 percent.[9] The Uniform Crime Reports themselves indicate that the police consistently release about half of all the juveniles they arrest without referring them to court.[10]

What this means is that the police, as well as the courts, are often inclined to support the benevolent, rather than the law-and-order, face of delinquency where nonserious offenses are involved. Consequently, the juvenile justice system acts like a large funnel: first, the police screen out large numbers of the children they

[9] Nathan Goldman, "The Differential Selection of Juvenile Offenders for Court Appearance," in *Crime and the Legal Process*, ed. William Chambliss (New York: McGraw-Hill, 1969); Malcolm W. Klein, "Police Processing of Juvenile Offenders: Toward the Development of Juvenile System Rates," Part III (Los Angeles: Los Angeles Sub-Regional Board, California Council of Criminal Justice, 1970); Donald J. Black and Albert J. Reiss, Jr., "Police Control of Juveniles, *American Sociological Review* 35 (February 1970): 63–77.

[10] Cf. Federal Bureau of Investigation (FBI), *Crime in the United States: Uniform Crime Reports, 1966* (Washington, D.C.: U.S. Government Printing Office, 1967), p. 110, and FBI, *Crime in the United States: Uniform Crime Reports, 1973* Washington, D.C.: U.S. Government Printing Office, 1974), p. 119.

apprehend, and then the courts repeat the process with the remainder. The actual number of children who are formally tried in court, therefore, is only a fraction of the total number who are apprehended. As a result, it is virtually impossible to determine what the relation is between the number of officially recorded court cases and the actual rate at which children violate the law.

Some of the same problems are inherent in trying to interpret the latest information on the number of dependency and neglect cases in the United States. The Office of Youth Development reported a total of 158,000 cases in 1973, an increase in 12 percent over 1972.[11] Although the number of such cases is much smaller than the reported number of delinquency cases (1.1 million vs. 158,000), this increase represents a sharp reversal of a downward trend that began in 1967. Again, however, it is impossible to know with any precision what this increase means. In short, while official information on the courts gives an estimate of the total number of cases being handled, it is not of much value in estimating the actual incidence of dependency and neglect cases or of delinquent acts.

Official Arrest Data

Because the police have first contact with any illegal event and because the juvenile justice system acts like a large filter, crimes reported to the police or arrests are more representative of the actual number of crimes committed than are cases recorded by the court. The Uniform Crime Reports indicate that law enforcement agencies made an estimated nine million arrests during 1973, excluding traffic offenses.[12] As the arrest curve in Figure 2 indicates, the majority of those arrests continue to involve young people. Before age ten the arrest rate is low. Then it accelerates sharply until it reaches a peak between ages fifteen and nineteen, after which it decelerates rapidly and gradually wanes for people in the remaining phases of the life cycle. Arrest rates in 1973 were

[11] Office of Youth Development, *Juvenile Court Statistics, 1973.*
[12] FBI, *Uniform Crime Reports, 1973,* pp. 30–34.

## Figure 2. Arrest Curve by Age

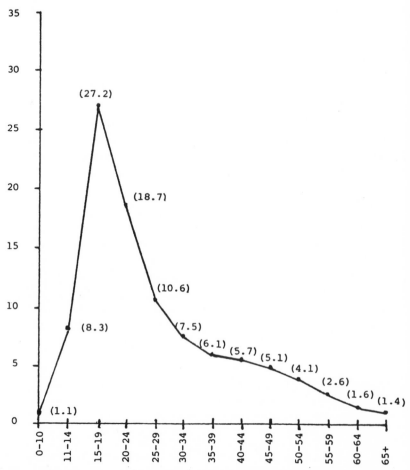

PERCENT OF
ALL ARRESTS

Source: Federal Bureau of Investigation, *Crime in the United States: Uniform Crime Reports, 1973.* (Washington, D.C.: U.S. Government Printing Office, 1974), pp. 128–29.

typical: 26 percent of all arrestees were under age eighteen; forty-one percent were under twenty-one; and 55 percent under twenty-five. More arrests were made of children, ages eleven to fourteen, than were made of adults, ages thirty to thirty-four.

More significant is the finding that juveniles ages ten to seventeen, who constitute less than 20 percent of the population, were arrested for almost half (45%) of the seven serious felonies that comprise the FBI's Crime Index Offenses (Table 1). However, children are not as likely to be arrested for murder, rape, and violent assault as people over eighteen, but they do constitute large proportions of the people arrested for auto theft (57%), burglary (54%), and larceny (48%). Their most common crimes, in short, are property crimes.

*Arrest of girls.* The arrest of girls is of increasing interest because of the widespread effort to achieve equality for females and because girls have received little attention in the delinquency literature. Two kinds of information, therefore, are useful: (1) information that contrasts the number of girls arrested with the number of boys; and (2) information that contrasts the number of arrests of girls under eighteen with the number of females over eighteen. In some cases, the information is striking.

In 1973 arrests of females, young and old, accounted for only 15 percent of all arrests; 85 percent were male. Thus, girls under eighteen accounted for only 8 percent of all the arrests for the seven serious Index offenses, versus 37 percent of the total for boys (Table 1). On only one non-Index offense—running away— were girls (57%) arrested more frequently than boys (44%), and this difference may be due to the traditional double standard. Hence, it is clear that arrests for serious traditional crimes are still predominantly male, typically young males, not females.

When girls are compared with older women over eighteen, however, the picture changes considerably. The reason is that arrests of girls constitute a higher proportion of all female arrests (38%) than arrests of boys do of all male arrests (25%). When only the serious Index crimes are considered, as shown in Table 2, girls constitute an even higher proportion of the female total (42%). Like boys, girls rank high among all females on arrests for auto theft (59%), burglary (51%), larceny (44%), and robbery (35%). In short, arrests among females, like arrests among males, are also a youthful phenomenon.

*Arrest trends.* The latest Uniform Crime Reports, like juvenile court statistics, suggest that the official delinquency rate is still

*Table 1.* Juvenile arrests for Index crimes, 1973

| Arrest offenses | All ages | Juveniles under 18 | Males under 18 | Females under 18 |
|---|---|---|---|---|
| Criminal homicide | | | | |
| Murder and | | | | |
| nonnegligent | | | | |
| manslaughter | 13,837 | 10.4 | 9.5 | 0.9 |
| Manslaughter by | | | | |
| negligence | 2,793 | 11.7 | 11.0 | 0.7 |
| Forcible rape | 18,387 | 19.8 | 19.8 | 0.0 |
| Robbery | 98,869 | 34.1 | 31.7 | 2.4 |
| Aggravated assault | 146,023 | 17.1 | 14.6 | 2.5 |
| Burglary: breaking | | | | |
| or entering | 300,923 | 54.2 | 51.4 | 2.8 |
| Larceny: theft | | | | |
| (except auto) | 613,934 | 48.4 | 34.4 | 14.0 |
| Auto theft | 113,369 | 56.9 | 53.4 | 3.5 |
| Total arrests | | | | |
| Number | 1,308,135 | 588,712 | 484,382 | 104,330 |
| Percent | 100 | 45.0 | 37.0 | 8.0 |

SOURCE: Federal Bureau of Investigation, *Crime in the United States: Uniform Crime Reports, 1973.* (Washington, D.C.: U.S. Government Printing Office, 1974), p. 132.

continuing to rise.[13] Between 1960 and 1973 the arrest of juveniles under eighteen increased by 144 percent even though the youth population increased by only 32 percent. Most striking is the fact that the greatest increase occurred in violent crimes. In the ten-year period between 1964 and 1973, the rate per 100,000 children went from a low of 130 to a high of 290, an increase of 123 percent.[14]

A notable part of this growth can be attributed to a surging number of arrests among girls. Between 1960 and 1973 arrests of girls increased by 264 percent as contrasted with an increase of 124 percent for boys. Even more striking was the increase

[13] Office of Youth Development, *Juvenile Court Statistics, 1973,* p. 1.

[14] Cf. U.S. Census Reports 1960–70, U.S. Department of Commerce, *Bureau of Census Reports, 1950–1970* (Washington, D.C.: U.S. Government Printing Office, 1971) and FBI, *Uniform Crime Reports, 1964–1973.*

*Table 2.* Arrest rates of girls and boys as proportions of all female and male Index arrests

| Arrest offense | Girls under 18 | | Boys under 18 | |
| --- | --- | --- | --- | --- |
| | Number arrested | Percent of all female arrests | Number arrested | Percent of all male arrests |
| Criminal homicide | | | | |
| Murder and nonnegligent manslaughter | 127 | 6.1 | 1,315 | 11.2 |
| Manslaughter by negligence | 21 | 6.5 | 306 | 12.4 |
| Forcible rape | — | — | 3,632 | 19.7 |
| Robbery | 2,340 | 35.1 | 31,372 | 34.0 |
| Aggravated assault | 3,626 | 18.7 | 21,286 | 16.8 |
| Burglary: breaking or entering | 8,330 | 51.2 | 154,885 | 54.4 |
| Larceny: theft (except auto) | 85,891 | 44.3 | 211,032 | 50.2 |
| Auto theft | 3,995 | 59.2 | 60,154 | 56.8 |
| Total | 104,330 | 42.4% | 484,382 | 45.6% |

SOURCE: Federal Bureau of Investigation, *Crime in the United States: Uniform Crime Reports, 1973.* (Washington, D.C.: U.S. Government Printing Office, 1974), p. 132.

among girls for violent crimes (393%) and for property crimes (334%) as contrasted to increases among boys of 236 percent and 82 percent, respectively. When these two types of Index crimes are combined, therefore, the increases are 337 percent for girls versus 92 percent for boys.

Official figures like these provide ammunition for those people who would resolve the societal ambivalence over children by implementing more stringent controls. Indeed some states have already written provisions into their statutes which lower the age of childhood or which require that older children be tried in adult court for serious crimes. In both instances, the length of the protective status for children is decreased. But caution must be observed in interpreting these official rates. Because the Uniform Crime Reports count the number of arrests in any time period, and not the number of children who are involved, one cannot be certain whether more and more youth are committing crime or whether it is only a few children who are committing most of it.

One recent study suggests that it is the latter.[15] Information from police and court records was collected on 9,945 boys born in 1945 who lived in Philadelphia from the time they were ten until they were eighteen. Thus, the total number of delinquent acts for this entire cohort was accumulated and determination made as to whether they were committed by large numbers of youth or by only a few repeat offenders. It was found that 35 percent of the entire cohort had at least one police contact during childhood, while 65 percent had none.[16] Thus, if generalized to all boys, the findings would suggest that for every 100,000 of them, 35,000 would become delinquent sometime during childhood.

But this was not the most significant finding. Instead, it was discovered that there was a chronic group of only 627 boys— only 6 percent of the total—who were responsible for *over half* of all the offenses. Included in their delinquent records were most of the serious assaults, property offenses, and robberies. Clearly, the findings seemed to suggest that the number of children who become serious career offenders are only a tiny proportion of all children. Furthermore, they indicated that poor and nonwhite children were grossly overrepresented in the chronic offender group. The evidence seemed to lend twentieth-century support to the nineteenth-century belief that it is poverty and ethnic depravity which produces crime.

Such evidence is compelling if taken at face value. Indeed, the investigators who produced it concluded that, of all the groups on which delinquency reduction effort might be concentrated, the one most likely to produce definitive results would be the nonwhite, lower-class group.[17] Such an effort might not only reduce

[15] Marvin E. Wolfgang, Robert Figlio, and Thorsten Sellin, *Delinquency in a Birth Cohort* (Chicago: University of Chicago Press, 1972).

[16] Ibid., p. 54.

[17] Ibid., p. 87.

law-breaking in general but drastically curtail the acts of violence and assault over which society has been so concerned. Since this is a pivotal conclusion, it merits close scrutiny when our remaining measures of delinquency are considered. As will be seen, it is neither confirmed nor disconfirmed.

## Self-reported Delinquency

In contrast to official methods of collecting data on delinquent behavior, a growing number of social scientists have gone to juveniles themselves to discover how many law violations they have committed and what led to them. They have done this by administering anonymous questionnaires, by interviewing youngsters, and by simply observing their behavior. Their findings reflect on a series of crucial questions that official measures raise but cannot answer.

1. *How widespread is law violation among juveniles?* Virtually all self-report studies indicate that the amount of undetected law violation is enormous.[18] Almost every child has broken the law at

[18] Maynard L. Erickson and LaMar T. Empey, "Court Records, Undetected Delinquency, and Decision-making," *Journal of Criminal Law, Criminology and Police Science* 54 (December 1963): 456–69; Martin Gold, "Undetected Delinquent Behavior," *Journal of Research in Crime and Delinquency* 3 (January 1966): 27–46; Martin Gold, *Delinquent Behavior in an American City* (Belmont, Calif.: Brooks/Cole Publishing Co., 1970); Illinois Institute for Juvenile Research, *Juvenile Delinquency in Illinois* (Chicago: Illinois Department of Mental Health, 1972); Fred J. Murphy et al., "The Incidence of Hidden Delinquency," *American Journal of Orthopsychiatry*, October 1946, pp. 686–96; A. L. Porterfield, *Youth in Trouble* (Fort Worth, Tex.: Leo Potishman Foundation, 1946); James F. Short, Jr., and F. Ivan Nye, "Extent of Unrecorded Delinquency, Tentative Conclusions," *Journal of Criminal Law, Criminology and Police Science* 49 (November-December 1958): 296–302; J. A. Wallerstein and C. J. Wyle, "Our Law-abiding Law-breakers," *Federal Probation* 25 (April 1947): 107–12; J. R. Williams and Martin Gold, "From Delinquent Behavior to Official Delinquency," *Social Problems* 20 (Fall 1972):209–29.

some time or another, sometimes repeatedly. This finding, moreover, is not limited to the United States but has been reported in other countries as well.[19]

2. *What kinds of offenses are reported most commonly?* Large proportions of the youth population admit having committed a number of *status offenses:* truancy and drinking rank first, with anywhere from half to two-thirds of all adolescents having committed them; defying parents and fornication rank second; running away ranks last. Girls report fewer offenses, but their pattern is generally the same.

Such *property crimes* as petty theft, shoplifting, and destroying property are about as common as drinking and truancy. Breaking and entering is also quite common, while auto theft is the least common and is reported by about only 10 percent of all respondents.

*Crimes against persons* are much less common among adolescents than are status or property crimes. There are only two exceptions: fistfighting and gang fighting. These appear to be about as common as drinking, truancy, petty theft, and destroying property. By contrast, only about one in ten adolescents admits to acts of aggravated assault, armed robbery, or carrying a concealed weapon. Nonetheless, this proportion is still higher than that reported in official records.

3. *How large is the "dark figure" of crime—the number of offenses that never become a part of the official record?* Studies indicate that at least nine out of ten illegal acts either go undetected or unacted upon by anyone in authority.[20] For example, after having checked the official record against the self-reports of a national sample, Williams and Gold found that "less than one

[19] Nils Christie et al., "A Study of Self-reported Crime," in *Scandinavian Studies in Criminology*, vol. 2, ed. K. O. Christiansen (London: Tavistock Publication, 1965); K. Elmhorn, "Study in Self-reported Delinquency among School Children in Stockholm," ibid.

[20] Erickson and Empey, "Court Records, Undetected Delinquency, and Decision-making"; Gold, "Undetected Delinquency Behavior"; Murphy et al., "The Incidence of Hidden Delinquency"; Williams and Gold, "From Delinquent Behavior to Official Delinquency."

percent of the chargeable offenses committed in the three years prior to the interviews were recorded as official delinquency." [21] Serious Index crimes are the most likely to be officially recorded, but even then eight out of ten go undetected and nine out of ten do not result in court action.[22]

4. *Is the amount of undetected delinquency increasing?* So large is the "dark figure" of delinquency that led Murphy to remark thirty years ago that "even a moderate increase in the amount of attention paid to [it] by law enforcement authorities could create the semblance of a 'delinquency wave' without there being the slightest change in adolescent behavior." [23] If all adolescent crimes became a part of the official record, the results would be unprecedented.

But this does not necessarily mean that the rate of delinquency is increasing. After comparing the results of two national surveys, Gold and Reimer found no overall increase in self-reported delinquency between 1967 and 1972.[24] More drugs, principally marijuana, were being used, but the overall rate did not increase. While this evidence is limited, therefore, it does raise the possibility that the sharp increases in *official* delinquency noted in recent years may be due, at least in part, to improved recordkeeping on the parts of officials, particularly since several national commissions recommended that improvements were needed.

5. *Do all young people report being equally delinquent or are some more delinquent than others?* All young people are not equally delinquent. Without expection, every study of the subject suggests that law-violating behavior is not an either-or thing but

[21] William and Gold, "From Delinquent Behavior to Official Delinquency," p. 221.

[22] Erickson and Empey, "Court Records, Undetected Delinquency, and Decision-making," p. 485; Williams and Gold, "From Delinquent Behavior to Official Delinquency," pp. 221–22.

[23] Murphy et al., "The Incidence of Hidden Delinquency."

[24] Martin Gold and D. J. Reimer, "Changing Patterns of Delinquent Behavior among Americans 13–16 Years Old: 1967–1972," *National Survey of Youth, Report No. 1,* University of Michigan Institute for Social Research (1974), Mimeo, p. 13.

that it is a more-or-less thing.[25] On one end of the continuum are the majority of young people who have committed a number of minor acts, with an occasional serious one mixed in. Then, as one proceeds farther along the continuum, one encounters fewer and fewer children who, at the same time, are more and more delinquent. Thus, at the extreme opposite end are a small minority who are both frequent and serious offenders.

6. *Who gets caught? Are official records at all accurate in identifying those who, by their own admission, are the most delinquent?* There is some evidence that the possession of an official record is not entirely a chance thing. In their nationwide study Williams and Gold found a small but nonetheless significant relationship between frequency and seriousness of offense and likelihood of arrest.[26] A second set of studies found an even stronger relationship between frequency of offense and appearance in court.[27] Finally, a third set indicates that the incarcerated delinquents are individuals who, by their own admission, fit on the most delinquent end of the contiuum.[28] This evidence, in fact, is very much like that presented in the Philadelphia cohort study mentioned earlier.[29] Just as it was found there that a small but chronic group of offenders was unusually delinquent, so these self-report studies find that incarcerated delinquents admit so far more illegal acts than do onetime offenders or persons who have never been arrested.

What these finding suggest, then, is that the juvenile justice

[25] Elmhorn, "Study in Self-reported Delinquency"; Erickson and Empey, "Court Records, Undetected Delinquency, and Decision-making"; Gwynn Nettler, *Explaining Crime* (New York: McGraw-Hill, 1974); Short and Nye, "Extent of Unrecorded Delinquency"; Williams and Gold, "From Delinquent Behavior to Official Delinquency"; Gold, *Delinquent Behavior.*

[26] Williams and Gold, "From Delinquent Behavior to Official Delinquency," p. 219.

[27] Erickson and Empey, "Court Records, Undetected Delinquency, and Decision-making," p. 147; Maynard L. Erickson, "The Changing Relationship between Official and Self-reported Measures of Delinquency: An Exploratory Predictive Study," *Journal of Criminal Law, Criminology and Police Science* 3 (September-October, 1972):394.

[28] Erickson and Empey, "Court Records, Undetected Delinquency, and Decision-making"; Short and Nye, "Extent of Unrecorded Delinquency."

[29] Wolfgang et al., *Delinquency in a Birth Cohort.*

system is like a coarse net dragged in a large ocean.[30] The chances are small that most fish will be caught and, even when some are caught, they manage to escape or are released because they are too small. But a few bigger, more active fish are caught more than once. Despite odds in their favor, their sheer size and activity repeatedly get them in trouble. Each time this occurs, the chances that they will escape, or be thrown back, are lessened. Officials are less willing to give them the benefit of the doubt. At the very end, therefore, it tends only to be the biggest and most active fish who end up in the can. When they reach that point, they are a very select group, clearly different from most of the fish still in the ocean.

7. *Are most delinquent children members of the lower class?* The President's Commission on Law Enforcement and Administration of Justice asserted that "there is still no reason to doubt that delinquency, and especially the most serious delinquency, is committed disproportionately by slum and lower class youth." [31] This assertion notwithstanding, there is little in the self-report literature to support it. Study after study suggests that the relation between social class and law-violating behavior is either small or nonexistent.[32] From a scientific standpoint, the best conclusion is that class membership is not a good way to separate law violators from nonviolators.

Does this mean then, that official records are biased? In part,

[30] Nettler, *Explaining Crime*, p. 90.

[31] PCLEAJ, *Task Force Report: Crime and Its Impact* (Washington, D.C.: U.S. Government Printing Office, 1967), p. 57.

[32] Ronald L. Akers, "Socio-economic Status and Delinquent Behavior: A Retest," *Journal of Research in Crime and Delinquency* 1 (January 1964): 38–46; R. A. Dentler and L. J. Monroe, "Social Correlates of Early Adolescent Theft," *American Sociological Review* 26 (October 1961):733–43; LaMar Empey and Maynard L. Erickson, "Hidden Delinquency and Social Status," *Social Forces* 44 (June 1966):546–54; Travis Hirschi, *Causes of Delinquency* (Berkeley: University of California Press, 1969); Illinois Institute for Juvenile Research, *Juvenile Delinquency in Illinois;* Short and Nye, "Extent of Unrecorded Delinquency"; Williams and Gold, "From Delinquent Behavior to Official Delinquency"; Harwin L. Voss, "Socio-economic Status and Reported Delinquent Behavior," *Social Problems* 13 (Winter 1966):314–24.

the answer is yes. But the bias is not a simple case of official bigotry, though bigotry is often present. Rather, it is due to our traditional failure to distinguish clearly between *official delinquency*—what official records measure—and *law-violating behavior*—what self-reports measure. These are not the same things.

*Official delinquency* is an ambiguous term reflecting three things: (1) the behavior of children; (2) the social backgrounds and characteristics of these children; and (3) the responses of officials to both behavior and circumstance. *Law-violating behavior*, by contrast, involves only one of these—the delinquent act itself. A gross error is committed, therefore, when official accounts of delinquency are equated with law-violating behavior.

The benevolent face of the juvenile court has contributed to the error. Existing laws have traditionally required officials to respond to the conditions of deprivation to which lower-class law violators are the most vulnerable. In those circumstances where a middle-class law violator might be treated leniently because he or she has family resources and is in school and conforms better to the ideal concept of childhood, the lower-class child might be arrested, made a formal ward of the court, and even removed from home. Thus, it is often the case that lower-class children become a part of official statistics, not just because of deliberate or unthinking prejudice, but because officials are expected to correct undesirable social conditions for children as well as their criminal behavior. In any comparison of *official delinquency* and informal *law-violating* rates, therefore, this fact must be kept in mind. Since official delinquency rates reflect the child-saving nature of social rules and official practices, as well as the behavior of children, interpretation which equates them with rates of law-violating behavior are seriously misleading.

8. *Are the most delinquent children members of minority groups?* This question cannot be answered for all minority groups due to the lack of self-report studies among them. Any conclusions, therefore, will have to be limited to contrasts between black and white Americans.

In opposite ends of the country official records indicate that black boys are far more likely to be defined as *officially* delinquent.[33] But when self-reported measures are used, differences between blacks and whites are greatly reduced. The overall frequency of law violation may be slightly higher for blacks, if it is higher, it is not much higher.[34] There are some important qualitative differences, however. Black children are more inclined to report committing serious offenses resulting in personal injury and serious property loss than are white ones.[35] Whites, meanwhile, may have an edge over blacks in automobile offenses—driving recklessly, joyriding, or stripping cars.[36] But even then the differences between the races in self-report studies are smaller than the differences in official accounts. Why?

The explanation is probably much the same as it was when social-class differences were being considered. To be sure, higher rates of some serious crimes among blacks are more likely to increase the probability of arrest and trial. But because proportionately more black children suffer from poverty, malnutrition, and learning disabilities, as well as being possessed of minority status, they are in a double bind. More than ever legal agents are charged with recording them as official cases and seeking remedies. Hence, in order to avoid perpetuating long-standing misconceptions about the relation of race to law-violating behavior, rather than official delinquency, it is wise to recall the findings of Shaw and McKay.[37] For half a century they found that the population composition of the high delinquency areas in our largest cities has changed again and again as successive, highly different

---

[33] Cf. Wolfgang et al., *Delinquency in a Birth Cohort;* Hirschi, *Causes of Delinquency;* and FBI, *Uniform Crime Reports, 1973,* p. 135.

[34] Gold, *Delinquent Behavior;* Hirschi, *Causes of Delinquency;* Illinois Institute for Juvenile Research, *Juvenile Delinquency in Illinois;* Williams and Gold, "From Delinquent Behavior to Official Delinquency."

[35] Illinois Institute for Juvenile Research, *Juvenile Delinquency in Illinois,* pp. 23–24; Williams and Gold, "From Delinquent Behavior to Official Delinquency," p. 217; Gold and Reimer, "Changing Patterns of Delinquent Behavior," p. 17.

[36] Illinois Institute for Juvenile Research, *Juvenile Delinquency in Illinois,* pp. 23–24.

[37] Clifford Shaw and Henry D. McKay, *Juvenile Delinquency and Urban Areas,* rev. ed. (Chicago: University of Chicago Press, 1972).

ethnic groups moved through them. Yet the official delinquency rates remained the same—high. Changes in race and nationality did not alter them. But as each successive group moved outward into more desirable areas, its official delinquency rate declined. Thus, the indications are that delinquency rates—high or low— are associated more with the kinds of neighborhoods in which people live than with their racial or ethnic backgrounds. It is deteriorated neighborhoods and poverty, not ethnic depravity, with which official delinquency is most strongly associated.

9. *What do self-report studies show about girls?* Self-report studies tend to confirm official findings that delinquency rates are lower among girls than among boys. But here the similarities end. Historically, such offenses as incorrigibility, running away, and fornication have come to be considered "girls' offenses." Self-report studies indicate, however, that such offenses account for only a small proportion of their total.[38] Considerably more common are drinking, shoplifting, truancy, theft, illegal entry, drug use, property destruction, and even assault. Secondly, there is some evidence that law-violating behavior among girls in increasing rather rapidly.[39] Finally, there is a possibility that black girls are more violent than white girls but, again, differences along racial lines have probably been exaggerated.

In summary, self-report studies indicate that official records grossly underestimate the extent of juvenile lawbreaking; that most juveniles are law violators, not just poor and minority children; that among all adolescents there is a chronic group of persistent serious offenders; and that serious distortions are inherent in the traditional tendency to equate official delinquency with law-violating behavior. Of crucial significance, therefore, is whether victimization studies paint a totally different picture, or whether they tend to agree with one or the other of the first two accounts.

[38] Gold, "Undetected Delinquent Behavior"; Gold and Reimer, "Changing Patterns of Delinquent Behavior"; Illinois Institute for Juvenile Research, *Juvenile Delinquency in Illinois.*

[39] Illinois Institute for Juvenile Research, *Juvenile Delinquency in Illinois;* Gold and Reimer, "Changing Patterns of Delinquent Behavior."

## Victimization Studies

Two major national commissions expressed the conviction that information on the nature and extent of crime could be improved by collecting data from crime victims.[40] Hence, the first National Crime Survey was conducted in 1973.[41] Information was gathered from a probability sample of approximately 125,000 people located in 60,000 households and 15,000 businesses in the entire nation. Information of three types was collected: (1) *crimes against persons*—rape, robbery, assault, and personal larceny; (2) *crimes against households*—burglary, household larceny, and vehicle theft; and (3) *crimes against commercial establishments* —burglary and robbery. For our purposes, the most significant findings were these:

1. *Number of victims.* The National Criminal Information Service estimated that there were approximately thirty-seven million victims of successful, or attempted, crimes in 1973.[42] This figure was well over four times as large as the number of similar crimes (8.6 million) reported by the police for the same year.[43] This large discrepancy must be discounted to some degree because, on some occasions, there are multiple victims of a single crime. Hence, one would expect to find more victims than crimes. Yet even when this difference is taken into account, important discrepancies persist. Counting only incidents, not victims, the NCIS found that victim-reported crimes exceeded police-recorded crimes by large numbers: rape, three times; robbery, three times; aggravated assault, three times; burglary, three times;

---

[40] PCLEAJ, *Crime and its Impact;* National Advisory Commission on Criminal Justice Standards and Goals (NACCJSG), "Victimization Surveying: Its History, Uses, and Limitations," *Report on the Criminal Justice System* (Washington, D.C.: U.S. Government Printing Office, 1973).

[41] National Criminal Justice Information and Statistics Service (NCIS), *Criminal Victimization in the United States: 1973, Advance Report* 1 (May) (Washington, D.C.; U.S. Government Printing Office, 1975).

[42] Ibid., p. 1.

[43] FBI, *Uniform Crime Reports, 1973,* p. 1.

*Table 3.* Victim- and police-reported rates for crime against persons, 1973

| Type of crime | Victim survey [*] | Uniform crime report [†] |
|---|---|---|
| Crimes of violence | | 20.5 |
| Murder | −[‡] | |
| Rape | 1.0 | |
| Robbery | 6.9 | 0.1 |
| with injury | 2.4 | 0.2 |
| without injury | 4.6 | 1.8 |
| Aggravated assault | 10.4 | |
| Simple assault | 15.6 | 4.9 |
| Total | 33.9 | −[‡] |
| Personal larceny | | 4.1 |
| Larceny with contact | 3.2 | |
| Larceny without contact | 90.3 | |
| Total | 93.4 | |

SOURCES: National Criminal Justice Information and Statistics Service, *Criminal Victimization in the United States, 1973. Advance Report.* (Washington, D.C.: Law Enforcement Assistance Administration, 1975), p. 12; Federal Bureau of Investigation, *Crime in the United States: Uniform Crime Reports, 1973.* (Washington, D.C.: U.S. Government Printing Office, 1974), p. 1.

NOTE: Rates and subrates may not add to total because of rounding.

[*] Rate per 1,000 population, age 12 and over.

[†] Rate per 1,000 population, all ages.

[‡] Not reported.

larceny, six times; and auto theft, one time.[44] Thus victim reports, like self-reports, lend support to the notion that official accounts grossly underestimate the actual number of criminal incidents.

2. *Vulnerability to crime.* The law-and-order face of delinquency receives support because of rampant fears of violent, personal crime. Table 3 provides data on that subject. It contrasts the rates of various personal crimes reported by victims with those reported by the police. According to the police, there were about four victims of violent crimes per 1,000 people in 1973. By contrast, the victim survey puts the rates at about thirty-four

[44] NCIS, "Typical Crime Victim is Young, Poor and Black," *LEAA Newsletter* 4 (December 1974):5.

per 1,000, a rate that is over eight times as great. For personal larceny the differences were also large, 21 versus 93 per 1,000.

Such findings could be interpreted as suggesting that the risks of being victimized are overwhelming, but a careful perusal of the table suggests otherwise. In any given year, the chances that the "average" person will be victimized are small. If that person is victimized, moreover, it is much more likely that she or he will have money or property stolen than that she or he will be assaulted, raped, or robbed by force. The notion that most crimes are characterized by direct, violent contact between victim and criminal is inaccurate. One thing to be remembered, however, is that if yearly rates are projected over a lifetime, the likelihood of victimization goes up considerably.[45] Furthermore, the chances that one's household or business will be victimized are greater than the chances that one will be victimized personally. It is in these settings, in fact, that the risks are greatest.[46]

3. *Special vulnerability.* In a very real sense it is misleading to discuss the vulnerability of the "average" person to crime because vulnerability is affected profoundly by the age, sex, race, and residence of the victim.

Consider *age.* Contrary to the prevailing assumption that it is the elderly who are most likely to be victimized, Figure 3 indicates that it is the *young.* Just as the high crime-producing years occur during adolescence, so it is that young people, age twelve to nineteen, are the most likely to be victimized. After adolescence, in fact, the risks of victimization decrease steadily, with each age group reporting a lower rate than its predecessor. Indeed, after age sixty-five, risks decline to a rate—three per hundred—that is almost eight times lower than that for twelve to nineteen-year-olds.

There are also some striking findings when we consider the types of crimes for which youngsters are victimized. We have already seen that juveniles are more likely to commit property than violent crimes. Hence, it is not surprising that they are the most

[45] Cf. Arnold Barnett and Daniel J. Kleitman, "Urban Violence and Risk to the Individual," *Journal of Research in Crime and Delinquency* 10 (July 1973): 111–16.
[46] NCIS, *Criminal Victimization,* pp. 19, 23.

Figure 3. Victimization Rates for Personal Crimes

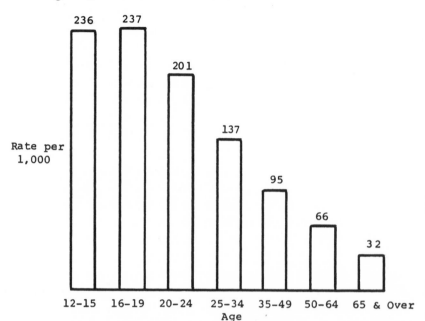

Source: National Criminal Justice Information and Statistics Service, *Criminal Victimization in the United States, 1973. Advance Report.* (Washington, D.C.: Law Enforcement Assistance Administration, 1975), p. 15.

common victims of such crimes, particularly larceny. But what is surprising is that they are also the ones most likely to be victimized in cases of rape, robbery, and assault.[47] Moreover, the same pronounced pattern is also characteristic of crimes against households.[48] *Almost half* of the households headed by teenagers were victimized in 1973. By contrast, the rate for people over sixty-five was only 109 per 1,000. Hence, such findings suggest that, if any segment of our society is close to living in a predatory jungle, it is the young, not the old. Not only may they be more likely to commit crime but they are more likely to suffer its consequences.

Consider *sex*. As a group, males are far more vulnerable to crime than are females, particularly to violent crime.[49] The only exception is rape. But when the effects of age and sex are

[47] Ibid., pp. 15–16.     [48] Ibid., p. 20.     [49] Ibid., pp. 15–16.

combined, some striking findings emerge. Although differences between the sexes persist as people grow older, they are of decreasing magnitude. Thus, by ages fifty to sixty-four the difference has diminished to 68 per 1,000 for men versus 54 for women. Contrast these relatively low rates with those for teenagers: 286 for boys and 189 for girls. Obviously, the risks that older men and women run are not only much lower than those for adolescent boys *but for adolescent girls as well.* What all of this means is that males run greater risks than females only when age is held constant; that is, only when males and females of the same age are compared. But when they are not, the conclusion that men are more vulnerable than women breaks down. Indeed, adolescent girls ages sixteen to nineteen have higher victimization rates than do males ages twenty-five to thirty-four, 189 versus 161 per 1,000.

Consider *race.* Overall, vulnerability to personal crimes is about equal for blacks and white—132 per 1,000 for blacks versus 127 for whites. However, within these overall rates are some highly important differences. Whites are typically victimized in crimes where weapons and injury are not involved. By contrast, the rates at which blacks are victimized for rape, robbery, and aggravated assault are from two to three times greater than for whites.[50] Furthermore, the murder rate among blacks is staggeringly high when compared to that of whites. Although blacks constitute only about 11 percent of the total population, approximately 52 percent of all murder victims nationwide are black.[51]

Again, the persons who suffer most are black males. Ranking considerably below them are white males, followed closely by black females, who are almost as likely to be victimized in violent crime. Even more numbing is recent evidence regarding violence among adolescents. Historically, the victims of murder have tended to be young and middle-aged adults.[52] In Chicago, however, Block and Zimring found that the most dramatic single increase in murder victimization rates between 1965 and 1970 was among young black males, ages fifteen to twenty-four. They went

[50] Ibid., p. 14.    [51] FBI, *Uniform Crime Reports, 1973*, p. 6.
[52] Donald Mulvihill et al., *Crimes of Violence: A Staff Report Submitted to the National Commission on the Causes and Prevention of Violence*, vol. 11 (Washington, D.C.: U.S. Government Printing Office, 1969), p. 210.

from 54 per 100,000 in 1965 to 298 in 1970. Hence, by 1970 the most vulnerable group to murder was black youth ages fifteen to twenty-four.[53]

Parenthetically, it should be noted that comparisons *across* races reveal that blacks, no matter what their income, are more likely than whites who have the same income to suffer from all types of crime—violence, larceny, and household crimes.[54] Furthermore, evidence suggests that traditional forms of crime are predominantly *intra*racial, not interracial. Most people are victimized by someone of their own race, particularly in violent crimes.[55]

Consider *place of residence.* Official accounts have long tended to confirm the nineteenth-century American belief that the city, particularly in its deteriorated core, is where the greatest amount of crime is spawned. Victimization studies lend support to these accounts.[56] Generally, as one moves from the central city to the suburbs and out into smaller towns and rural areas, victimization rates decline, especially those involving violence. With this final finding, therefore, we are in a position to draw some conclusions from our effort to take bearings upon the delinquency problem from different angles.

## Conclusions and Implications

Our triangulating survey provides provocative information in several areas, each of which is fraught with implications.

### Extent of Delinquent Behavior

There are compelling reasons to conclude that official records grossly underestimate the actual amount of law violation.

[53] Richard Block and Franklin E. Zimring, "Homicide in Chicago, 1965–70," *Journal of Research in Crime and Delinquency* 10 (January 1973):5.

[54] NCIS, *Criminal Victimization,* pp. 18, 22.

[55] Philip H. Ennis, *Criminal Victimization in the United States: A Report of a National Survey* (Chicago: University of Chicago, National Opinion Research Center, 1967), p. 36; Mulvihill, *Crimes of Violence,* pp. 208–15.

[56] Ennis, *Criminal Victimization in the United States,* pp. 23–30.

It is difficult to be precise about the size of this underestimation but it is possible to derive an approximation:

1. Self-report studies indicate that only about 10 percent of all delinquent acts are detected; 90 percent go undiscovered.

2. Studies of the police indicate that of the 10 percent that are discovered only a small proportion result in formal arrest.

3. Uniform Crime Reports indicate that of those acts that do result in arrest about half are handled entirely by the police. At most, therefore, only 5 percent of all acts are pushed into the system beyond the police level.

4. Court statistics indicate that of this small residue less than half actually result in trial, at most 2.5 percent; at worst, much less than that. What, then, are the implications?

It has been suggested that much of our crime could be controlled if we concentrated on suppressing the delinquent acts of those chronic offenders whom the juvenile justice system does apprehend. Even though the system is a coarse net, there is both official and self-report information that some of the most serious offenders are being detected and incarcerated. But what if only 1, or 2, or even 10 percent of all their criminal acts become a matter of official record?

The answer seems obvious. Although society might be better protected if means were found for dealing more effectively with chronic official delinquents, it is clear that many, if not most, criminal acts would not be affected. So long as most of them remain undetected, the system of juvenile justice cannot possibly be an efficient protector of society, to say nothing of the expectation that it can also be society's superparent. If society wishes greater protection from juvenile crime, then the present legal net is too coarse. Either it must become more repressive or other nonlegal means must be used to supplement it.

In recent years officials at all levels in the field of juvenile justice have become preoccupied with implementing a series of three "reforms": [57]

[57] LaMar T. Empey, "Juvenile Justice Reform: Diversion, Due Process, and Deinstitutionalization," in *Prisoners in America,* ed. Lloyd E. Ohlin (Englewood Cliffs, N.J.: Prentice-Hall, 1973), pp. 13–48.

1. *Diversion.* Divert more first-time and nonserious offenders from legal processing.

2. *Due process.* Extend the constitutional protections of due process to juveniles, not only in cases involving charges of criminal conduct but in cases involving issues of dependency, neglect, or moral turpitude.

3. *Deinstitutionalization.* Remove correctional programs from places of confinement and locate them in open community settings.

These reforms are rooted in two major seedbeds: one seedbed, which seriously questions whether correctional programs have any desirable effect;[58] and a second, which suggests that it is official labeling and processing which make career delinquents out of misbehaving youngsters, not anything that is inherently peculiar to them or their environments.[59] But if the net of the juvenile justice system is as coarse as the evidence suggests, such "reforms" are likely to be irrelevant with respect to making significant reductions in the crime rate. Hence, they have to be justified on other grounds—humaneness and benevolence, not crime control.

Juvenile Status Offenses

The implications relative to juvenile status offenses are similar, except that they are more pronounced. Since many of the illegal acts of juveniles are status offenses, it is useful to ask whether legal means should be used to deal with them. Our analysis has shown that the commission of status offenses is not an either-or thing, like having the measles or not having them. Rather, it is a

[58] Douglas Lipton et al., *The Effectiveness of Correctional Treatment* (New York: Praeger, 1975); Robert Martinson, "What Works?—Questions and Answers about Prison Reform," *Public Interest* 35 (Spring, 1974): 22–54.

[59] Howard S. Becker, *Outsiders: Studies in the Sociology of Deviance* (Glencoe, Ill.: Free Press, 1963); Edwin M. Schur, *Radical Nonintervention: Rethinking the Delinquency Problem* (Englewood Cliffs, N.J.: Prentice-Hall, 1973); Frank Tannenbaum, *Crime and the Community* (New York: McGraw-Hill, 1936).

more-or-less thing, since most, or all, young people commit them.

The issue is a difficult one because of rather persistent beliefs that such things as truancy, drinking, sexual promiscuity, and incorrigibility are socially undesirable. There is reason to suspect, however, that the police and courts are, themselves, uncertain on this issue. Many of the status offenders whom they do apprehend are counseled and released rather than arrested and processed through the system. The face that officials operate in this way suggests either that they do not consider status offenses particularly serious or that they believe that other means would be preferable to legal ones, such as the "reforms" mentioned above.

In the last analysis, the basic issue is whether the juvenile justice system is the best means for insuring the conformity of the young to an increasingly ambiguous and unsupported concept of childhood. Not only would legal agents be more free to concern themselves with predatory crimes but more attention might be devoted to the obvious need for new social inventions by which juvenile crime might be prevented. Certainly, we need social institutions that are better adapted to adolescent life in the twentieth century than are the educational, welfare, and penal institutions we inherited from the nineteenth century. The issues, in short, go far beyond our traditional preoccupation with benevolent child saving or coercive legal structures.

Increases in Law Violation

The three measures of delinquent behavior described above are less than definitive as to whether serious crimes by juveniles are increasing. Official accounts suggest that they are, but self-report and victimization studies cannot speak efficiently to the issue because they have not been conducted on an annual basis. Yet in a very real sense conclusive information is almost irrelevant in the present context. The reason is that, along with current beliefs about crime, the collection of self-report and victimization data only adds to the impression that illegal acts are on the increase. Because the actual extent of juvenile law violation was unknown until these data were available, the finding that it is much higher than previously thought has helped to construct an image of delinquent behavior that can only be viewed as increasingly ominous. This kind of process is a common one. Initial concerns over some problem—poverty, mental illness, or ecology, as well as delinquency—lead to an understandable desire for better information by which to comprehend and deal with it. Once developed, the new information almost inevitably makes the problem seem worse because people are made a party to details they were previously unaware of or unconcerned with. New details, in turn, lead to new explanations, to new methods of remedy and control, and to larger numbers of specialists whose concern is with clarifying and ameliorating the problem. But, as the number of specialists grows, so does the problem. A widening spiral is generated which is not reduced until, through the mysterious processes of social change, some new problem becomes ascendant and the former one drifts to some lesser level in the hierarchy of social concerns.

The recognition of this process as applied to delinquent behavior tends to leave one with conflicting impressions and feelings. On one hand, it is difficult to disregard the extent of criminal behavior and victimization among children. Though it is highly likely that such behavior has been common for a long time, it scarcely becomes more palatable upon being discovered. On the other hand, the recognition that delinquency is also a changing social construction, quite apart from what children do, leads to caution in interpretation.

The point is that any enlightened concern with delinquency requires that we step back far enough to see how our society is continually constructing and reconstructing the "problem," as well as to see how it manifests itself in the schools, the playgrounds, the streets, and the hangouts where children spend their time.

## Social Location of Delinquent Behavior

When we look at the social location of delinquent behavior, many of the same issues surface again. Despite differences in the way they get at delinquent behavior, arrest and victim studies provide some impressive, and perhaps surprising, similarities in their social location of those kinds of delinquent acts that are criminal. Official police records show that arrest rates are higher for the young than for the old, higher for males than for females, higher for blacks than for whites, higher for low income than for high income persons, and higher in the city than in the country. Victimization studies, though they look at crime from a totally different perspective, paint an identical picture: young people are more vulnerable to crime than older people; males are more vulnerable than females; blacks are more vulnerable than whites; poor people are more vulnerable than affluent people; and city dwellers are more vulnerable than country dwellers. Though arrest reports represent those who are caught and victim reports represent those who are preyed upon, they seem to be drawing from a common universe of behavior. Thus, despite their differences over the size of that universe, both methods are in general agreement regarding the social location of the crime.

The implications are many. The first is related to the protective stance we have taken toward children. Though we have proclaimed their innocence and supposedly developed elaborate procedures for nurturing and protecting them, evidence indicates that they not only remain inclined to violate legal rules but they are far more likely than mature adults to be the *victims* of crime. The situation is full of ironies, the most impressive of which is the tremendous gap between our idealized construction of childhood and what children actually do, or what actually occurs to them.

It is easy to see why ambivalence exists. Tension is inevitable in a society that on the one hand, is preoccupied with children but, on the other, is confronted with their criminality. That tension is further increased by the belief that delinquent acts must be suppressed but that their perpetrators must be helped and protected. Finally, tension reaches its apex when it is discovered that children and young adults are far more likely to be victimized than are older people. Such a state of affairs might have been expected in Western society during the Middle Ages, but in a society that comes close to worshipping its children, high rates of victimization among them are a surprising, if not shocking, contradiction. Somehow, despite all of our grandiose aspirations, childhood has not turned out to be a guarantine from evil.

The second implication is confounded by the disproportionate location of crime *and* victimization among the children of poor and minority groups. Americans are ambivalent over this validation because it is not only an embarrassment to a supposedly egalitarian society but because it is the result of a self-fulfilling racist prophecy. After centuries of slavery, the consequences of the prophecy are not easily rectified. Even more than white children, black children still occupy a subordinate status in American society. Thus, the white majority sees itself placed in the position of fearing a "criminal" group whom they would like to see suppressed but for whom they also feel an increasing sense of guilt and responsibility.

The search for a solution is made even more difficult by our social construction of crime. The types of crime recorded in arrest, self-report, and victim surveys include few, if any, types of white collar crime. It is as though they did not exist. This only exacerbates the self-fulfilling prophecy. Since the only crimes that are recorded by officials are those most commonly committed by the young, the black, and the poor, those groups are found to be the most criminal. Most affluent groups are protected from being viewed as law violators because data on their crimes are not systematically gathered.

Finally, there is something to be said for some law and some order. Legally, adolescents are "children" in most states until they reach eighteen. Yet it is among these "children" that many serious forms of crime are concentrated. Thus, in fairness to those who would suppress criminals, it is worth noting that there are relatively few differences in the amounts and types of crime committed by older adolescents, ages fifteen to seventeen, and those committed by young adults, eighteen to twenty-five. The fact that violence seems to be increasing among younger age groups only underscores this conclusion. The point is that age eighteen, as the magic dividing line between childhood and adulthood, does not have much meaning whether one is looking at either victimization or crime. Were it not for our present construction of childhood, in fact, our responses to adolescent offenders might be altered considerably. Indeed, there is ever more evidence that considerable reconstruction is already underway.[60]

During the 1960s college and minority youth protested their social and political impotence; the voting age was lowered; changing mores have not only stressed greater sexual freedoms but may signal important alterations in the institution of marriage, particularly as ever larger numbers of young women pursue both legitimate careers; a series of court decisions supports the view that children should be treated as persons in their own right; and legal changes in some states are lowering the age of accountability. The ideal image of childhood is changing and implies greater precociousness than earlier child savers would ever have thought possible.

But these are not the only changes of great significance. A decline in the birthrate, combined with an increase in life expectancy, is creating a societal population that is growing older. For the first time American society, along with other Western societies, is witness to a changing population pyramid that will likely grow increasingly heavy at the top, a phenomenon largely unknown in prior civilizations. For example, the growth in population from 1950 to 1970 was lowest for people under forty-five, 30.5 percent. By contrast, the growth in the number of people over sixty-five increased by 63 percent. Even more striking was the growth in the number of people over seventy-five, 97 percent—from 3.9 million in 1950 to 7.6 million in 1970.[61]

Such trends may hasten a decline in our protective stance toward the young. Ever larger numbers of older people will have to be supported by a proportionately smaller and younger segment of the population. Resources and attention formerly reserved for the young may have to be turned to the elderly, a possibility that could significantly affect efforts to assist those poor and minority segments of the youth population who need it most. A decrease in the privileged status of the young, moreover, may hasten increased demands for accountability, particularly where serious

[60] LaMar T. Empey, *American Delinquency: Its Meaning and Construction* (Homewood, Ill.: Dorsey, 1978), chap. 19.

[61] U.S. Department of Commerce, *Bureau of Census Reports, 1950–1970.*

criminal acts are involved. Magnified demands for retribution are not an impossibility.

In short, we are on the watershed of a series of societal trends that are likely to produce revolutionary changes in our social construction of childhood and our treatment of children. The basic question, therefore, is whether our efforts both to save children and yet reduce their predatory acts can be related to these trends so that the results are somewhat more rational and humane than they have been in the past.

# Delinquency in Cross-cultural Perspective

## Jackson Toby

THE bad news received global attention at the second United Nations Congress on the Prevention of Crime and the Treatment of Offenders in London in 1960. Adolescent delinquency was an increasingly serious problem throughout the world, not only quantitatively greater than before but qualitatively worse: more violent, more likely to involve groups of youngsters (gangs), and more likely to occur at younger ages. In 1965 in Stockholm the third United Nations Congress heard similar reports, as did the fourth Congress in Kyoto in 1970 and the fifth Congress in Geneva in 1975. Economic growth, though it raised living standards, did not seem to reduce crime rates, especially among adolescents. Some criminologists went further: Development itself was a causal factor in the worsening crime and delinquency problems of contemporary societies.

Why should economic development tend to *increase* crime rates? After all, study after study in many countries reports a correlation between disadvantaged socioeconomic status and arrest, conviction, and punishment for crime, including predatory crime. Moreover, it seems plausible that those with the least economic resources are most subject to the temptation to steal. If, indeed, poverty causes crime—or, at least, theft, which in one form or another constitutes the bulk of crime—why should delinquency and crime *increase* when societies become more affluent?

In order to explain this seeming paradox, we must first consider the specific mechanism by which disadvantaged socioeconomic status gives rise to theft. Do most thieves steal because they are starving or cold or in rags? Although Victor Hugo's influential novel *Les Misérables* shows Jean Valjean stealing a loaf of bread because he is hungry, Hugo was statistically incorrect. Even in poor countries, the run-of-the-mill thief arrested by the police is not starving before his crime any more than the average prostitute is before she begins selling her sexual services. To put it another way, it is not *absolute* poverty but *relative* poverty that motivates theft.

This may not seem an important distinction, especially if one is discussing theft in Uganda, where the relatively poor may also be poor by nutritional standards. But in more affluent societies like Israel or Japan or Sweden it becomes clearer that although thieves are motivated by a strong desire for money and the material possessions money can buy, they do not fit the romantic stereotype of the starving victim of circumstances. Consider first an interview with an incarcerated thief in Uganda.

I stole a car during the daytime on———Road in Kampala. This car belonged to an Asian. Previously, I had given 500 shillings to the driver [chauffeur] of that car. He then gave me the key and I copied its model. So I went back and made exactly the same key. So one day when I saw that he had parked his car on———Road, about ten in the morning, I stole it. It was the owner who was driving, not the chauffeur. I had planned to steal the car. You know, such things take a long time to plan. We have to trace the car for quite a long time. This time was I who was to trace this car. I did it quite satisfactorily and got it. Later, along with seven people, one of them my brother, we chased a car which was taking money from a bank for about twenty miles. We were well equipped with pangas [large knives like machetes]. It was about 11:00 in the morning. We used a car which I had stolen. We beat this Asian and took his 1,800 shillings. This was on———Road. Another time, we were five people in the group, all friends. We chased and stopped an Asian's car on———Road. We were all equipped with pangas. It was about 11:00 in the morning. We took about 9,000 shillings from the man. We used the same car I had stolen before. We knew that the car was taking money. This takes months and months until we study or trace the movements of these people. For each case it took two months to trace the factory owners, or to know where, when, how, in what car they transferred the money. In some cases, we bribe the driver or cooperate together. This time it was all our business. We did everything ourselves. We did not use the drivers of those managers to tell us when they would be taking to money. We were discovered because of the Malayan [prostitutes] who reported us! I happened to be a friend of a young, nice looking and attractive lady. She used to spend nights with me and I always had sex with her. She was a very nice woman. But I didn't know that she was a member of the C.I.D., for she loved me very much for about two months. Then one day she took the duplicates of the keys of my car to the police. She reported me. I was finished. Then one evening as we were drinking in a bar with my friends we saw two policemen come in, and they arrested us. It was easily found out that it was the same group which had done all the crimes. But I pleaded not guilty and now I am serving a four-year sentence for theft of a motor car. I learned it from my friends. My brothers had done this for quite a number of years. I was persuaded to join them. We had a brother of ours who sells spare parts of different vehicles so we used to give him all the money we stole. He would use this money to buy spare parts. I hear he is still doing well in our business. But I am afraid he may not have enough money with which to buy more spare parts. He depended too much on our financial help. This business was paying us quite well. But when I go back it seems that I may do the same work [stealing] because all my business [garage] will be in its worst situation. So it seems it will take me years to bring it to the former standards. The best way will be to steal.[1]

Of course, one case study does not establish a statistical generalization. Although Clinard and Abbott report other interviews with prison inmates in Uganda that sound much the same, prisoners are a selected sample of those who commit crimes; they must be caught, convicted, and sentenced to imprisonment. They are probably more dedicated to a criminal way of life than offenders who are not apprehended and therefore less typical of the ordinary thief in Uganda. Nevertheless, it seems noteworthy that in a relatively undeveloped society a thief could become so much like thieves in American prisons and reformatories.

Consider the next case, a twenty-year-old inmate of an Israeli reformatory, interviewed in 1964 (with the aid of an interpreter). Happy is an Yemenite Jew, part of the "Oriental" minority within Israel. On the average, Oriental Jews are as disadvantaged educationally and occupationally, compared with Jews from European

[1] Marshall B. Clinard and Daniel J. Abbott, *Crime in Developing Countries: A Comparative Perspective* (New York: Wiley, 1973), pp. 206–7. Reprinted by permission.

or American backgrounds, as blacks and Hispanics are in the United States, compared with native-born whites. The consequence of this disadvantage is reflected in higher crime and delinquency rates. For example, youngsters born in Israel, Europe, or the United States had in 1960 a delinquency rate only one-half the delinquency rates of youngsters born in Asia and one-third the rate of youngsters born in Africa.[2] Still, Happy lived up to his nickname; he seemed to enjoy the predatory way of life he and his friends engaged in.

Happy's parents came to Israel in 1939 from a town in Yemen when they were young adults. Born in 1944, Happy does not seem to have many pleasant childhood memories. He mentioned two birthday parties when he was very young. I think he mentioned them to suggest how little his parents did for him as he grew older. He stopped going to synagogue at the age of 10. By the age of 15, he began smoking and gambling on the Sabbath. This was shocking behavior to his Orthodox parents, and they objected. "But I did not hear." Happy finished elementary school at 15 and went for a year to a vocational school.

When he was free, he lived in Tel-Aviv. He would wake up about 10:30 A.M. Although his mother was in the house, he would take something to eat for himself. Then we would go to a street with trees and benches where he would meet his friends. If any of the boys had money, they would go to play snooker [a form of pool] or to a day performance in the movies, taking a girl if possible. If there were unaccompanied girls near the meeting place, who didn't work and had nothing to do, they might be picked up. If the boys had no money, they sat, talked, got bored, and annoyed people. If there was a plan to steal a car in the evening and break in, they talked about the job. If no job was planned, they talked about girls, about jobs they did pull or would pull.

Happy wanted to be considered *bomba* [tough] rather than *fryer* [a sucker]. A *fryer* wants to be accepted by the gang, but he never succeeds. "This kind of boy hasn't had the kind of childhood we had,

[2] Central Bureau of Statistics, *Statistical Abstract of Israel, 1963* (Jerusalem: Israeli Government Printing Office, 1962), p. 688. For a discussion of ethnic stratification in Israel, see Henry Toledano, "Time to Stir the Melting Pot," in Michael Curtis and Mordeczi Chertoff, eds., *Israel: Social Structure and Change* (New Brunswick, N.J.: Transaction, 1973), pp. 333–47.

and he doesn't know how to take care of himself." He is permitted to associate with the *chevra* [gang] because he gets money [presumably from his parents] for gasoline, for a party, or to pay the bill in a restaurant. A *bomba*, on the other hand, is daring and aggressive. He steals the latest model cars, and he is successful with *fryereet* [girls who are easy to seduce].

The *chevra* gambled three or four evenings a week for about 5 hours at a time, playing poker, rummy, 21, coin tossing, dice, or a game with a numbered board called "7 times 3." Happy was not usually very lucky. He lost as much as $50 in an evening. Gambling usually started on Friday evening, stopped at 2 or 3 A.M. and began again at about 10:30 A.M. on Saturday morning. The gambling stopped by Saturday evening when the *chevra* went to the movies or to a dance club. Sometimes a boy won too much, and the others suspected him of cheating. They might beat him up and take his money.

Happy and his friends drank liquor at every opportunity, sometimes during a card game, sometimes at a coffee shop, sometimes at a party. They drank Stock 84, for which they paid $1.20 to $1.40 for a half pint. When they had little money, they bought a big bottle of medicinal brandy for 70 cents.

Alcohol increased the probability of fights. "When you are a little drunk, sometimes you start pushing someone around." Once Happy kicked a dog when he was "high." The lady who owned the dog shouted at him; he shouted back. The owner's husband joined the argument. Soon the *doda* [literally "aunts" in Hebrew but meaning "police"] were called. But fights occurred for other reasons. Happy recalled one time when he was playing cards out-of-doors on a Saturday afternoon. A member of an extremely Orthodox sect came over to the *chevra* and told them to stop gambling on the Sabbath. In the course of the furious argument that ensued, the Orthodox man threw a nearby bicycle in the middle of the game. They stopped the game and beat him up badly. If members of the *chevra* made remarks about a girl in the movies, and her boyfriend resented them, this could start a fight. Or sometimes a member of the group took a couple of friends and *laredet alay* [literally "went down on" but meaning "beat up"] a boy who was saying insulting things about him or about the group.

On Happy's right hand is a tattoo consisting of a half-moon and three stars, which [he said] means, "we are against the law." Although he made this tattoo in the reformatory, this could well have been the motto of his *chevra* in the community. Car thefts were a favorite activity. At first cars were stolen only for joyrides. The competition consisted of stealing newer model cars and large cars. "The car is always full—as many as the car will hold." Girls were sometimes reluctant to come for fear of getting involved. Once Happy left his straw hat with a feather in a car he had tried to start unsuccessfully. The gang went back to get the hat after having stolen another car. The *doda* gave chase; but Uri, the driver, outdistanced them. After a while they decided to use the cars they stole to help in burglaries. For example, they broke into a supermarket through air vents in the back—forcing the grill—and took cigarettes and cognac and chocolate away in the car. Then they went back to the room of one of the boys and had a party.

Once, when they passed a Willys station wagon filled with appliances, they stole them and sold them to a *client* [fence] recommended by a friend. The loot consisted of: Clothes, irons, fans, transistor radios, and electric shavers. Four boys each got $200. Happy hid his share under a tile in the courtyard of his house and continued to ask his mother for a pound or two [33 or 66 cents] for spending money. Happy spent all of his share in a month. (He kept the clothes he bought in a pal's house so as not to arouse his mother's suspicions.) This success aroused the interest of the *chevra* in transistor radios, and they broke into appliance stores, preferably from the back but sometimes from the front when the street was clear. Sometimes they also broke into dry goods stores—but this was not so profitable. From every car they stole, they took the radio. Sometimes they stripped cars without moving them.[3]

In some ways the crimes of Happy and his gang are commonplace. They remind American criminologists of the Irish, Polish, and Italian juvenile gangs in Chicago a half century ago—or of black gangs today in Philadelphia, New York, or Cleveland. What is intellectually problematic is the social-psychological mechanism whereby socioeconomic disadvantage leads to criminal motivation. *Envy* rather than desperation seemed to motivate Happy and his friends; similarly, envy seems to underlie the style of life of Yukio, a nineteen-year-old Japanese delinquent interviewed in a reformatory outside of Tokyo in 1963.

[3] President's Commission on Law Enforcement and Administration of Justice, *Task Force Report: Juvenile Delinquency and Youth Crime* (Washington, D.C.: Government Printing Office, 1967), pp. 136–37.

At 15, Yukio graduated from junior high school and enrolled in a vocational school to learn how to drive and repair cars. He stayed six months although the course was supposed to last one year. He said that his friends urged him to quit in order to "live an adult life." He wanted to smoke, to stay out late at night in the entertainment districts of Tokyo, to play *pachinko* [a popular Japanese slot machine game], and to wear fashionable clothing. Before he was imprisoned Yukio wore bell-bottomed trousers and short jackets, the costume of a *chimpira* gang. He and his friends wished to feel superior to other Japanese and therefore wore what they thought to be American-style clothing. Yukio's mother disapproved, but his father, a hard-working clerk, did not say anything. Like his friends, Yukio wore thin underwear instead of the heavy underwear worn by the older generation. [There is very little central heating in Japan, and heavy underwear is protection against a cold, damp climate.]

After leaving the vocational school, Yukio and his friends maintained their interest in cars. They broke into at least eleven cars over a period of several weeks, using a master key to get inside and shorting the ignition wires to start them. They picked up bread in the early morning from in front of grocery stores and ate it while driving around. When the gasoline was used up, they would abandon the cars—first taking care to remove the radios, which they sold for as much as 2,000 yen [$5.50] each.

Yukio and his friends also broke into shops at night. They would select a little shop without a watchman. It would have to be located where a car, previously stolen for the purpose, could be parked nearby while the break-in was in progress. There were usually three to five in the group, one or two looking out for the police. They would either jimmy the door or apply a chemical paste to a window and set it aflame, enabling it to break easily and quietly.

Sometimes they picked a quarrel with a drunk, beat him up, and went through his pockets. Aside from drunks, however, they did not usually bother conventional people. More usually, they would extort money from members of rival *chimpira* groups. Yukio would walk down the street until he saw a likely victim. Two confederates would be nearby but not visible. "Hello, fine fellow. Lend me your face." This was a challenge for the victim to go to a less busy place for a fight. Not seeing Yukio's friends, the victim would agree; he was angry. After the fight started, the confederates would join in, using wooden bats as well as fists. Soon the victim had enough and was willing to agree to give the victors what they wanted. They preferred money. But the victim might not have any. If not, they would take his fountain pen, watch, railroad ticket, and even his clothing. If he had on expensive shoes or a new suit, they might accompany him to a pawn shop where he would exchange these things for old clothes and cash, the latter for Yukio and his friends. They would give a small amount to the victim, 10 percent or less.

Since Yukio was stealing and extorting *yen* with his friends, he had enough money to spend long evenings in the entertainment districts of Tokyo. Subways and buses stopped running at midnight, whereas he did not usually leave his favorite bars until 2 A.M., so he was forced to pay expensive night-rates to taxis in order to get home. This dissatisfied him; he preferred to pay for beer and whiskey or, if he was looking for cut-rate intoxication, for sleeping pills, rather than for transportation. He asked his father to buy him a car so that he might drive himself home in the small hours of the morning. His father was outraged. Yukio did not work; he slept until noon or later every day; he spent his nights in the bars of Shibuya [an entertainment district]; and he had the effrontery to ask his father, a poorly paid clerk, to buy him a car. (His father did not himself have a car.) A violent argument ensued in the course of which his father hit him; he hit his father back.

This blow must have been even more surprising to Yukio's father than the original request for a car. While paternal authority is not now what it was once in Japan, it is still considerable. In traditional homes the wife and children do not eat with the father, who is served in solitary grandeur. That a son would dare to argue openly with his father is a sign of the increased equality between the generations in urban Japan. That a son would hit his father, no matter what the provocation, is, to a Japanese, almost unbelievable.

Yukio's father ordered him out of the house. He left home and moved in with a friend where he stayed for a week. Then he came home and apologized. His father would not forgive him. For a few weeks he stayed first with one *chimpira* and then with another. As soon as he found a girl who worked in a bar as a hostess and could help support him, he rented an apartment. (Such a girl is called *dambe* in Japanese slang, meaning "one who pulls money on a string.") It was important to him that she not become pregnant because she could not continue to work, so Yukio was careful to use contraceptives during sexual intercourse. This was not his usual practice with casual pick-ups.[4]

The interview with Yukio does not explain *why* he became delinquent; but it is probably impossible to explain a single case with confidence. Clearly, though, Yukio was unwilling to accept the traditional Japanese subordination of the young to the old. He wanted to share in the new postwar affluence that mass-produced cars, transitor radios, television sets, and stylish new clothes. And why not? Isn't the revolution of rising expectations a worldwide phenomenon? But adolescents in Japan are caught in a cultural bind. Far more than adolescents in other countries, Japanese adolescents are impoverished compared with adults. Despite tremendous economic growth during the 1960s, despite the more than six million cars registered in Japan when Yukio was in his teens, he had little chance to earn enough to buy one. The Japanese custom is to pay workers mainly in accordance with their age rather than in accordance with their skill. Adolescent workers cannot buy cars —unless they happen to have rich parents willing to subsidize them. Thus, Japanese adolescents have more reason to be envious than adolescents in other affluent societies.

The cases I have presented from Uganda, Israel, and Japan point to *relative* deprivation rather than absolute deprivation as a factor in the explosive growth of youthful property crime. My final case, a twenty-year-old safecracker interviewed in a youth prison in Uppsala, Sweden, in 1960, adds further support to the relative-deprivation hypothesis because Sweden has not been burdened with the social turmoil and economic problems presumed to cause crime. Sweden, the richest country in Europe, was not a belligerent during World War II and did not suffer the disruptive effects of bombing, population loss, and foreign occupation, as did Japan. Sweden has no ethnic minorities, except for Lapp reindeer herders in the northern section, and therefore need not be concerned about prejudice and discimination as an indirect cause of crime (through unequal educational and occupational opportunity). Sweden is culturally homogeneous; except for temporary

[4] Ibid., pp. 135–36.

workers from Latin countries, there has been no large-scale immigration for centuries. Poverty in the old sense of hunger, ragged clothes, and disease does not exist. In the United States and Great Britain, on the other hand, an appreciable part of the crime problem can be attributed to the limited economic and social opportunities of racial minorities. In Israel, too, much crime results from the "melting pot" problems of immigrants from the Middle East and Africa. As in many countries, there has been a housing shortage in Sweden, especially in the cities, dating from the post–World War II rise in the birthrate. But existing housing is modern and pleasant. Slums cannot be the breeding place of crime in Stockholm, Malmö, or Gothenburg, the three largest cities of Sweden, because there are no slums. From the viewpoint of crime prevention Sweden seems ideal; yet delinquency has been a growing problem. The case of Lappen suggests why. Envy is at least as likely in an affluent, welfare-minded society as in societies with lower standards of living and deprived population segments.

Lappen was an unwanted child. He arrived just as the marriage of his parents was breaking up. Shortly after Lappen's birth, his father left his mother for another woman and Lappen was temporarily sent to live with his maternal grandparents in Lapland; his mother could not take care of both children. Lappen's mother earned 600 crowns a month [about $120] in a butcher shop. By Swedish standards this was a low income, and Lappen reported that he envied the clothes and spending money of some of his friends whose family earned 1,600 crowns a month [the man of the family earned a thousand and the woman 600]. When Lappen was 9 or 10 years old, he and three friends from relatively poor families began stealing candy and fruit from local stores so that they could have the same things as the other boys in the neighborhood. (Stig was 1 year older than Lappen, Borje 1 year older, and Jan 1 year younger.) The other neighborhood boys admired the courage of the thieves. "We took greater and greater chances because we had to show that we were just as good as those whose parents had a lot of money." The boys who did not need to steal stole anyway out of a sense of adventure. Lappen and his three friends became the leaders of a gang. Lappen's gang controlled 10 or 15 square blocks. Between the ages of 10 and 15, Lappen participated in many fights. As many as 200 boys were involved in some of the biggest fights. The fights were with gangs from outside the neighborhood and were usually over "honor and girls, if I may say so." Lappen differentiated between two types of boys from outside the neighborhood: boys who came from essentially the same class and boys who were *sossar* [important]. Fights with boys from the same social level were relatively friendly. "We only fought to show who was best. After the fight, we were all friends." In addition to fighting, Lappen and his friends increased the scope of their stealing activities. They "borrowed" rowboats and bicycles. They also "borrowed" automobiles for joyrides.

At the age of 15, just about the time he quit school, Lappen had his first sexual experience. His gang [the south End Club] had obtained a meeting room in a local youth club. Lappen had carefully observed the caretaker's keys, and he had made a duplicate from memory. Consequently, he, Stig, and Borje had a key to the meeting room. One evening he took a girl friend into the room and locked the door. Stig and Borje were outside to see that members of the youth club did not try to come in. Other members of the gang were in the game rooms of the club to keep the caretaker busy enough so that he would not disturb Lappen. Since there was no bed or sofa in the room, his first experience with *knulla* [intercourse] occurred on a table. Subsequently, he engaged in *knulla* frequently, usually in the home of girls whose parents were working. Although he and his friends were *raggarbrud* [promiscuous], they resented it when girls were unfaithful. He told me of one member of the gang who was in love with a girl. When he discovered that he had been sharing her with numerous others, he was enraged. He told his friends. On some pretext the jealous lover and seven of his friends, including Lappen, rowed to a deserted island near Stockholm with the girl. They confronted her with her infidelity and, as punishment, forced her to remove her clothes, and then all except the injured boy friend had sexual relations with her in turn, They rowed back to the mainland leaving her to swim back as best she could.

When he left school, Lappen got a job as a car mechanic. On and off for the next 3 or 4 years, he worked in his occupation, earning 200–250 crowns a week [$40–$50]. Like many other Swedish boys of similar social background, he is fascinated by cars, especially big American cars. He eventually became a member of one of the four most important *raggare* clubs of Stockholm, the Road Devils. Lappen and his friends drank heavily, drove recklessly, and cruised around the city of Stockholm picking up girls who were "looking for a good time." They held noisy parties and dances. Some members stole accessories for their cars. Those who did not own a car "borrowed" cars for joyrides. Lappen was probably more delinquent than most of the *raggare*. He rolled homosexuals and drunks. He burglarized stores with one or two confederates—usually using *schmacha* [the smash and grab technique]. His last *schmacha* was a jewelry store window. He got enough jewelry and watches to sell to a fence for 2,000 crowns. With this money he bought his own car and gave up stealing.

As Lappen described his life as a *raggare* boy, it was a life of fun, of laughs. "I lived an expensive life and I done exactly what I want. If I wanted to go to Copenhagen, I gotta go to Copenhagen. When we would drive to a little town, the girls knew we came from Stockholm and looked up to us." There was dancing and singing in the streets. "When I want to dance, I dance." Every weekend there would be parties in the homes of various girls or boys that he knew. He would start out on a Saturday evening at one party and would move on to others as the inclination moved him. He would usually bring vodka or Scotch or Spanish brandy as his contribution to the merriment. Ten to twenty young people would be present at a given party at one time, but there would be constant comings and goings. For example, Lappen would usually get to three or four parties by Sunday morning. "If I didn't have fun, I'd get home by 3 or 4 A.M. If I had fun, I'd get home by 6 or 7." Sometimes, however, the parties lasted all through Sunday.

In 1957 Lappen was convicted for breaking and entering and sent to Fagared, a youth prison near Gothenburg. When he was released, he did not return to Stockholm. Instead he took a room in Gothenburg and got a job as an auto mechanic. Somehow, while he was in the institution, he had fallen in love with a local girl. He distinguished his love for this 17-year-old girl from the many intimate relationships that he had with girls in his neighborhood and in the *raggare*. (Girls are also members of the *raggare* clubs, but they rarely own cars.) "That year 1958 I shall never forget. It was the happiest year of my life. For the first time, I had a family. I played cards with her father and listened to the radio." The girl's father, an office worker, took a liking to Lappen. He discovered that the boy was living in a lonely furnished room and offered to rent a room to him in their house. Lappen eagerly accepted. During the period when he lived in his girl friend's house, he was, according to his account, a model young man. He didn't drink; he went to bed early; he worked steadily; and he spent his spare time with his girl friend. Unfortunately, she became pregnant. When they told her parents, he at first thought that they would allow him to marry her, which is what both of them wanted. But a few days later the father told him that he "was no longer welcome in the house." Without further discussion, Lappen left. The girl. being only 17, could not marry without her parent's consent. They insisted that she go to a hospital and have an abortion. Lappen returned to Stockholm. His letters to her were returned unopened. Soon he went back to his old life with the *raggare*. Twice he and another Road Devil broke into safes although Lappen was very nervous, and he let his partner handle the explosives.

"The boys in this place are like gamblers. If we win, we get money. If we lose, we are locked up. Because we are good losers, we can smile." He recognized that, when he got out of prison, he faced a choice between two very different ways of life. "I know that the right kind of life is to work and have a family, something to hope at. Maybe I had it too easy the last year now and it is difficult to get back to normal life. On the one side, I found a lot of fun and on the other side, the right side, there was only a hard life." I asked Lappen what the chances were of his not getting into trouble any more. "If I learn to trust people, I won't have any more trouble." I think what he meant was that he would not commit further crimes if he developed another relationship like the one he had with the girl from Gothenburg and her family.[5]

Case studies like the foregoing ones illustrate the mechanism whereby poverty leads to crime: through arousing feelings of material deprivation that cannot be satisfied legitimately. Bear in mind, though, that adolescent delinquents are the minority of their age cohort in every country. Feelings of relative deprivation do not inevitably lead to crime. On the contrary, they are rarely acted upon. Under what conditions does the impulse to steal lead to theft? When affluence not only arouses predatory motives but offers the potential predator some prospect for "getting away with it," the probability increases that the motives will find expression in action. The reason why economic development tends to increase the rate of property crime is that economic development not only increases affluence; it also stimulates urbanization, which loosens social controls and thus provides the *opportunity* for delinquency and crime.

[5] Ibid., pp. 137–39.

### Urbanization and Crime

The notion that urban life gives rise to a distinct personality draws
on a long tradition, counting among its proponents such founding
fathers of sociology as Max Weber, Georg Simmel, and Robert E.
Park. But certainly it is not the asphalt or the high-rise buildings
of the city or even its congestion that produces a less tradition-
bound, more self-oriented individual. It is the character of urban
social interaction, especially its anonymity compared with rural
areas. Urban anonymity gives the individual an opportunity to escape social control, and stealing is a possible response to this opportunity. Certainly, if an individual is not personally known to
most of the people he meets on the street of a large city, his crime
has a better chance of escaping detection. Automobiles facilitate
further the evasion of this kind of personal control.

But there is another aspect of urban anonymity that also increases the temptation to steal: the anonymity of property. The
city is a place where the ownership of possessions is usually based
on an impersonal market transaction. I take money that I have
earned and walk into a store and buy a wristwatch or a suit. The
sales clerk is not interested in my character or my mental health;
the item is for sale to anyone with the money to pay for it. The
customer and the clerk do not ordinarily expect to haggle with
one another, as is customary in many societies when goods are
bought and sold. In fact, in a modern supermarket the shopper
need not speak at all to the checkout person at the cash register.
Not only goods but services are impersonally bought and sold in
contemporary cities. In a hotel, for example, I can obtain a bed
for the night from a complete stranger merely by paying money.
Such an arrangement might puzzle an aboriginal Murngin from
Australia because he lives in a society where sleeping accommodations are strictly determined by kinship; they are too personal to
sell. He would certainly find shocking the Western practice of paying nurses to take care of persons who are sick.

Thus, the market economy of the city contrasts with the subsistence economy of the rural areas of underdeveloped societies.
An appetite for money develops in the city because money is
needed to enter the market and obtain goods and services. That is

why persons in New York, Moscow, Stockholm, Nairobi, and Caracas are concerned about money. In preliterate societies, on the other hand, where very little consumption is organized through markets, lack of interest in money is understandable. The Trobriand Islanders, though excellent divers, could not be induced to dive for pearls because the monetary rewards offered to them by traders had little meaning in their society.[6] A similar situation prevails in underdeveloped countries starting to industrialize. High factory wages are not as effective an incentive as in fully industrialized societies because the population does not depend much on money to satisfy its wants.[7] The good things of life are not for sale in the marketplace.

Whereas the subsistence farmers of an underdeveloped society need not become involved in the market system, even though the society around them has a money economy, the logic of urban existence forces city dwellers into the marketplace. City dwellers, almost by definition, do not raise their own food and therefore must exchange something of value with an agricultural hinterland. Over the past three centuries a major part of that something has been industrial production. This emphasis on industrial production in modern cities explains why economic development and urbanization are thought of as concomitant processes. In point of fact, however, industrialization can take place in rural and suburban areas; and the concentration of population in cities can occur without sufficient economic development to involve the new migrants in the market economy. Insufficient economic development is relevant to the association between urbanization and crime. If rural migrants to the city cannot find jobs, they cannot enter the market system except as welfare dependents or thieves. They and their children may be tempted to take advantage of the anonymity of the city to steal what they cannot obtain on a more legitimate basis.

Greater migration into cities than urban economies can absorb —what demographers call overurbanization—has characterized recent decades of demographic history. Complex forces account for

[6] Dorothy Lee, *Freedom and Culture* (Englewood Cliffs, N.J.: Prentice-Hall, 1959), pp. 98–99.

[7] Wilbert E. Moore, "Primitives and Peasants in Industry," *Social Research* 15 (1948):44–81.

*Table 1.* Countries in which the population classified as urban at least doubled between 1950 and 1975

| Country * | 1975 population Total (in millions) | Growth rate (percent) | Percent urban† 1975 | 1950 | Percent change | Per capita income (in U.S. dollars) |
|---|---|---|---|---|---|---|
| Africa | | | | | | |
| Algeria | 16.8 | 2.2 | 49.9 | 21.4 | 133.2 | 295 |
| Angola | 6.3 | 2.1 | 18.3 | 5.8 | 215.5 | 280 |
| Burundi | 4.0 | 2.4 | 3.8 | 1.4 | 171.4 | 68 |
| Cameroon | 6.4 | 1.8 | 23.8 | 9.0 | 164.4 | 165 |
| Central African Republic | 1.8 | 2.3 | 35.9 | 10.6 | 238.7 | 122 |
| Chad | 4.0 | 2.1 | 13.9 | 4.0 | 247.5 | 70 |
| Dahomey | 3.0 | 1.4 | 18.0 | 5.9 | 205.1 | 81 |
| Ethiopia | 28.8 | 2.6 | 11.2 | 4.8 | 133.3 | 79 |
| Ghana | 9.9 | 3.0 | 32.4 | 14.5 | 123.4 | 217 |
| Guinea | 4.4 | 2.4 | 19.4 | 5.6 | 248.2 | 79 |
| Ivory Coast | 4.9 | 2.4 | 20.4 | 6.3 | 223.8 | 387 |
| Kenya | 13.3 | 3.4 | 11.3 | 5.6 | 101.8 | 167 |
| Lesotho | 1.0 | 2.0 | 3.1 | 0.8 | 287.5 | 77 |
| Liberia | 1.8 | 3.1 | 15.2 | 5.7 | 166.7 | 197 |
| Malagasy Republic | 7.6 | 2.3 | 17.8 | 7.8 | 128.2 | 138 |
| Malawi | 5.0 | 2.6 | 6.4 | 3.2 | 100.0 | 104 |
| Mauritania | 1.3 | 3.3 | 11.1 | 4.9 | 126.5 | 174 |
| Mozambique | 9.4 | 3.5 | 6.3 | 2.3 | 173.9 | 228 |
| Rwanda | 4.1 | 2.1 | 3.8 | 0.9 | 322.2 | 61 |
| Uganda | 11.5 | 3.3 | 8.4 | 2.9 | 189.7 | 132 |
| Upper Volta | 6.0 | 2.3 | 8.3 | 4.0 | 107.5 | 62 |
| Zaire | 24.9 | 2.8 | 26.2 | 7.9 | 231.6 | 118 |
| Zombia | 5.0 | 3.5 | 36.6 | 11.0 | 232.7 | 345 |
| Asia | | | | | | |
| Afghanistan | 19.1 | 2.3 | 12.3 | 6.0 | 105.0 | 83 |
| China | 942.0 | 2.4 | 23.3 | 11.1 | 111.7 | —‡ |
| Khmer Republic | 8.0 | 2.6 | 22.5 | 8.7 | 158.6 | 123 |
| Korea, Dem. Rep. of | 15.9 | 2.8 | 42.7 | 20.5 | 108.3 | —‡ |
| Korea, Rep. of | 34.0 | 1.7 | 47.4 | 18.4 | 157.6 | 344 |
| Lebanon | 3.3 | 3.4 | 59.8 | 24.5 | 144.1 | 631 |
| Mongolia | 1.4 | 3.0 | 51.5 | 22.4 | 129.9 | —‡ |
| Nepal | 12.6 | 2.3 | 4.8 | 2.1 | 128.6 | 90 |
| Saudi Arabia | 8.9 | 2.9 | 20.8 | 8.2 | 153.7 | 833 |
| Turkey | 39.9 | 2.5 | 43.1 | 21.3 | 102.3 | 435 |
| Yemen Arab Republic | 6.7 | 3.0 | 8.9 | 2.1 | 323.8 | 77 |
| Yemen Dem. Republic | 1.7 | 3.3 | 29.0 | 14.4 | 101.4 | 96 |
| Vietnam, Dem. Rep. of | 24.5 | 2.9 | 14.3 | 5.1 | 180.4 | —‡ |

*Table 1* (cont.)

| | 1975 population | | Percent urban † | | | Per capita |
| Country | Total (in millions) | Growth rate (percent) | 1975 | 1950 | Percent change | income (in U.S. dollars) |
|---|---|---|---|---|---|---|
| Latin America | | | | | | |
| Jamaica | 2.1 | 3.1 | 45.1 | 22.2 | 103.1 | 727 |
| Bulgaria | 8.7 | 0.5 | 57.9 | 27.6 | 109.8 | —‡ |
| Oceana | | | | | | |
| Papua/New Guinea | 2.7 | 2.4 | 12.9 | 1.2 | 975.0 | 477 |

SOURCES: "1975 World Population Estimates," The Environmental Fund, Washington D.C. (unpublished); United Nations, *Statistical Yearbook 1974* (New York: Department of Economics and Social Affairs, 1975), pp. 644–648.

\* Only countries with a 1975 population of at least one million inhabitants are included in this table.

† Percent of urban population is unfortunately defined somewhat differently in different countries, thereby necessitating countries in international comparisons.

‡ Not available.

overurbanization: rural poverty, higher living standards (including greater cultural and educational opportunities) in the cities compared with rural areas, and, above all, the pressure of the explosive growth of world population in response to lower death rates. In 1975 world population was growing at an annual rate of 2.2 percent; that is, at a rate sufficient to double every thirty-three years.[8] Rural areas traditionally have higher rates of natural increase; that is, an excess of births over deaths, than urban areas. But the pressure of this rapidly growing population in rural areas set off vast internal migration to cities all over the world. The problem is particularly acute in underdeveloped countries, where population increase tends to be greatest and where the economic growth is far too modest to integrate the newly arrived city dwellers from rural areas into the occupational system and the market for consumer goods and services. To put it another way, urban populations have grown very rapidly in underdeveloped countries; for such countries overurbanization is not merely a problem; it is a catastrophe. Table 1 documents overurbanization by listing all

[8] "1975 World Population Estimates," The Environmental Fund, Washington, D.C. (unpublished).

of the countries (with more than a million inhabitants in 1975) in which the proportion of the population living in urban areas at least doubled between 1950 and 1975. Note that most of these countries have extremely low per capita incomes.

Overurbanization produces in many underdeveloped countries two radically different ways of life: a tribal, or familistic, way of life in rural areas and a more individualistic way of life in the expanding cities. The cultural differences are enormous between the more personal social bonds in the rural areas and the anonymous patterns of the cities. These differences are much greater than in societies like the United States or Sweden, where economic development and urbanization have proceeded so far that the cultural differences between urban and rural areas have become blurred. A major factor in this blurring is the spread of the money economy into all corners of modern urban industrial societies. Thus, commercial farmers, unlike subsistence farmers, resemble urban businessmen in consciousness of costs, orientation to the market for the sale of farm products, investment in capital equipment, and even in the use of accounting. Commercial farms have been called "factories in the field."

There still remain substantial differences in crime rates between rural and urban areas, even in countries like Sweden and the United States. Table 2 shows the different rates of crimes known to the police in 1974 in the United States in cities of various sizes and in rural areas. Clearly, the larger cities had more serious crime problems than smaller cities and rural areas. However, the differences in rates between the largest cities and the rural areas for the most frequently occurring types of theft, burglary, and simple larceny were modest: 2.5 times larger for burglary and 2.6 times larger for simply larceny. For all property crimes together, cities of 1,000,000 or greater population had a rate 3.4 times the rate in rural areas. (There were 37 times as many armed robberies per 100,000 population in the largest cities as in the rural areas, but this violent property crime was less frequent than nonviolent crimes.)

In Uganda, on the other hand, the crime problem in Kampala, the capital and largest city (300,000 inhabitants), contrasts more sharply than in urban industrial societies with the crime problems

*Table 2.* Crimes known to the police by community size per 100,000 population, United States, 1974

| Community size | Murder | Robbery | Burglary | Larceny-Theft | Auto-theft |
|---|---|---|---|---|---|
| 6 cities over | | | | | |
| 1,000,000 pop. | 24 | 837 | 2,012 | 2,532 | 1,055 |
| 21 cities 500,000 | | | | | |
| to 1,000,000 | 21 | 547 | 2,357 | 3,713 | 998 |
| 31 cities of 250,000 | | | | | |
| to 500,000 | 17 | 451 | 2,471 | 3,591 | 840 |
| 107 cities of 100,000 | | | | | |
| to 250,000 | 12 | 265 | 2,079 | 3,720 | 712 |
| 253 cities 50,000 | | | | | |
| to 100,000 | 7 | 168 | 1,568 | 3,256 | 518 |
| 519 cities 25,000 | | | | | |
| to 50,000 | 6 | 128 | 1,341 | 3,069 | 411 |
| 1300 cities 10,000 | | | | | |
| to 25,000 | 5 | 76 | 1,139 | 2,738 | 291 |
| 3631 cities under | | | | | |
| 10,000 | 4 | 47 | 980 | 2,406 | 214 |
| Rural areas | | | | | |
| (Population: | | | | | |
| 21,233,000) | 8 | 23 | 792 | 956 | 103 |

SOURCE: United States Department of Justice, *Crime in the United States: 1974* (Washington, D.C.: Government Printing Office, 1975), pp. 160–61.

of rural areas. Table 3 shows the rates for crimes against property and crimes against the person for Kampala and for the rest of Uganda in 1968. Property crimes were 12.6 times as frequent in Kampala per 100,000 population as they were in the rest of Uganda. Table 3 may not reveal the extent of the contrast between urban and rural crime in Uganda because four cities with populations over 10,000 are included in the data for "the rest of Uganda." Nevertheless, it shows rather clearly that property crime in Kampala is far more prevalent than in the rest of the country. Kampala also had 8.1 times as many crimes against the person (murder, rape, assault) in 1968 as the rest of Uganda; in the United States, the largest cities had a murder rate only 3.4 times the murder rate in rural areas. The contrast between Kampala and the rest of

*Table* 3. Property and personal crimes reported to police in Uganda, type by rate for 100,000 population in Kampala, the largest city, and the rest of the country, 1968

| Type of crime | Kampala | | Rest of Uganda | |
|---|---|---|---|---|
| | Number reported | Rate | Number reported | Rate |
| Against property | 13,125 | 4,187 | 29,767 | 333 |
| Against the person | 5,651 | 1,803 | 19,924 | 223 |
| Total | 20,574 | 6,565 | 60,292 | 675 |

SOURCE: Marshall B. Clinard and Daniel J. Abbott, *Crimes in Developing Countries: A Comparative Perspective* (New York: Wiley, 1973), p. 91.

Uganda apparently holds for crimes against the person as well as for property crimes—although not to the same extent. Some of these crimes against the person in Uganda, as in the United States, occur in the course of thefts; but it is not possible to disentangle predatory from nonpredatory motivations in official criminal statistics.[9]

To sum up: The contrasting ways of life in urban and rural areas make for greater urban crime rates, especially property crime rates. Overurbanization complicates the situation by bringing into cities rural migrants with no opportunities in the economic system. Overurbanization is particularly serious in underdeveloped societies with spectacular rates of population growth and, consequently, big flows of population into cities overwhelmed by the socioeconomic problems the migrants pose. But the wealthy urban industrial societies can suffer from overurbanization too. Over-

[9] Criminological studies have found in the past that the majority of murderers knew the victim before the fatal incident. The murder occurred in the course of a quarrel between friends, drinking companions, or family members. For example, see Marvin E. Wolfgang, *Patterns in Criminal Homicide* (Philadelphia: University of Pennsylvania Press, 1958). However, it is estimated that the majority of murders in the largest American cities *now* involve strangers, e.g., victims of robberies. This mixture of motives is probably the case in Kampala also. If not for this confounding of predatory and nonpredatory motives in crimes against the person, the differences between urban and rural rates for crimes against the person would probably be smaller than they are.

urbanization is possible (and indeed likely) because the socio-economic factors *pushing* rural persons out of agriculture are not necessarily matched by educational and occupational opportunities awaiting them in the cities.[10] Thus, in the United States the further mechanization of agriculture after World War II drove millions of unskilled farm workers out of rural areas into cities, creating in the process an urban crisis, including in the 1960s a steeply rising crime rate. One reason for the urban crisis in the United States was the lack of a migration policy which sought to achieve a balance between the absorptive capacity of the cities and the industrialization of agriculture.

Table 4 documents the extent to which urban societies—here defined as countries with two-thirds of their populations living in urban areas—urbanized further between 1950 and 1975. The United Kingdom is unique among urban societies in becoming slightly *less* urbanized over that twenty-five-year period. The United States, with an increase of 19 percent in its urban population, urbanized to a much smaller extent than Japan, Chile, Venezuela, France, and Spain. Hong Kong, Italy, and Denmark were closest to the United States in rate of urban growth. Some of these urban societies, such as Japan, avoided overurbanization (1) because their rates of economic growth were sufficient to absorb rural migrants into the economy and (2) because the rural migrants to the cities were especially adaptable. But it is doubtful whether any society, urban or underdeveloped, has a rational policy toward internal migration.

Even urban societies need a migration policy because segments of their rural populations lack the educational preparation and the occupational skills required in the urban economy. But in urban societies rural populations are more involved in the money economy than they are in underdeveloped societies, and this contributes to cultural homogeneity. For instance, not only has rural electrification eliminated such laborious tasks as pumping water and milking cows by hand on Swedish and American farms; it has

[10] Demographers have for a long time explained internal migration in terms of both pushes and pulls. See, for example, Samuel A. Stouffer, "Intevening Opportunities: A Theory Relating Mobility and Distance," *American Sociological Review* 5 (1940): 845–67.

*Table 4.* Urban societies

| Country | 1975 population | | Percent urban | | | Per capita income U.S. dollars) |
|---|---|---|---|---|---|---|
| | Total | Growth rate | 1975 | 1950 | % change | |
| Asia | | | | | | |
| Hong Kong | 4.3 | 2.0 | 94.9 | 79.1 | 20.0 | 735 |
| Japan | 111.9 | 1.3 | 75.2 | 50.3 | 49.5 | 3,292 |
| Kuwait | 1.0 | 4.8 | 88.6 | 55.9 | 58.5 | 3,890 |
| Singapore | 2.3 | 1.9 | 90.2 | 47.4 | 90.3 | 1,265 |
| North America | | | | | | |
| Canada | 22.7 | 1.3 | 78.4 | 60.7 | 29.2 | 4,751 |
| U.S.A. | 219.7 | 1.0 | 76.3 | 63.9 | 19.4 | 5,554 |
| Latin America | | | | | | |
| Argentina | 25.0 | 1.5 | 80.0 | 64.2 | 24.6 | 1,191 |
| Chile | 10.7 | 1.9 | 83.0 | 58.1 | 42.9 | 590 |
| Uruguay | 3.1 | 1.0 | 80.6 | 65.4 | 23.2 | 759 |
| Venezuela | 12.0 | 2.9 | 82.4 | 55.2 | 49.3 | 1,307 |
| Europe | | | | | | |
| Belgium | 9.9 | 0.5 | 71.8 | 63.4 | 13.2 | 3,346 |
| Denmark | 5.1 | 0.8 | 82.0 | 67.9 | 20.8 | 5,004 |
| Dem. Rep. of Germany | 16.8 | —0.4 | 74.9 | 70.8 | 5.8 | — |
| Fed. Rep. of Germany | 62.5 | 0.5 | 83.4 | 70.8 | 17.8 | 5,040 |
| France | 53.0 | 0.8 | 76.1 | 56.0 | 35.9 | 3,403 |
| Italy | 56.0 | 1.0 | 66.7 | 64.4 | 22.6 | 2,298 |
| Netherlands | 13.7 | 0.8 | 79.4 | 73.2 | 8.5 | 4,103 |
| Spain | 35.6 | 1.1 | 69.5 | 52.6 | 32.1 | 1,606 |
| Sweden | 8.2 | 0.2 | 83.7 | 65.9 | 27.0 | 5,596 |
| United Kingdom | 56.2 | 0.2 | 78.2 | 79.1 | —1.1 | 2,503 |
| Oceania | | | | | | |
| Australia | 13.5 | 1.3 | 86.0 | 80.2 | 7.2 | 3,426 |
| New Zealand | 3.1 | 2.1 | 83.4 | 72.2 | 15.5 | 3,711 |

SOURCE: "1975 World Population Estimates," The Environmental Fund, Washington, D.C. (unpublished); United Nations, *Statistical Yearbook 1974* (New York: Department of Economic and Social Affairs, 1975), pp. 644–48.
NOTE: For the purpose of this table a country is considered an urban society if two-thirds or more of its population were urban in 1975 and it contained more than one million inhabitants in 1975.

also enabled farm families to listen to the same radio programs and view the same television programs as urban families. In underdeveloped societies, on the other hand, the cultural gap between rural and urban areas is so great that a migration policy is crucial if the new urbanites are to have a reasonable prospect of integration into urban life.

### Economic Development and Reduced Control
### over Adolescents

Economic development tends to increase predatory crime indirectly through fostering the growth of cities—and especially through *over-stimulating* urban growth; the anonymity and individualism of city life provide greater opportunity than rural areas do for the commission of crimes. Economic development simultaneously tends to increase crime through loosening the tight family bonds that prevail in tribal or peasant societies. Bear in mind that urban industrial societies are highly differentiated societies in which roles in the economy or in government are assigned to persons as individuals rather than as representatives of families or tribes. Thus an *occupational* role can be played well or poorly quite independently of the person's role in his *family*. A woman, for example, can get a job and support herself and her children if she is not satisfied with the way her husband treats her. The possibility of employment for women does not automatically lead to a high divorce rate or to an equalitarian ideal for married couples, but the role structure is conducive to female independence. For the same reason a differentiated role structure is also conducive to *adolescent* independence. If Johnny leaves home, he has a place to go and the means of supporting himself. The individualistic organization of industrial societies therefore is an obstacle to patriarchal domination. Unlike the situation in biblical times, wives and children can survive socially and economically if they do not obey the would-be patriarch.

The individual is the unit of social participation far more than in underdeveloped societies because the family is no longer the dominant institution of society; it is one of many institutions (economic, political, religious, recreational, educational) in which the individual plays roles. The individual still thinks of himself as a family member, especially in Japan, where family obligations are considered more important than personal happiness, but the or-

ganization of the role structure encourages him to think of his own
accomplishments and the rewards these accomplishments gain for
him. Monetary rewards are important not only as a means of purchasing intrinsically desirable goods and services but as a symbol
of accomplishment, the approval of others, and even of personal
fulfillment. The contemporary individual is prone to ask whether
he is having as much fun as others do, which often translates into
a monetary question. Fun in industrial societies has become pur-
chasable in the marketplace; commercial recreation offers the possibility of enjoying life through skiing weekends, sailboat charters,
a flight to Las Vegas, a visit to Disneyland—as well as by watching
movies or playing golf.

One reason the family has less control over the individual in
modern societies is that he now allocates his commitments over a
bigger range of institutions. The other reason—and probably the
more important one—is that the nuclear family of urban industrial
societies is not embedded in an extended family to the extent that
the nuclear family is in preindustrial societies. The nuclear family
is isolated physically and emotionally from other relatives. This
isolation of the nuclear family has special complications for the
adolescent stage of the life cycle; it makes adolescence in industrial societies a situation of minimal familial guidance.

Consider why this should be so. Unlike families in tribal societies, which proceed in an unbroken line for generations, families
in industrial societies pass through a cycle of establishment, de-

*Table 5.* Arrest rates for different age groups: United States 1965
(arrests per 100,000 population)

| Age groups | Arrest rates for larceny, burglary, motor vehicle theft |
|---|---|
| 11–14 | 1,293 |
| 15–17 | 2,467 |
| 18–20 | 1,452 |
| 21–24 | 834 |
| 25–29 | 507 |

Source: *The Challenge of Crime in a Free Society,* A Report by The President's
Commission on Law Enforcement and Administration of Justice (Washington.
D.C.: U.S. Government Printing Office, February 1967), Table 1, p. 56.

*Table 6.* Nontraffic penal code offenders investigated by the Japanese police, by age, 1970

| Age | Number | Rate (per 1,000) |
|---|---|---|
| 14–15 | 37,818 | 11.5 |
| 16–17 | 40,606 | 11.6 |
| 18–19 | 35,657 | 9.0 |
| 20–24 | 87,816 | 8.1 |

SOURCE: Government of Japan, *Summary of the White Paper on Crime,* 1971 (Tokyo: Research and Training Institute, Ministry of Justice, 1972), p. 36.

velopment, and, when the children leave to establish their own households and the parents die, dissolution. Thus, an individual typically is a member of *two* families, not one: first the family into which he is born and then the family he creates by marriage. Adolescence in modern societies is the period of transition between these two families. In the course of the process of emotional and physical disengagement from the family into which he was born, the adolescent is temporarily adrift; family control over him is not reestablished until he voluntarily commits himself to marriage and parenthood. During this limbo period, delinquency rates are characteristically high. Tables 5, 6, and 7 show the pattern of rising delinquency rates in adolescence and falling rates in young adulthood in the United States, Sweden, and Japan.[11] As one commentator put it, "Delinquency is an episode, not a disease."

[11] This pattern of high delinquency rates for adolescents is *not* characteristic of the underdeveloped societies, although these societies are growing alarmed at the disproportionate *increase* in adolescent crime. Countries like Nepal, Malaysia, Uganda, and India have not yet reached the stage where adolescents commit a disproportionate share of most crimes. See B. K. Bantawa, "Juvenile Delinquency in Nepal," *Resource Material Series, No. 10* (Tokyo: United Nations Asia and Far East Institute for the Prevention of Crime and the Treatment of Offenders, 1975), p. 117; M. H. B. Yunos, "Problems of Delinquency in a Multi-Racial Society—Malaysia," *Resource Material Series, No. 4* (Tokyo: UNIFEI, 1972), pp. 152–53; John Lobo, "Some Aspects of Juvenile Deviant Behavior and Delinquency in a Developing Country," *Resource Material Series, No. 4* (Tokyo: UNIFEI, 1972), p. 143; and Clinard and Abbott, *Crime in Developing Countries,* p. 95.

*Table 7.* Persons convicted* of offenses against the penal code per 100,000 population, Sweden, 1935–67

| Year of conviction | Age of offenders | | |
|---|---|---|---|
| | 15–17 | 18–20 | 21 and over |
| 1935–1939 | 316 | 234 | 102 |
| 1940–1944 | 580 | 538 | 159 |
| 1945–1949 | 478 | 498 | 147 |
| 1950–1954 | 625 | 677 | 192 |
| 1955–1959 | 947 | 940 | 268 |
| 1960–1964 | 1,334 | 1,187 | 288 |
| 1965–1967 | 1,216 | 1,219 | 301 |

SOURCE: Carl-Gunnar Janson, "Juvenile Delinquency in Sweden," *Youth and Society* II (1970), 208.

* Or given a suspension of prosecution in accordance with the law of 1944 governing such suspensions.

Of course, control is a matter of degree. Even in urban industrial societies, some parents are more effective than others in maintaining control over their children, including adolescent children. The greater the concern of parents about their children's comings and goings, the more likely they are to establish guidelines for bedtime, homework, mealtimes, and general whereabouts. Children who accept this parental control as legitimate have less opportunity to engage in delinquent behavior. Children need not experience parental supervision as oppressive, and parents may not intend it to be so. Many years ago, while interviewing a group of teenagers in a slum neighborhood, I asked whether their parents required them to be home by a definite time. I received various replies: 11, 12, 1, 2. One fifteen-year-old girl said she had no definite time to be home. But when I asked when she *usually* got home, she explained that she *always* was home by midnight. "Why is that?" I asked. "Because I know that, if I'm not home by midnight, my mother will start to worry." The image of her mother restlessly pacing the apartment and waiting for her daughter to return brought this young woman home by midnight without fail. The mother was exercising extremely effective control. Even concerned parents find it difficult to control their own children if

*Table 8.* The relationship between coming from a broken home and appearing in juvenile court, by color and sex: Philadelphia, 1960

| Girls | Nonwhites | | Whites | |
|---|---|---|---|---|
| | From broken homes | From intact homes | From broken homes | From intact homes |
| Juvenile court appearance | 699 | 317 | 196 | 278 |
| No juvenile court appearance | 26,925 | 64,367 | 16,880 | 182,904 |
| Total population | 27,594 | 64,684 | 17,076 | 183,182 |
| Delinquency per 10,000 population | 242 | 49 | 115 | 15 |
| | ⌊4.9 times greater⌋ | | ⌊7.7 times greater⌋ | |

| Boys | Nonwhites | | Whites | |
|---|---|---|---|---|
| | From broken homes | From intact homes | From broken homes | From intact homes |
| Juvenile court appearance | 2,081 | 1,660 | 732 | 1,730 |
| No juvenile court appearance | 24,859 | 61,490 | 16,482 | 182,892 |
| Total population | 26,940 | 63,150 | 17,214 | 184,622 |
| Delinquency per 10,000 population | 773 | 263 | 425 | 94 |
| | ⌊2.9 times greater⌋ | | ⌊4.5 times greater⌋ | |

SOURCES: The data on juvenile court appearance in Philadelphia comes from the *Forty-Seventh Annual Report of the County Court of Philadelphia* (1960), pp. 122–23; the data on the family composition of the population of Philadelphia County come from United States Bureau of Census, *U.S. Census of Population: 1960,* Volume 1, Part 40 (Pennsylvania) (Washington, D.C.: U.S. Government Printing Office, 1961), p. 620; the rates computed are considerably lower than the true rates because the base population contains *all* children under eighteen whereas the juvenile court statistics refer with minor exceptions to children under eighteen but over seven.

other people's children in the local community are uncontrolled. One reason why the urban slum is associated with delinquency is the concentration in such neighborhoods of families with serious health and welfare problems, problems interfering with effective socialization of and control over children.[12]

Under urban industrial conditions family control is always precarious; other institutions compete with the family, and the child is ultimately expected to become emotionally independent of the

*Table 9.* Delinquency in two cohorts of Stockholm boys, by occupational status of their fathers (mothers) and by the presence of both parents in the home

| Occupational status of fathers (mothers) when boys were eleven | 2,442 boys born in 1925 | | 1,900 boys born in 1940 | |
|---|---|---|---|---|
| | Percent delinquent from intact homes | Percent delinquent from broken homes | Percent delinquent from intact homes | Percent delinquent from broken homes |
| Upper class | 2.0 | 3.0 | 2.9 | 5.4 |
| Middle class | 3.3 | 5.0 | 9.7 | 17.3 |
| Working class | 7.8 | 12.3 | 14.3 | 22.6 |

SOURCE: Unpublished tabulations made available by Professor Carl-Gunnar Janson of the University of Stockholm.

family into which he or she was born. Although children less frequently become orphans in urban industrial societies, where the life expectancy is greater than in underdeveloped societies, a child in an industrial society has a better chance of having his biological parents alive and well during his or her adolescence; on the other

[12] Sociologists at the University of Chicago in the 1920s spoke of "interstitial areas" where "disorganized families" were concentrated on the basis of ecological studies of delinquency and delinquent gangs in Chicago. See Frederic M. Thrasher, *The Gang* (Chicago: University of Chicago Press, 1927) and Clifford R. Shaw and Henry D. McKay, *Juvenile Delinquency and Urban Areas*, rev. ed. (Chicago: University of Chicago Press, 1969).

*Table 10.* Juvenile arrests of Tokyo males born in 1950 by extent of family control

| Number of arrests | Extent of family control | | | | | |
|---|---|---|---|---|---|---|
| | Weak control | | Medium control | | Strong control | |
| | Number | Percent | Number | Percent | Number | Percent |
| 0 | 2,126 | 93 | 2,164 | 95 | 1,684 | 97 |
| 1 | 101 | 4 | 81 | 4 | 38 | 2 |
| 2 or more | 63 | 3 | 30 | 1 | 12 | 1 |
| Total | 2,290 | 100 | 2,275 | 100 | 1,734 | 100 |

SOURCE: Michael S. Wasserman, "Personality System, Social System, and Cultural System Influences on Juvenile Delinquency: A Tokyo Birth Cohort Analysis" (Ph.D. Diss. Rutgers 1975), pp. 60–61.
NOTE: Family control is measured by written responses in 1965 to three questionnaire items: (1) "How important is it to your family that you get good grades?" (2) "What does your family think of your going to high school?" (3) "Does your mother work other than housework?"

hand, divorce, separation, mental illness, alcoholism, and other disabling circumstances occur that distract parents from the task of child socialization—or remove one or another of the parents from the home. Since nuclear families in contemporary societies are not reinforced by the support of extended kin, problems

*Table 11.* Intact and broken homes among delinquents and nondelinquents, Ghana, 1957–60

| Type of home arrangement | 164 delinquents * | 169 Non-delinquents |
|---|---|---|
| Broken home | | |
| By death of one or both parents | 22 | 8 |
| By separation or divorce | 41 | 21 |
| Subtotal | 63 | 29 |
| Intact home | 37 | 71 |
| Total | 100 | 100 |

SOURCE: S. Kirson Weinberg, "Juvenile Delinquency in Ghana: A Comparative Analysis of Delinquents and Non-delinquents," *Journal of Criminal Law, Criminology, and Police Science* 55 (1964): 474.
* The family situations of ten cases were unknown.

in the nuclear family quickly manifest themselves in further re-
laxation of control over children. Thus, it seems reasonable to expect children from broken or otherwise disorganized homes to
have higher delinquency rates in industrial societies than children
from more advantaged family situations. Tables 8, 9, and 10 confirm this prediction for the United States, Sweden, and Japan.
Similar relationships are found between family disorganization
and delinquency in developing societies, doubtless because the
detribalization process fostered by industrialization has eroded
the control of the extended family, especially in the cities. Tables
11 and 12 show the relationship between family disorganization
and delinquency in Ghana and Uganda. Such data as these demonstrate that "problem" families have less effective control over
adolescents than "normal" families in most societies, but under

*Table 12.* Differential contact of offenders and nonoffenders with
relatives, Kampala, Uganda, 1968

|                             | Nonoffenders | | Offenders | |
| --------------------------- | --- | ----- | --- | ----- |
|                             | No. | %     | No. | %     |
| Contact with relatives      | 148 | 96.1  | 72  | 66.7  |
| No contact with relatives   | 6   | 3.9   | 36  | 33.3  |
| Total with relatives        | 154 | 100.0 | 108 | 100.0 |
| No relatives in Kampala     | 52  | 25.0  | 56  | 34.2  |
| Total                       | 206 | 100.0 | 164 | 100.0 |

SOURCE: Clinard and Abbott, *Crime in Developing Countries*, p. 124.

urban industrial conditions *all* families have weak control over
adolescents, especially over *boys*.[13] This weakness of adult control,
more obvious under pathological circumstances such as slum
neighborhoods or broken homes, is ultimately due to the increasing social fluidity resulting from the isolation of the nuclear family and the allocation of education, recreation, work, and family
life to separate institutional contexts. These changes in social or-

[13] Family control is normally greater for female children and adolescents.
See Jackson Toby, "The Differential Impact of Family Disorganization,"
*American Sociological Review* 22 (1957):505–12.

ganization affect everyone in contemporary societies, but their impact is especially great on adolescents.

### Economic Development and Teenage Gangs

In more than a dozen countries new words have been coined to describe adolescents, nondelinquent as well as delinquent, who wear distinctive clothing and hair styles, listen to special types of music, frequent amusement areas and other gathering places, and generally annoy adults: bar gangs (Argentina), *blousons noirs* (France), bodgies (Australia), *chimpira* (Japan), *halbstarke* (West Germany), hooligans (Poland), *nozem* (Netherlands), *raggare* (Sweden), *stilyagi* (Soviet Union), *tapkaroschi* (Yugoslavia), *tau-pau* (Formosa), teddy boys (Great Britain), *vitelloni* (Italy), *tsotsis* (South Africa). In short, adolescence has come to be regarded, by experts as well as by the general public, as a period of potential antisocial behavior. This is a recent image of adolescence; the turbulence traditionally associated with adolescence was an inner state resulting from sexual maturation and the search for an adult identity.[14] In the *new* perspective on adolescence, delinquent gangs tend to be interpreted as extreme manifestations of teenage culture rather than as juvenile divisions of adult criminal gangs.[15]

The emergence of teenage culture is partly the result of affluence. Adults in the United States, Sweden, Great Britain, the Soviet Union, Israel, and other industrial societies give adolescents substantial discretionary purchasing power, which enables adolescents to demand (and obtain) distinctive clothing, motion pictures, phonograph records, recreational facilities, and eating and drinking places.[16] Teenage culture helps to ease the transition be-

[14] Erik H. Erikson, "Youth: Fidelity and Diversity," *Daedalus* 91 (1962): 5–27.

[15] John Mays, "Teenage Culture in Contemporary Britain and Europe," *Annals of the American Academy of Political and Social Science* 338 (1961):22–23.

[16] Mark Abrams, *The Teenage Consumer* (London: London Press Exchange, 1960).

tween the family into which the child was born and the family the young adult will create by marriage. Peers give the adolescent temporary emotional security, but they constitute an unpredictable influence. The adolescent peer group is not necessarily rebellious, but it is usually structurally unstable. Its members grow older, and, unless younger adolescents are admitted to membership, the group disintegrates. Groups which enjoy adult sponsorship or support—boys' clubs, settlement house youth groups, scouts, church youth clubs—do not disintegrate in this way. They recruit younger adolescents to take the place of the older adolescents who lost interest. Hence these adult-sponsored youth groups are permanent. Although the membership is constantly changing, the basic structure of the group remains intact. Youth groups that develop spontaneously on street corners are less likely to be age-graded and thus less capable of preserving group identity beyond the current membership. Millions of these spontaneous groups come into being, exist for several years as vehicles for expressing the interests and the solidarity of a particular group of adolescents, and then disintegrate. This flux is conducive to nonconformity because such autonomous groups are structurally isolated from adults whose responsibilities in the larger society are likely to make them sympathetic interpreters of conventional values.[17]

Unless adolescents are organized under adult sponsorship, they may mutually encourage one another to engage in a wide variety of unconventional or rebellious behavior. Delinquent gangs represent an antisocial development of adolescent autonomy; they are of course less pleasing to adults than scouting or church youth groups. Gangs form in contemporary societies partly because the institutional structure, in adjusting to the requirements of urban industrial life, has (unintentionally) undermined effective adult supervision of adolescents. Even the technology of industrial societies emphasizes the independence of the adolescent from parental observation. In the age of the automobile, an adolescent's home may be the place where he sleeps and little else. The car is not the only means of avoiding adult surveillance, but the car

[17] Sophia M. Robison, "Autonomous Groups: An Unsolved Problem in Group Loyalties and Conflicts," *Journal of Educational Sociology* 20 (1946):154–62.

symbolizes the looseness of the ties between adults and adolescents because it is such an effective instrument for escaping the eyes of adults. Some peer groups are actively organized to promote delinquent activities: fighting gangs, drug-using cliques, car thieves. But much adolescent nonconformity is tolerated rather than required by peers. In the *raggare* clubs of Stockholm (the Road Devils, the Car Angels, the Car Comets, and the Teddy Boys were the names of the main groups in 1960) it was prestigeful to have an American car in which to cruise around the city looking for girls. A boy who stole a squirrel tail to hang on the aerial of his car would probably not be disapproved of by his friends. And he would be able to signal to boys in other cars, by raising or lowering the squirrel tail, indicating how he was making out in his quest.

Criminologists for a long time have regarded the peer group as an immediate, precipitating factor in delinquency. Individual needs and social forces may underlie delinquency in a fundamental way, but the delinquent is not himself aware of these needs and forces. However, he is aware of the influence of his friends and companions. Thus, one American delinquent whom I interviewed in a youth treatment center (Highfields) explained why he stole cars. He said, that he would get a thrill out of the approval of his friends when he would drive up in a stolen Lincoln Continental to the street corner where they hung out and would call, "Pile in." Although he realized that a sixteen-year-old boy ran greater risks of apprehension by driving an expensive car that was beyond his financial means, he could not obtain the same response from his friends if he stole smaller, older cars for joyrides with them. So he continued to steal Lincolns. When he finally aroused the suspicions of the police, he was driving his eightieth stolen Lincoln Continental. The following autobiographical statement, written by another sixteen-year-old delinquent at the same youth treatment center, also reflects the role of peer approval in the motivation to engage in law violations.

I was born October 25th 1950 in the Bronx [N.Y.]. The neighborhood wasn't too rough or too calm. Well, at any rate I made out all right living my years there. When I was seven years old we moved from our two-family house there to a house of our own in Teaneck, N.J. The schools in Teaneck were about one-half year ahead of the Bronx schools so I barely passed the 2nd grade (I never quite got back to par although that may not have been the reason). Being an asthma sufferer and pretty skinny anyway I was pretty much of a weakling, thus mocked and ribbed many a time by other boys. This continued until I got to be around fourteen years old and in the 9th grade. Then I began to look around for other company and after some time got into a group with long hair, black leather jackets, etc. I made this group my goal since in my mind I felt that the more intelligently scholastic boys in school more or less feared and held a certain respect for these boys. Soon, after acquiring a motorcycle jacket, letting my hair grow, etc., I felt I had to do something illegal to "feel the part" more. Thus began my career which was to eventually end me up in Highfields! It began with dopey little things like pushing over bus stop benches, rolling public trash cans into the street, taking the paint off cars with instant shaving cream bombs, robbing glove compartments of cars, etc. etc. etc. After over a year of this type of thing I began to fear the police less and less. Then in September 1966 I made my first big move; several other boys and I decided that robbing houses and stores would be a profitable venture. Between September and December '66 I broke into eleven places and was in on three car thefts—although the whole gang was responsible for about forty break and entries of which there were several narrow escapes. Then on January 10th 1967 one of the gang was picked up in a stolen car. Early the next morning he told the police about some of our activities and consequently we were all picked up.

The ultimate question, of course, is why some youngsters crave peer approval so desperately that they will risk adult disapproval and formal punishment to get it. A further question is why some youngsters seek and obtain recognition from conventional peers whereas others can only obtain status among outcasts.

## Educational Commitment and Delinquency

Although diminished adult control over adolescents and increased individualism may explain the increase in delinquency *rates,* the principle of *relative deprivation* is more useful in explaining *recruitment* into delinquent groups. Some adolescents feel more at a disadvantage than others. Thus, the principle of relative deprivation helps account for the disproportionate representation of ethnic minorities in delinquent gangs. It also explains why school failures and those who withdraw from school before completing a course of study are more likely to become delinquents than students doing well in school. In contemporary societies, the system of formal education is an important mechanism for allocating youngsters to positions in the occupational system; students who do poorly at school have reason to grow discouraged about their futures. Such discouragement is often antecedent to rebellion.[18] Consider the following autobiographical account of the school experiences of a school dropout in the United States:

> When I was in the classroom I never did nothing. And then I did want to do something, like get in a discussion with all the kids. I'd raise my hand and the teacher would say, "I don't want to hear you. Go back to sleep."
>
> I didn't want to get kicked out, but I didn't want to go to school. I just had to go to school because my mother told me to go. And I didn't want to go out and work, so I figured I would stay in school.
>
> The year before that they kicked me out of school because I wasn't there all the time. They wouldn't let me come back 'til the next year. So it took me two years to get out of eighth grade. Later, they said that I missed too much time in school. I wasn't passing nothing, so they asked me to leave.
>
> To me, I thought the teachers was lazy, because we'd go into class and the teacher would put one thing down for all her classes that would come in. It would be on the board, and all the kids had to do it. Some of the kids used to take seven books home a night. And I knew if I had taken one of them books home, I never would have got out. I would have been home doing my homework all night. And I figure that you only go to school from nine to three; that's it. I don't want to hear about homework because I want to go out when I get home.
>
> If I went to another school I'd be a freshman. And I heard that if you're a freshman they make you do all kinds of stuff. I wouldn't have did it. I would start fighting with them, and I would get suspended from that school too.

[18] Arthur L. Stinchcombe, *Rebellion in a High School* (Chicago: Quadrange, 1964); Jackson Toby, "Educational Maladjustment as a Predisposing Factor in Criminal Careers: A Comparative Study of Ethnic Groups" (Ph.D. Diss. Harvard 1950).

I went to school. I didn't like school. I figured, "What the heck! I was stupid." I went to school to fool around.

I never listened to the teachers anyway. I just went there to fool around.

When I was first kicked out, I was ashamed for a while. When somebody else started fooling around I'd say, "Be careful or you'll get thrown out of class." But after a while you get fed up and start horsing around yourself.

Some subjects that you're interested in, you put your mind to it. Say, if it's science, and you're not interested, you don't pay attention. You got nothing to do so you start fooling around. And that's how you get in trouble.

The first time I got suspended my mother never said nothing, nobody said nothing to me. They let me go a second time. Nobody said nothing. So I figured I had nothing to worry about. I thought if I got kicked out, maybe I'd get hit or something.

I was going to a reading class. I really wanted to go in order to read better. I was doing all right. So I got a pass one day to go to the boys' room. I was dying for a cigarette, so I lit up the cigarette and I was smoking. When I went back to the classroom I had the cigarette in my pocket. I walked in there and started reading. The teacher says, "Have you been smoking?" I says, "Yeah," because I had been smoking and she smelled it on me. She says, "I don't want to hear your nonsense." She wrote me out a slip and I went to the office. I tried to explain to the principal because I really wanted to go to the reading class, but he threw me out of the reading class for that. It was my fault for smoking, but she could have let it go, I thought, maybe.

When I went back to school I got real far back on my work, and I didn't know what they were talking about after a while in the classes. So I just started talking and fooling around with the girls.[19]

Lack of commitment to school does not inevitably lead to delinquency; but educational failure reduces the individual's *stake in conformity*. Some boys become accessible to socialization by adolescent gangs because they feel, rightly or wrongly, that "they have no future." The gang offers "pleasures of the moment" instead

[19] Based on transcripts of group discussions with boys on probation in connection with a special rehabilitation project sponsored by the Sociology Department of Rutgers University and the Middlesex County, N.J., Probation Department.

of the future that more fortunate youngsters look forward to. Presumably, the gang would have trouble recruiting new members if all the boys in the neighborhood stayed in high school until graduation and were confident about getting a good job or going to college afterwards. This explanation of the attractions of an illegitimate role assumes that it is adopted after a legitimate role is perceived as unavailable. Another way of stating the foregoing explanation of the attractions of a delinquent peer group is this: People want to conform. They prefer legitimate roles. However, when legitimate roles are unattainable or are thought to be unattainable, people seek an illegitimate role or unconsciously accept a definition of self that makes an illegitimate role commitment more likely.

Consistent evidence from various countries suggests that the longer a youngster stays in school, the smaller are the chances that he will commit crimes. For example, Table 13 presents some Swedish data showing that the criminal conviction rate for boys born in Stockholm in 1940 was ten times as great if they completed primary school than if they completed *gymnasium*. The data in Table 13 are unusually clear-cut; few countries have as good criminal records as Sweden, where it was possible to trace 94 percent of the cohort of Stockholm boys from birth until the age of twenty-one.

Table 13 shows that educational accomplishment tends to pre-

*Table 13.* Boys born in Stockholm in 1940 who, by the age of 21, acquired a record in the criminal register, by educational attainment

| Highest educational attainment | Boys with criminal records | | All boys |
|---|---|---|---|
| | Number | Percent | |
| Gymnasium | 10 | 2.0 | 488 |
| Realskola | 34 | 9.9 | 445 |
| Primary School | 185 | 20.2 | 918 |
| Unknown | 7 | 14.3 | 49 |
| Total | 236 | 12.4 | 1,900 |

SOURCE: Jackson Toby, "Affluence and Adolescent Crime," *Task Force Report: Juvenile Delinquency and Youth Crime* (Washington, D.C.: President's Commission on Law Enforcement and Administration of Justice, 1967), p. 142.

vent criminality, but it does not tell why. Therefore it does not immediately suggest policy recommendations. Raising the age for compulsory school attendance would not necessarily reduce adolescent delinquency unless mere custody of children in school is the reason for the correlation between educational attainment and nondelinquency. This is rather unlikely to be the case. The correlation almost certainly reflects the motivations of young people themselves. That is to say, the significance of graduation from *gymnasium* is that graduation from *gymnasium* fulfills the aspirations of Swedish young people. Some of them are interested in obtaining business and professional occupations. Some are interested in education for its own sake. But committing crimes would be incompatible with the fulfillment of either of these goals. Arrests label a boy to himself as well as to his classmates and teachers as belonging to a different world, a world where values are opposed to those of the school and incompatible with it.

Table 14 is a refinement of the data of Table 13, taking into account the fact that the 1,900 boys came from different socioeconomic circumstances. It is known that boys from working-class families are less likely to seek higher education than boys from business, professional, and white collar families. It is also known that boys from working-class families are more likely to be arrested for delinquent behavior than boys from more elite occupational backgrounds. Table 14 examines the joint effect of socioeconomic background and educational attainment on criminality, thus providing an answer to the question, Which takes precedence? The answer is fairly clear. Those Stockholm boys who graduated from *gymnasium* had a low offense rate, and it did not make much difference whether their fathers were high status or low status. Three of the 71 working-class boys who completed *gymnasium* had a criminal record as compared with 2 of the 235 boys from upper-class families. At the *minimal* education level, on the other hand, parental status had an appreciable effect on criminality. Whereas 21 percent of the 618 working-class boys with minimal education had a criminal record, *none* of the 25 upper-class boys with minimal education had one. One implication of these findings is that a youngster who commits himself to education is unlikely to become delinquent *regardless of his family background.*

*Table 14.* Criminality of boys born in Stockholm in 1940, by their educational attainment and the socioeconomic status of their families

| Highest educational attainment | Boys with criminal records | | | | | |
| | Upper class | | Middle class | | Working class | |
| | Number of delin- quents | Percent delin- quent | Number of delin- quents | Percent delin- quent | Number of delin- quents | Percent delin- quent |
|---|---|---|---|---|---|---|
| Gymnasium | 4 | 1.7 | 3 | 1.6 | 3 | 4.2 |
| Realskola | 4 | 5.3 | 15 | 8.3 | 15 | 8.0 |
| Primary school | 0 | — | 57 | 20.4 | 128 | 20.7 |
| Total delinquents | 8 | 2.4 | 75 | 11.8 | 146 | 16.6 |

SOURCE: Jackson Toby, "Affluence and Adolescent Crime," *Task Force Report: Juvenile Delinquency and Youth Crime* (Washington, D.C.: President's Commission on Law Enforcement and Administration of Justice, 1967), p. 143. NOTE: There were 49 cases where the education was unknown.

But *why* does educational commitment have this effect? Criminologists do not know for sure. One likely possibility is that youngsters who pursue successful careers at school are consciously doing so in order to enjoy the "good life" as adults. They desire to share in the material rewards of an affluent society, just as delinquents do, but they utilize a legitimate path to socioeconomic advancement. This is probably not the whole explanation. Whatever the initial motivation for desiring success at school—to please concerned parents, to obtain a well-paying job as an adult, to learn —involvement in the school program has consequences for the student's conception of the world. Compared with a university student, a relatively uneducated delinquent does not know as much about the pleasures an affluent society can offer. The university student may obtain pleasure out of reading a book, attending a concert or ballet, visiting a museum, appreciating natural beauty, fighting for social justice—as well as out of driving a powerful car, getting "high," and wearing fashionable clothes. Delinquents in affluent societies characteristically desire material pleasures intensely—so much so that they are willing to risk freedom for them —but they are aware only of a small part of the opportunities for gratification that their societies offer. Furthermore, opportunities they are unaware of are those that are awakened or cultivated by the educational system. These considerations suggest that another reason that education prevents crime is that education broadens the range of desires of young people and stimulates some desires that bear little relation to income. This is, of course, speculation. Research is needed to establish the precise mechanism whereby educational achievement prevents crime.

### Occupational Commitment and Delinquency

In the industrialized societies compulsory school attendance laws have exposed adolescents to longer and longer educational careers. This pattern of educational upgrading is spreading to the developing societies. Although for many youngsters education is an opportunity to develop verbal and other skills necessary for work in a complex society, for others it is a blind alley, a source of chronic frustration. They drop out of school at the first opportunity and seek a more direct entry into the adult world of work. Unfortunately, failure at school is predictive of failure in the labor market. For many early school leavers, work does *not* provide a fresh start, a basis for commitment to a conventional life. In the following autobiographical account an adolescent delinquent from New Jersey describes his experiences in the American occupational system.

With me, every job I went for I really wanted, but after I was working at it, I didn't feel like getting up in the morning, so I quit. You have to have an interest in the job in the first place.

The first three months was kind of hard. They didn't have no merchandise or nothin' inside, and I helped them put flooring in. I went to bed about 7 o'clock or 7:30. After three or four months the place got straightened out, I didn't have much to do. I just walk around with mop or broom like I was doin' something. Then I got out at 5 o'clock and got home about 5:30. I would eat, wash up and change my clothes, and I would go out and stay out till about 1 o'clock, then come back home and go to bed.

If I find a job, I hope I can stick to it for a few months. It depends if I like the job. If I like it, I stick to it. If I don't like it [heck] with it. I'd just quit.

They [my friends] always told me to quit 'cause they were never working themselves. Then when I was working in Amboy, they always told me to quit. "You have to get up early in the morning to work, and you have to find a ride down there." After a while I started thinkin' about it. It's cold early in the morning. I have to wait on the corner. . . . In the winter, when I hitchhike back from work, it's cold out. I thought to myself, the best thing to do is quit. So I quit.

(In answer to question "What makes a guy want a job?") One reason is 'cause I need the money.

I try to work for a while. Work a few months. Maybe you get disgusted with that. Go back to your old ways.

I was workin'. I didn't like it. I used to work after school. I'd go just to fool around. I didn't like the job very much anyway.

My friend Tom told me to quit school and not to work because "You should have fun now, while you're young."

I mean I'd rather go out than work. I don't have the time to work. You'll work all your life when you get older.

. . . I know a few people who think that they don't have to work . . . at least not for a while. The guy who just came out of the service is collecting money for a bum leg. He gets enough money to live on from his leg. Another guy he's always got money, but he never works.[20]

Lack of commitment to the occupational system may be the *result* of criminality rather than its cause. If a youngster wants to be a safecracker or an armed robber, the availability of vocational training programs for conventional jobs will not attract him. Studies of convicted criminals in both industrialized and developing societies consistently show poor work records: frequent changes of jobs, long periods of unemployment, lack of interest in legiti-

---

[20] Based on transcripts of a group discussion with boys on probation in connection with a special rehabilitation project sponsored by the Sociology Department of Rutgers University and the Middlesex County, N.J., Probation Department.

mate occupations.[21] But they do not clarify the crucial question of what precedes what. Does occupational maladjustment lead to a feeling that crime is their only chance, or does commitment to criminal activities foreclose a more conventional attitude toward work? Only through longitudinal study of a cohort of youngsters can a definitive answer to these questions be secured.[22]

Although we do not yet know whether it is rationalization or causal factor, a large proportion of offenders have an antiwork ideology. "Only suckers work" is a saying of American offenders. Given their poor educational histories and low levels of conventional work skills, they certainly are unqualified for high-paying, prestigious jobs. But many persons in similar situations take low-paying, menial jobs. The following is the frank explanation of a young British prisoner of his preference for crime over honest work; he entitled his essay "Does It Pay to be Honest?"

I do not know if honesty pays or not. Because I have not tried it. But I have made a lot of money out of being crooked. To be honest, you have to work and work five or six days a week for £12 or £13 a week [£ is the English pound and is currently worth $2.40].* You hear some blokes say they like work. I'd like work, too, if I could sit and look at it all day and not get bored.

When I get out I *might try* to be honest, but when I think of going to a job five days a week, nine hours a day, getting up at 6:30 A.M. for £12 or £13 a week, I feel sick.

I do not like work very much. I live up to the old motto, "Death before work." Why get up at 6 or 7 o'clock in the morning and work hard until 6 at night for a lousy £12 a week? When you can get up at 11 o'clock, go to the cafe with your mates and have a good time, then

---

[21] See, for example, Daniel Glaser, *The Effectiveness of a Prison and Parole System* (Indianapolis: Bobbs-Merrill, 1964), chap. 11, for a discussion of the work histories of American offenders, and Clinard and Abbott, *Crime in Developing Countries*, pp. 96–98, for data on the work histories of offenders in Uganda.

[22] Professor Carl-Gunnar Janson is engaged in a monumental study of 15,000 Swedes born in 1953 and living in Stockholm in 1963 (Project Metropolitan). They and their families are being studied carefully, including relating personal interviews with official records of various kinds. The research plan calls for continuation of this monitoring until 1983 (when cohort members will be 30 years of age).

* At the time this was written

at 12 o'clock go to the pub and have a beer or two, then go out on our motor bikes. And when we need money, do a bit of the old villainy and if the coppers get you, it is hard luck. Be a bit more careful next time. But if you are honest and want to work day in, day out, nine hours a day for a lousy £12 a week—when you get paid, say £12, you have to pay:

Tax, say £2 [$4.80]

N.H., 10/6 [National health insurance: 10 shillings, sixpence or $1.26]

Pension, 3/6 [3 shillings, sixpence or $0.42]

Union, 2/6 [Union dues, 2 shillings, sixpence or $0.30]

Savings, 10/– [10 shillings or $1.20]

Tea money, 2/6 [2 shillings, sixpence or $0.20]

So out of £12, you take home £8–11/–. When you get home with your £8–11/– you worked hard all week for:

Good Old Mum takes 3 quid [3 pounds or $7.20]

That leaves you with £5–11/– [5 pounds, 11 shillings or $13.32].

H.P. on bike, 31/1 [Hire-purchase installment payment on bike, 31 shillings or $3.72]

Christmas Club, 10/– [10 shillings or $1.20]

Clothes, 10/– [10 shillings or $1.20]

Holiday money, £1 [Vacation money, $2.40]

You pay that and you got £2. Your cigs for the week, say:

15 bob [15 shillings or $1.80]

Petrol [gasoline] for the weekend, 15 bob [15 shillings or $1.80]
What have you got to your self? 10 bob [10 shillings, or $1.20], and you have worked all week for 10 bob.

Does it pay to be honest? [23]

Whether it is a sour-grapes type of rationalization or not, offenders in many societies express contempt for legitimate work. Derisive slang terms apply to "suckers"; in Japanese the phrase is *majimena hito wa richigimono;* in Swedish the word is *knegare*.[24] A *knegare* is a poor dumb clod who goes to work early in the morn-

---

[23] Written in the British borstal, Huntercombe. Jackson Toby, "Are Criminals Germs?" in *The Administration of Justice in America* (Newark, University of Delaware, 1970), pp. 13–14.

[24] See Professor Hara's comments in Jackson Toby, "Adolescent Delinquency in Japan," *Asahi Journal* 9 (December 1967):38–42; see Professor Janson's discussion of *knega*—a colloquial verb meaning to carry such a heavy burden that one's knees bend in walking—in Carl-Gunnar Janson, "Juvenile Delinquency in Sweden," *Youth and Society* 2 (1970):214.

ing, works hard all day for low pay, and comes home in the evening too tired to have any fun; he reads the newspaper or watches television and goes to sleep. Next morning he repeats the same routine—and continues to do so till the end of his life. He dies without having lived. From the viewpoint of a Swedish criminal, a *knegare* is a negative role model because he lacks the capacity to enjoy the good life. The criminal prefers to gamble with his freedom by committing crimes.

## Conclusion

Widespread poverty is nothing new. It is widespread affluence that is new. But the relationship between subjective dissatisfaction and objective deprivation is more complicated than was at first thought. Poverty does not cause crime but resentment of poverty does, and resentment of poverty is at least as likely to develop among the *relatively* deprived of a rich society as among the *objectively* deprived in a poor society. Industrial societies are also urbanized societies; and urbanized societies offer greater opportunities to steal and get away with it. Social control of adolescents is especially weak, thus explaining the world epidemic of adolescent crime.

Formal education is not new, either. But *mass* education, extending to the late teens, has new implications that go beyond its direct goal of transmitting the content of the cultural tradition. One implication is that segregating youngsters in schools and adults in the occupational system increases the differentiation between the teenage and the overall culture. Another is that the gap has widened between those youngsters who successfully upgrade their verbal and quantitative skills in the schools and those who develop serious educational disabilities. For academically successful adolescents, school is a bridge between the world of childhood and that of adulthood. For children unwilling or unable to learn, school is a place where the battle against society is likely to begin.

Orientation to consumption seems to be an increasing characteristic of all societies. It permeates all age groups, not merely that of adolescents, and it contributes to other phenomena besides delinquency, such as ostentatious expenditures for food, clothing, travel, housing. However, the impact of commercialism is more criminogenic for working-class adolescents because the impact on them of the educational system is less positive than for middle-class youth. If they leave school as soon as they legally may, they have less opportunity to experience art, literature, serious music, science, religion, and meaningful work than they have of being attracted to the gadgets and entertainments available in the marketplace. This isolation of school-leaving youths from what are generally conceded to be the accomplishments of industrial civilization may partially account for their predatory crimes. As Nelson Algren put it in his paraphrase of a literary idea of Richard Wright, "When a crime is committed by a man who has been excluded from civilization, civilization is an accomplice of the crime." [25] Selective exposure to industrial society is not merely an internal problem. Anthropologists have called attention to the selective diffusion of culture traits to underdeveloped societies. The appetite for trinkets, tools, hard liquor, and Coca Cola are easier to export than arts and sciences or even religion, and that appetite motivates predatory behavior. Crime, like peace and justice, is indivisible; its rate varies from society to society but the basic causes seem remarkably similar.

[25] Nelson Algren, "Remembering Richard Wright," *Nation* 192 (1961): 85.

# American Concerns: Keeping Order versus Fighting Crime

## Paul Lerman

### Introduction

IN the 1960s public concern about crime appears to have increased dramatically. For the first time in modern American history the presidential election of 1964 featured "crime in the streets" as a major campaign issue. Subsequent to that election, and the ghetto disorders of the mid-1960s, the first federal grant-in-aid program was enacted, and provided funds to states and localities to combat crime.

Amidst these developments a Presidential Commission on Law Enforcement and the Administration of Justice issued a series of reports to the nation, including a summary volume, *The Challenge of Crime in a Free Society.* In this report the commission summarized an array of facts about the crime problem. One set of striking facts concerning juveniles has aroused minimal public interest: *a majority of recorded juvenile arrests were for behaviors that involved little or no harm to persons or property.* The paradox of a mounting public concern about serious crime while police were emphasizing the arrests of nonharmful offenders deserves much greater study than is evident in either the criminological or mass media literature—since the paradox continues into the 1970s.

The facts reported by the President's Commission are a useful starting point for introducing a discussion of the issues. In 1967 the Commission concluded the following: "although juveniles account for more than their share of arrests for many serious crimes, these arrests are a small part of all juvenile arrests. Juveniles are *most frequently* arrested or referred to court for petty larceny, fighting, disorderly conduct, liquor-related offenses, and conduct not in violation of the criminal law such as curfew violation, truancy, incorrigibility, or running away from home." [1]

A current commission would probably reach a similar conclusion, except that the possession, use, and sale of marijuana and nonalcohol drugs would have to be added to the list of most frequent arrests. This list of frequent offenses is instructive, since (with the exception of larceny) it provides empirical evidence that the American system of law enforcement appears to be more involved in juvenile "order-keeping" than classical "law-keeping." If we are interested in understanding, explaining, and possibly providing guidance for dealing with juvenile delinquency, then it seems reasonable to pay attention to the everyday boundaries of the official practices that are engaged in "most frequently."

The American concern about "order" includes behaviors that are usually conceived as two distinct categories: (1) juvenile status offenses and (2) victimless crimes. Juvenile status offenses refer to actions that are deemed to justify an arrest or a court petition only if committed by a juvenile—since adults are not usually stigmatized or penalized for merely possessing or consuming alcohol, violating a curfew, being absent from school, acting incorrigible or stubborn, or running away from home. These behaviors can be conceptualized as "order offenses" because they symbolize unapproved status behaviors of youth vis à vis adult superiors and violate adult-sponsored conceptions of acceptable juvenile activities. Victimless crimes can include drug consumption, but it can also include prostitution, gambling, homosexuality, and pornography. Both categories of offenses (status and victimless), unlike classical criminal offenses, rarely involve a clear victim, nor is a direct personal or property harm (or threat) readily apparent. Instead, order offenses can refer to the improper behavior of youth in family and school institutions, lack of deferential status behaviors to adults and officials, improper behavior in public places, and activities deemed morally offensive. Order offenses define the permissible legal boundaries of everyday

[1] President's Commission on Law Enforcement and the Administration of Justice *Task Force Report: Corrections* (Washington, D.C.: U.S. Government Printing Office, 1967), p. 56.

youthful activities, separate and distinct from such traditional crimes as theft, robbery, burglary, and assault.

Until the early 1960s no American state explicitly recognized in its statutes that juvenile order offenders were different from criminal offenders. About fifteen years ago a new juvenile legal category, Persons in Need of Supervision (PINS), or an equivalent (MINS, JINS, or CINS), was created in New York and California as a separate jurisdictional basis for arresting, detaining, adjudicating, and correcting youth. This development primarily redefined juvenile status offenders but also included grounds of immorality (such as "growing up in idleness" and associating with "immoral persons"). By 1974 there were thirty-four states that distinguished between criminal-type delinquency and at least some of the status offenses. However, only eleven states explicitly prohibited institutionalizing status offenders in traditional state training schools that housed criminal offenders. At present only one state, New Jersey, has legally prohibited Juveniles in Need of Supervision from also being detained in the same secure facilities as formal delinquents.

Despite these changes in the laws, juveniles can still be coercively arrested, detained, and adjudicated, and removed from their homes for *all* of the order offenses. Whether the new legal labels or the separate places of confinement will yield less stigmatization and reduce the type, degree, and duration of institutionalization than occurred before the statutory changes is, at present, uncertain. It would be necessary to examine actual practices—regardless of the label—and not just the intentions of public policies, if the impact of legal changes were the focus of study and discussion.

A discussion about noncriminal offenders could also focus on why American youth are not as orderly as adults and law enforcement officials would like them to be. In addition, the largest category of juvenile arrests could generate questions concerning the nature of the adult responses. Three questions that seem useful and will guide the ensuing discussion, are:

1. Are the many youths arrested for order offenses—regardless of the legal label—merely admonished and reprimanded by offi-

cials, or do they receive other types of sanctions – similar to the types received by juvenile crime offenders?

2. Does the recent emphasis on "community treatment," coupled with increased resources for local corrections, provide any empirical evidence that the American handling of order offenses is likely to change?

3. Why have American adults and their publicly supported enforcement agencies exhibited such a disproportionate concern about order offenders?

All three of the questions are related to the scope and rationale of the American conception of juvenile crime and pose potential implications for theory and public policy. In addition, the kinds of answers that are generated by these questions can help us develop a broader understanding of the American response to the developmental problems of youth.

### Community Treatment and Order Offenses in California: A Case Study

During the 1960s (as well as today) California was deemed to be one of the major leaders in the field of juvenile corrections. As noted earlier, California was one of the early states to make a legal distinction between delinquency and status offenses. Two presidential commissions singled out California approaches to community treatment as worthy of imitation in other parts of the country.[2] In 1965 California also began to pay special subsidies to the counties if rates of commitment to state institutions were decreased.[3] From fiscal 1966 through fiscal 1972, California paid out of its state treasury a total of nearly $60 million over and above any previous payments to the counties. There are few, if any states, that can duplicate this massive infusion of unmatched state funds to pay for increased personnel and correctional re-

[2] Ibid., p. 179.

[3] Robert L. Smith, *A Quiet Revolution: Probation Subsidy*, Department of Health, Education and Welfare Publication no. (SRS) 72–26011 (Washington, D.C.: U.S. Government Printing Office, 1972).

sources at a local level. In addition to these advantages California had also developed one of the best state reporting systems in the nation. Using this available data, we can try to discern what occurred in the actual processing of youth before and after the heavy investment in new community treatment resources on a statewide basis.

The California Bureau of Criminal Statistics classifies juvenile offenses according to carefully defined categorical codes. These categories are quite similar to the distinctions used in this paper. The codes are as follows:

1. *Specific criminal offenses:* homicide, robbery, aggravated and other assault, burglary, theft (auto and nonauto), sex offenses (except girls' illicit sex or victims of rape), weapons laws, drunk driving, hit and run (auto), and all other offenses not specified in any of the other categories (such as tampering with autos, fish and game violations, etc.).

2. *Drug offenses:* sale, possession, or use of narcotics, marijuana, or dangerous drugs, but not glue sniffing.

3. *Delinquent tendencies:* truancy; runaways from home, county camp, custody of an officer or state institution, but excluding forcible escapes, to be included in specific crimes, all other; incorrigibles; curfew violation; transients (out-of-state); malicious mischief; disturbing the peace; liquor laws and being drunk; glue sniffing; other offenses not deemed specific crimes, including arson, vagrancy, loitering, school suspension, etc.

It is evident from this classification that the term *delinquent tendencies* includes most of what we have called order offenses; the only omission is for drug offenses, but they are classified separately. It is clear, too, that only the term *specific criminal offenses* refers to classic criminal law violations. In 1960 the arrest rates per 100,000 youth, ages ten through seventeen, for the three categories were as follows:

| | |
|---|---|
| Specific criminal offenses | 3,232 per 100,000 youth |
| Drugs only | 59 per 100,000 youth |
| Delinquent tendencies | 5,340 per 100,000 youth |

It is clear that at the beginning of the decade the highest arrest category was that of delinquent tendencies. The specific criminal

*Table 1.* Juvenile arrests: specific rates for 1960, 1965, and 1970 (in rates per 100,000 youth, ages 10–17, and percent distribution for each year)

| Arrest category | Rates | | | Percent distribution | | |
|---|---|---|---|---|---|---|
| | 1960 [a] | 1965 [a] | 1970 [b] | 1960 | 1965 | 1970 |
| Specific crime offenses | 3,232 | 3,636 | 4,214 | 37.4 | 35.8 | 33.9 |
| Drugs only | 59 | 87 | 1,189 | 0.7 | 0.9 | 9.6 |
| Delinquent tendencies | 5,340 | 6,421 | 7,014 | 61.9 | 63.3 | 56.5 |
| Total arrest rates | 8,631 | 10,144 | 12,417 | 100.0 | 100.0 | 100.0 |
| Number of arrests | 182,715 | 277,649 | 382,935 | | | |

[a] Numbers arrested and computed rates for 1960 and 1965 can be found in *Crime and Delinquency in California, 1969* (Sacramento: Bureau of Criminal Statistics, 1969), table I–2, p. 10, and table I–14, p. 44.

[b] Numbers arrested used in rate computations can be found in *Crime and Arrests: Reference Tables, 1970* (Sacramento: Bureau of Criminal Statistics, 1970), table VI, p. 61; population figure used in computations can be found in *Juvenile Probation and Detention: Reference Tables, 1970* (Sacramento: Bureau of Criminal Statistics, 1970, table 1, p. 5).

offenses accounted for only about 37 percent of all arrests (3,232 out of 8,631). Before the onset of a decade of legal changes and community treatment activities, particularly the subsidy scheme launched in 1965, the order offenses accounted for a preponderant majority of the arrests—63 percent. Table 1 attempts to portray what occurred in 1965 and 1970, so that the five years before and after massive community subsidies can be examined.

Table 1 indicates that the rates for each category increased, controlling for population increases of the specific age group. The most dramatic change occurred in reference to drug arrests—mainly for marijuana possession and smoking (59 to 87 to 1,189). In 1970 arrests for drugs comprised 9.6 percent, compared to less than 1 percent for 1960 and 1965. While the proportion of delinquent-tendencies arrests decreased in 1970, the combined order-offense categories accounted for 66.1 percent in 1970, 64.2 percent in 1965, and 62.6 percent in 1960. While the combined increase is about 2 percent for 1960 to 1965 and a similar amount for 1965 to 1970, it is important to note that the proportion of arrests for classical crimes *decreased* throughout the decade. Clearly, the infusion of massive resources did not change the state's ability to focus on "real" delinquency incidents at the first stage of official juvenile processing.

## Patterns of Decision-making in California

Besides arrests, youth can be processed by the official system in a variety of informal and formal pathways—including a period in a detention facility pending or following a final judicial decision. It is possible to gain some insight into the priority that potent criminal-type sanctions—via a detention stay—possesses within the total police/court/correctional system. Since for each year the arrests for order offenses varied between 62.6 and 66.1 percent, it is possible to gain insight into what are the dominant postarrest responses afforded to a majority of arrested youth.

Table 2 is based on official data reported to the Bureau of Criminal Statistics by local police departments or county probation departments. In Part A, the raw data found in annual reports have been converted into annual rates per population risk, youth ten to seventeen years of age, for 1960, 1965, and 1970. Besides detention rates, rates have been computed for arrests, referrals to probation by police, initial referrals received by probation from all sources, filing of new petitions, declaration of wardship, admissions to camps, and commitments to the California Youth Authority (CYA). Part B attempts to compare the degree of change for all of these indicators of adult responses. This permits an assessment of detention within the context of other reponses and provides a historical baseline for the assessment of all of the major indicators of social decisions that are available.

Table 2 discloses that the police arrest rate increased by 18 percent between 1960 and 1965, but it increased by a comparable amount during the subsidy period 1965–70. However, the rates of referrals to probation by the local police departments changed appreciably. The subsidy years are associated with a 53 percent

*Table 2.* California police, probation, and court responses to youth behavior for 1960–65 and 1965–70 (by rates per 100,000 youth, ages 10–17, and by percent changes in rates)

| Response category | A. Rates | | | B. Rate changes (percent) | |
|---|---|---|---|---|---|
| | 1960 [a] | 1965 [a] | 1970 [a] | 1960–65 | 1965–70 |
| Police arrests | 8,631 | 10,144 | 12,417 | 18% | 18% |
| Police probation referrals [b] | 3,612 | 4,543 | 6,948 | 26 | 53 |
| All new referrals to probation | 2,775 | 3,540 | 5,204 | 28 | 47 |
| All delinquent detention admissions [c] | 2,978 | 3,261 | 4,866 | 10 | 49 |
| Initial petitions filed | 1,342 | 1,301 | 1,725 | −03 | 33 |
| Initial declarations for court wardships | 918 | 937 | 1,040 | 02 | 12 |
| New probation admissions to county camps, ranches and schools [d] | 117 | 183 | 226 | 56 | 23 |
| New CYA commitments | 158 | 169 | 72 | 07 | −57 |

[a] Unless otherwise noted, all rates for 1960 and 1965 are taken from *Crime and Delinquency in California, 1969* (Sacramento: Bureau of Criminal Statistics, 1969), (table I–14, p. 44, and table I–15, p. 45. Computations for 1970 (except arrest data) are based on data reported in *Juvenile Probation and Detention: Reference Tables, 1970* (Sacramento: Bureau of Criminal Statistics, 1970), table 1, p. 5, and table 30, p. 42; data on police obtained from *Crime and Arrests: Reference Tables, 1970* (Sacramento: Bureau of Criminal Statistics, 1970), table 5–A, p. 9.

[b] These rates are computed for 1960 and 1970 on the basis of raw data appearing in Bureau of Criminal Statistics annual publications, and population figures provided in *Juvenile Probation and Detention, 1970*, p. 5; the rate for 1965 is estimated on the basis of the stability of rates of new referrals/all probation referrals. In 1960 the proportion of new referrals/all referrals was 0.765, in 1966 it was 0.749, and in 1970 it was 0.747. The mid-point proportion of 0.757 was used for 1965 and the following equation (based on 1965 data for new referrals appearing in the 1969 Bureau of Criminal Statistics): $\frac{3540}{x} = \frac{757}{100} = 4{,}543/$ 100,000 youth population.

[c] See table 12 for sources on independent computations of detention rates. All detention rates in this and subsequent tables *exclude* dependent-neglect cases.

[d] Systematic statewide reporting of new commitments to juvenile county institutions (camps, ranches, and schools) began on 1 January 1966, according to *Crime and Delinquency in California, 1966* (Sacramento: Bureau of Criminal Statistics, 1966), p. 236; data for 1970 are computed on basis of *Juvenile Probation and Detention: Reference Tables, 1970*, table 1, p. 5, and table 32, p. 49. See table 9 for sources of estimate for 1960 and 1965

rate increase, while the presubsidy period rose 26 percent. The new referrals to probation (from all sources) displayed a comparable trend—up 28 percent in 1960–65, and 47 percent for 1965–70. The rates of detention admissions (regardless of court status, and whether the admission was for a new or old referral) rose only 10 percent in 1960–65, or less than the arrest or referral rates. However, the detention rates in the subsidy years rose substantially and appeared to keep up with the referral rates.

The rate of initial petitions filed also changed, dipping slightly in 1960–65 but showing a substantial increase during the subsidy period (33 percent). However, the actual rates of declaring court wardships of the new petitions did not keep pace with either the referral, detention, or filing rates in either period. Trend data for camp admissions indicate a lower rate of increase for 1965–70. Unlike the other indicators, CYA commitments decreased during the subsidy period.

In general, it appears that the police response shifted to directing many more youth to be processed by the courts (via referrals). While during the subsidy years the filing of petitions also increased (perhaps related to decisions by probation officers), the judges did not appear to respond in kind. The rates of court wardship declared rose, but far below the change in rates of police activity, filing decisions, and, significantly, detention.

Looking at the rate figures in Part A for each year, it is quite clear that CYA commitments, even in 1960, comprised only a very small part of the decision workload of the probation departments and juvenile courts. There is also a wide disparity in police referral rates and initial filing rates, indicating that there is probably much informal, nonjudicial handling of the cases being processed in the probation system. Whether the police would want their referrals to be taken more seriously is unknown, using available data.

What is most striking, however, is the similarity in disparity between detention-admission rates and any of the rates of official handling by probation officers or judges. The disparity between rates of detention and rates of filing or declaration of wardship increases over time. Evidently many youth are, in fact, detained without even being deemed worthy of having a petition filed regarding their alleged deviance. It is quite likely that detention can be associated with an informal disposition, as well as with formal dispositions. It is noteworthy that rates of detention far exceed those for any other form of correctional response, for all years.

Since the detention data cannot be broken down to indicate whether a petition is filed, whether it is a new or old case, or whether youngsters are currently on probation, we cannot determine precisely how detention is associated with informal handling and official dispositions. Despite these shortcomings in the data, it is apparent that detention has been–and is–the most significant element of the county correctional program. It was growing before 1965, but during the subsidy years it increased appreciably. During both periods it appears quite likely that more youth received detention than received adjudication or formal treatment services. At the county level the dominant form of official response appears to be detention–not treatment–since the risk of being detained is much higher than the combined risk of being a probation case, a camp commitment, and a CYA ward.

## Community Treatment and Detention Decision by Offense Categories

Since more youth received detention than a formal court hearing or formal probation, it seems much more accurate to term the stages of police/court processing a *social-control system*–rather than a juvenile justice, correctional, or treatment system. Given that detention is the dominant postarrest response, it is still possible that the delinquency definitional changes and the infusion of community-treatment resources shifted the proportion of youth detained for order offenses. Table 3 presents data on admissions, by reason for detention, for each of the relevant years.

(This table *excludes* youth detained in an "administrative/ other" category. According to the Bureau of Criminal Statistics, this category refers to youngsters "whose present detention is an outgrowth of some prior situation and not the result of any new acts of delinquency," as well as traffic offenses. Since the reasons for their "prior situation" are unknown, they are deleted from Table 3.)

The data of Table 3 indicate that the biggest changes in the population detained have occurred with drugs and specific criminal offenses. In 1970 only 36.2 percent of youth detained for a known offense were held in custody because of a specific criminal activity, a decrease of nearly 9 percent since 1965, and almost 14 percent since 1960. It is evident that a decade of community-treatment emphasis is associated with a higher rate of detention admissions (Table 2), as well as a disproportionate number of detentions that are noncriminal (Table 3).

It appears that order offenses can be dealt with in practice as if they were actually types of criminal offenses. In addition, the experience of California indicates that additional resources can be correlated with an increase of this mode of handling non-criminal offenses. These two statements summarize the reasonable answers linked to two of the major questions posed earlier: (1) are order offenses responded to seriously and (2) will a

*Table 3.* California detention: specific rates for 1960, 1965, 1970 (in rates per 100,000 youth, ages 10–17, for each year and percent distribution)

| | Rates | | | Percent distribution | | |
|---|---|---|---|---|---|---|
| Reason for Detention [b] | 1960 | 1965 | 1970 [a] | 1960 | 1965 | 1970 |
| Specific criminal offenses | 1,368 | 1,317 | 1,604 | 49.8 | 45.4 | 36.2 |
| Drug offenses | 48 | 57 | 571 | 1.7 | 2.0 | 12.9 |
| Delinquent tendencies | 1,331 | 1,524 | 2,253 | 48.5 | 52.6 | 50.9 |
| Total rates per year | 2,747 | 2,898 | 4,428 | 100.0 | 100.0 | 100.0 |

[a] For population figures, *Juvenile Probation and Detention Reference Tables, 1970* (Sacramento: Bureau of Criminal Statistics) table 1, p. 5; for actual numbers detained, by reason, for each year, *Crime and Delinquency in California, 1969* (Sacramento: Bureau of Criminal Statistics), table X–13, p. 174, and table X–14, p. 177; and for 1970 data, *Reference Tables, 1970*, table 28, p. 40 and table 30, p. 42.

[b] Excludes "administrative/other reasons," as defined in the text. The rates for each year for this category were: 1960—231; 1965—363; and 1970—438.

community-treatment emphasis and additional resources reduce the severity of handling noncriminal offenders?

### The Comparability of the California Findings

Even though I cited special reasons for paying attention to the results of the data from California, it is conceivable that the results are atypical of the rest of the country. There are several lines of evidence that indicate that the California findings are probably valid for many other jurisdictions.

The dominance of local detention as the *primary* response of juvenile social-control systems is true on a nationwide basis, not only in California. In 1967 the National Council on Crime and Delinquency reported the results of the first nationwide study of corrections. This study was prepared for the President's Commission on Law Enforcement and the Administration of Justice. Some of the study's most significant findings have yet to be fully absorbed into an empirically based conception of what public policy actually offers American youth on a national scale:

In 1965 the total number admitted to detention facilities was more than 409,000, or approximately two-thirds of all juveniles apprehended. . . . These youngsters were held in detention homes and jails for an estimated national average stay of 12 days at a total cost of more than $53,000,000—an average cost of $130 per child.

The statistics show 409,218 children detained but only 242,275 children placed on probation or committed to an institution.[4]

The figures clearly indicate that on a national level the dominant public response to arrested juveniles is likely to be a local twelve-day lockup. Since about one-half of those formally arrested (about 300,000 of the 600,000) are not even officially handled by the court, but are screened out, the national data also indicate that more youth receive community-based institutional-

---

[4] President's Commission on Law Enforcement and the Administration of Justice, *The Challenge of Crime in a Free Society* (Washington, D.C.: U.S. Government Printing Office, 1967), pp. 121, 129.

ization than are even formally adjudicated as delinquent.[5] In addition, only about 189,000 youth received probation in 1965, but over twice as many were detained. It seems extremely unlikely these 189,000 youth received twelve full days of treatment services during the year, since not even intensive programs provide this level of service. The data indicate that more arrested youth are locked up than receive juvenile justice or probationary treatment. These facts lead to the inference that restraint is still the dominant public-policy response toward youth—not rehabilitative and reintegrative services.

Recent data suggest that a greater emphasis on due process within the juvenile court has not yet had an appreciable impact on detention usage. In 1970 California data reveal that statutory changes and Supreme Court decisions have not decreased the relative dominance of social control. A recently completed national survey, conducted by Sarri and other University of Michigan researchers, provides the following empirical estimates: in 1973 at least 100,000 children spent at least one day in an adult jail, while nearly 500,000 other youth were confined in local detention facilities. Between 1965 and 1973 the number of youth detained grew from roughly 400,000 to 600,000—a gain of 50 percent. This gain is greater than the growth in the age-specific growth population that faces the risk of detention.[6]

A recent study offers some insights into how difficult it can be to try to reverse the steady rise in detention rates. In 1967 the Chief Judge of Cuyahoga County (based in Cleveland, Ohio), launched a determined effort to reduce detention. He comments about his efforts as follows:

Social workers, probation officers, and police officers, who had previously for all practical purposes made the decision as to the necessity of detaining the child, reacted strenuously to our screening process.

Naturally, these criticisms, those from within the court and more

[5] U.S. Department of Health, Education and Welfare, *Juvenile Court Statistics 1970* DHEW Publication no. (SRS) 72–03452 (Washington, D.C.: U.S. Government Printing Office, 1972), p. 12.

[6] DHEW, Office of Public Information, Office of Youth Development, *Youth Reporter* (November 1973), p. 2, (January 1974), p. 7.

especially those from outside agencies, mitigated against acceptance of our new policy. . . .

The social agencies which staunchly proclaimed their non-punitive philosophy wanted us to detain children as part of their "treatment" process. . . .

Helpful in discouraging one of the social agencies from the overuse of detention was our new requirement that an official complaint must be filed concerning each child placed in the detention home. . . .

It had been a common practice for a probation officer to place a child in detention who was uncooperative, who failed to keep appointments, who truanted from school, or when upon a complaint of the parents was considered out of control at home. . . . The 380 children admitted by probation officers in 1967 was reduced to 125 in 1971, a reduction of 60 percent. . . .

As we began our initial effort to reduce population, we found that many children were being detained, awaiting acceptance by various state, county, and private facilities who, often arbitrarily and for their own convenience, imposed quotas and admission requirements on the court.[7]

This unusually frank report indicates that detention can be used as a multipurpose resource for a variety of preventive, treatment, and administrative reasons in Ohio as well as in California. For three years (1967–69) Judge Whitlatch was unable to demonstrate that the Chief Judge could administratively regulate the use of detention by police, probation officers, treatment agencies, and correctional organizations. Finally, in 1970 and 1971, his detention-reduction policy began to show signs of success—particularly with police and his own probation staff. However, a separate reading of the 1971 Annual Report of the Cuyahoga County Court reveals that more local youth still received formal detention than received formal probation—3,430 to 2,387.[8]

In addition to national data about the prevalence of local detention, there exists evidence that about one-half of the youth detained in 1965 were in fact charged with a juvenile status offense. Sheridan, using federal data for ten jurisdictions, re-

[7] W. C. Whitlatch, "Practical Aspects of Reducing Detention Home Population," *Juvenile Justice* 24 (1973):17–30.

[8] County of Cuyahoga, *Cuyahoga County Juvenile Annual Report 1971* (Cleveland: Cuyahoga County Juvenile Court, 1971), pp. 26, 27.

ported this type of finding.[9] Lerman, in a special secondary analysis of New York City data, found that youth charged with crimes were much less likely to be detained than status offenders. In addition, status offenders were much more likely to stay for more than 30 days once they were detained than was true for regular delinquents.[10]

The national handling of the order arrests around 1970 is best summarized by the following set of facts: (1) order offenders were arrested "most frequently," (2) about one-half of all youth detained were in custody because of a juvenile status charge, (3) at least one-fourth of all juvenile court petitions occurred because of a juvenile status charge, (4) about 25 to 30 percent of all institutionalized juveniles in state correctional facilities were there because of a juvenile status charge, and (5) juvenile status offenders tended to be detained *and* institutionalized for longer periods of time.[11] A federal report, prepared in 1974, relied on this set of facts to estimate the varied modes of handling juvenile status offenders.[12] If drug arrests, which have undoubtedly increased across the nation, are added to these indicators of handling, then it seems reasonable to infer that the following conclusions can be made about current *national* trends:

1. Order offenses, besides being the most frequent basis for arresting a juvenile, also form the basis for detaining over one-half of the juveniles found in local custodial facilities.

2. Detention is the dominant response provided by American authorities to juveniles arrested for an order offense—whether they are charged or uncharged with the offense.

3. Changes of legal labels, community-treatment approaches, and massive infusion of new fiscal resources have yet to demonstrate that these "reforms" have changed these dominant trends.

[9] Paul Lerman, "Beyond Gault: Injustice and the Child," in *Delinquency and Social Policy,* ed Paul Lerman (New York: Praeger, 1970), pp. 70–71.

[10] Ibid., p. 245.

[11] President's Commission, *The Challenge of Crime;* and Lerman, "Beyond Gault."

[12] Law Enforcement Assistance Administration, *LEAA's Discretionary Funding Program to Reduce Detention and Institutionalization of Juvenile Status Offenders* (mimeo) (1974).

Given these trends, it is likely in the near future that order offenders will continue to be arrested *and* detained "most frequently." This dour—but quite reasonable—prediction may seem surprising to those expecting federal leadership to reverse the dominant social-control trends for juveniles via the mechanism of the 1974 federal Juvenile Justice and Delinquency Prevention Act of 1974. This Act requires all states receiving block grants under the Act to assume that, within a specified time period, no status offender would be detained or committed to institutions set up explicitly for criminal delinquents. A reading of a 1976 progress report and "plan" presented to the Congress indicates that this minimal ideal reform requirement does not even figure in the projected plans of the current leaders of the agency entrusted to implement the Act.[13]

If we set aside predictions about the near future and merely pay attention to the past and the present, the intriguing question remains: Why have American adults and their publicly supported enforcement agencies exhibited such a disproportionate concern about order offenders? The remainder of this essay will attempt to address the question by examining and assessing the reasons that appeared plausible at critical periods in history.

## Early Reasons

The American concern about order offenses is as old as the Plymouth Bay Colony. By 1660—only half a century after establishing a governing community—the leaders of the colony offered the following rationale for punishing deviant youth: "It appeareth, by too much experience, that diverse children and servants doe behave themselves disobediently and disorderly, towards their parents, masters, and Governors." [14]

---

[13] LEAA, *First Comprehensive Plan for Federal Juvenile Delinquency Programs* (Washington, D.C.: U.S. Department of Justice, LEAA Office of Juvenile Justice and Delinquency Prevention, March 1, 1976).

[14] Quoted in Joseph M. Hawes, *Children in Urban Society: Juvenile Delinquency in Nineteenth Century America* (New York: Oxford University Press, 1971), p. 14.

se that children, like servants, must "know their place"
lings with key adults is apparent in this preamble to the
rs. In a hierarchical society threats to any superordinate
bordinate were taken as a challenge to the legitimacy, as
s the religious, moral, and social bases, of Puritan society.
Relying on legal institutions and the mechanism of the criminal
law, the Puritan authorities responded to "order" challenges by
trying to detail the kinds of behaviors that could justify a communal punishment. For example, the following youthful behaviors
were deemed to be punishable noncapital offenses: acting rude,
stubborn, and unruly; lying; failure to observe the Sabbath; committing fornication; or contracting for marriage without permission of a master. In addition, juveniles were also subject to the
Poor Law that condemned idleness, begging, and vagrancy.[15]

When whipping and other forms of physical punishment were
replaced by institutionalization as a form of noncapital punishment and correction, shortly after the American Revolution, an
interest in maintaining order via the criminal law remained.[16] The
continuity with the 1660 laws is evident in the 1826 law incor-
porating the Boston House of Reformation for Juvenile Offenders.
According to the statute of incorporation, the House Directors
were enabled to "have power, at their discretion, to receive and
take into said house all such children who shall be convicted of
criminal offenses or taken up and committed under and by virtue
of an act of this Commonwealth 'for suppressing and punishing of
rogues, vagabonds, common beggars, and other idle, disorderly,
and lewd persons,' and who may . . . be proper objects therefore" [17]

Two years earlier New York had also incorporated a House of
Refuge that could receive "vagrants," as well as criminal offenders.

[15] Edwin Powers, *Crime and Punishment in Early Massachusetts* (Boston:
Beacon Press, 1966); Hawes, *Children in Urban Society;* R. H. Bremner,
J. Barnard, T. K. Hareven, and R. M. Mennel, *Children and Youth in
America: A Documentary History*, vol. 1 (Cambridge: Harvard University
Press, 1971).
[16] David Rothman, *The Discovery of the Asylum: Social Order and Dis-
order in the New Republic* (Boston: Little, Brown, 1971).
[17] Bremner et al., *Children and Youth in America*, 1:681.

In order to justify the institutionalization of youth for much longer than under the old system, as well as to justify the request for full legal guardianship, the founders of the New York Refuge set forth a new rationale for their proposal. The reformers argued that agents of government could then "stand towards the community in the moral light of guardians of virtue." [18]

Unlike the Puritans, who were primarily content to point out and punish specific examples of nonvirtue (when sermons and religious training had failed), the Refuge founders were willing to undertake, as an organization, the legal role of substitute parent for those deemed to be "proper objects." This unusual grant of authority and power was deemed necessary if crime, pauperism, vagrancy, idleness, intemperance, lewdness—and other undesirable behaviors and conditions—were to be eliminated.

It is possible to argue, as Rothman has, that the post–Revolutionary War generation was more concerned about the problems of order than earlier generations—and this provided the thrust to institutionalize a variety of undesirable persons, including the mentally ill and the poor as well as adult and juvenile criminals.[19] An alternative, or supplementary, view regarding the increased institutionalization of deviants is that the new concept of "reformation" required separation from the centers of moral corruption, crime, idleness, and intemperance—the nascent urban slums. The confident belief that a new "course of treatment" could be devised (as an alternative to Bridewell and the Almshouse) for handling juveniles provided a new rationale for enforcing broad statutes in a discretionary manner. If "proper objects" could be identified by the police magistrates, judges, or Commissioner of the Almshouse, then they could be received and "subjected to a course of treatment, that will afford a prompt and energetic corrective of their vicious propensities." [20]

The argument that they were dealing with "propensities," and not just with "trifling offenses," justified their asking the public, the city, and the state for contributions to develop and maintain

[18] Society for Reformation of Delinquents, *House of Refuge Documents* (New York: Mahlon Day, 1832), p. 13.

[19] Rothman, *Discovery of the Asylum.*

[20] *House of Refuge Documents*, p. 21.

a costlier and lengthier mode of separate institutionalization. Since the course of treatment, unlike the prison and the Almshouse, could be applied to a variety of forms of "vicious propensities," it seemed prudent and cost-effective to receive youth who were "vagrants, or houseless," as well as those charged with petty crimes. The new emphasis on an active attempt to reform individuals and the specific promise of preventing *future* pauperism, crime, and intemperance are components of a new ideological orientation for taking nonharmful crimes seriously. Besides the rationales of morality, protecting the hierarchical social order, and legitimating specific types of adult authority (provided by the Puritan heritage), the Refuge reformers provided an additional set of ideas that could guide a juvenile policy: guardianship and reformation of the individual as an object of treatment; preventive identification and correction of "propensities"; and the obliteration of a legal distinction between penalties for order offenses, petty crimes, and serious crimes. The quantum leap from a punishment of a maximum of 10 stripes for disorderly behavior in 1660 to a discretionary institutional stay of one year to three years (including stripes while residing in the Refuge) in 1825 could not have been accomplished without these potent ideological shifts.

### The Juvenile Court and the Broadening Definition of Delinquency

In the post–Civil War period sympathy for the plight of orphans and half orphans of Civil War soldiers fostered a movement to build special asylums for poor and homeless youth, thereby diverting some youth from a potential reformatory experience. In addition, the placing out of children, particularly in rural areas, was used to rescue children from "corrupting" living conditions. The spread of the free common schools also served to occupy some idle youth during the day. While these efforts may have diverted many idle and dependent youth from being placed in reformatories, the earlier diverse statutes remained on the books in the older states; and new midwest and western states, early in their statehood, enacted a broad correctional conception of delinquency through a variety of statutes that legitimated institutionalization in specific facilities.[21]

With the creation of the first Juvenile Court in Chicago at the turn of the twentieth century, there was an attempt to codify existing Illinois statutes by adding a dependent and neglect category distinct from a criminal delinquent classification. However, distinctions between dependent, neglected, status youth, and criminal offenders were often blurred in actual practice. Each type of youth could be detained in the same facility and sent to the same institution, even though the legislation and early judges gave a new emphasis to reforming worthy children in their own homes. In the original law of 1899, for example, youth could be sent to state training schools or held in detention for the following conditions and behaviors: being destitute, homeless, abandoned, or dependent; improper parental care; begging or receiving alms; living in a house of ill fame or with any vicious or disreputable person and living in an unfit place.[22]

As other states followed the lead of Illinois, they, too, made certain that the jurisdiction of the court was sufficiently broad to encompass, as a "proper object" for detention or reformation in a training school, a broad array of poor law, juvenile status, and criminal characteristics. The justification for these broad terms was set forth with clarity by a Chicago child-saving committee in 1901. They urged that an amended legal definition of what constituted a "condition of delinquency" include items that were implicit in the original dependency and neglect category or had been used in practice—"incorrigible"; "growing up in idleness and crime"; or "knowingly associating with thieves, vicious, or immoral persons." They argued that "the amendment is intended to include all children that are in need of government and care." [23] Since the use of local jails and prisons were forbidden, any separate juvenile correctional facilities were deemed places of government and care for the incorrigible and idle, as well as criminal offenders. The reformers were successful in enacting a statutory

---

[21] Bremner et al., *Children and Youth in America,* vols. 6 and 7.

[22] Ibid., 7:507.

[23] Hawes, *Children in Urban Society,* p. 185.

definition of delinquency that had been the historical practice for about 250 years.

By deliberately equating delinquency with any child "in need of government and care," the reformers believed that they could use the police powers of the state to coercively save children who might escape a narrow legal construction of dependency and neglect. To provide this control and care, they pushed through the legislature the creation of the first all-juvenile detention facilities, a truancy and parental school, paid probation officers, and state subsidies to existing religious-based institutions. They also initiated, before World War I, the creation of small pensions for worthy widows to allow them to keep their children at home. The court, with its broad jurisdictional boundaries, was primarily designed to serve the intake functions of a coercive welfare agency within the context of a modern juvenile, quasi-criminal court.

This overview of the juvenile court development indicates that the reformation paradigm initiated by the founders of the Refuge Movement remained intact. Probation and foster home placement had been added as newer, family-centered, noninstitutional forms of treatment. Instead of emphasizing the elimination of "vicious propensities," the newer, "progressive," ideas emphasized a concern for child development and child welfare via a concern to "include all children in need of government and care." Services were now to be imposed for the "best interests of the child," as well as the community. To make certain that the care was provided, according to the rationale, it was necessary to have boundaries that could technically include all children with problems. A 1946 statement by the official United States Working Group on Social Welfare Activities, organized to provide information and advice to the United Nations, echoed this line of reasoning as follows: "Many children . . . commit overt acts forbidden by the laws, mores, and customs of the particular state or society in which they live. For this reason, it becomes necessary in certain cases for the state to use its police powers as a tool of treatment. *This power should be used only in cases where it is absolutely necessary,* and the paramount objective of such use should be securing that treatment which will best meet the needs of the child." [24]

## Assessing Today's Reasons

From a historical perspective the following major reasons for maintaining broad boundaries of a delinquency definition, including nonharmful order offenses, have been identified:

1. Upholding morality
2. Protecting the broader social order
3. Defending the legitimacy of specified adult authorities
4. Reforming the individual
5. Preventing future crime and delinquency
6. Providing involuntary child welfare and treatment service

While today's system appears to publicly espouse rationales 4, 5, and 6, the operation of the system appears to indicate that the older rationales exhibit the greatest influence in practice. The current system appears to operate as if one-half of the arrests will *not* appear in court. It is difficult to envision that the half that does not appear have been arrested because officials are interested in reformation, prevention via treatment, or providing an involuntary service. Instead, it appears that other reasons must be influencing adult officials.

The fact that the dominant response of the entire system is detention—not treatment—provides evidence that the modern rationales do not fit the basic facts for a majority of youth. Instead, the rationales that appear to fit the data the best are those associated with the oldest practices—reasons of morality, being a threat to the social order, and maintenance of adult authority. Of the three reasons, the threat to adult authority is probably the most salient, since it is most often associated with the decision to arrest. Virtually every observational study of the police has

[24] United Nations, *Comparative Survey of Juvenile Delinquency, Part I: North America*, U.N. Sales no.:58.IV 2 (New York: U.S. Department of Economic and Social Affairs, 1958), p. 111. Italics in original.

found that disrespect of police authority will almost guarantee an arrest—regardless of the precipitating circumstances.[25]

Besides the authority of the police, youth are also subject to parents and new types of "governors"—probation and parole officials. Analyses of juvenile status data indicate that parents are primary initiators of PINS petitions, apparently attempting to enlist the power of an outside party, the state, in an attempt to control the behavior of their children. In addition, the example of the Cleveland judge, cited earlier, indicates that probation officers can place a child in detention "who was uncooperative, who failed to keep appointments, who truanted from school, or when upon a complaint of the parent was considered out of control at home." [26]

The findings of Cleveland are not unusual. In a special community-treatment project conducted by the California Youth Authority Parole Department the following reasons for "suspending parole" and detaining youth were offered:

*Table 4.* Parole suspension or detention

| Reasons | Suspensions/Detentions |
|---|---|
| Uncooperative attitudes | 53 |
| Missed group meetings | 14 |
| Home adjustment | 67 |
| Poor school adjustment | 78 |
| Simple runaway | 35 |
| Curfew, loitering, trespassing | 31 |
| Drinking, possession of alcohol | 19 |

[25] Nathan Goldman, *The Differential Selection of Juvenile Offenders for Court Appearances* (New York: National Council on Criminal Delinquency, 1963); Irving Pilliavin and Scott Briar, "Police Encounters with Juveniles," *American Journal of Sociology* 70 (1964):206–14; James Q. Wilson, *Varieties of Police Behavior* (Cambridge: Harvard University Press, 1968); Albert Reiss, *The Police and the Public* (New Haven: Yale University Press, 1971).

[26] Whitlatch, "Practical Aspects of Reducing Detention Home Population."

In addition to the everyday violations of adult authority, youth can also violate the treatment norms of their adult treaters for being uncooperative or missing a group meeting. The discretionary authority to arrest (or "suspend") and detain has been rationalized as a "tool of treatment"—but this appears to be an approach that escapes the presumed beneficiaries of the "treatment." When suspended youth were asked by outside interviews if they knew why they were being detained, it was found that youth "were generally unaware of any predetermined goals of treatment." [27] They appeared to view their detention for violation of adult treatment norms as just another form of punishment—since the typical response of youth was, "no, no one likes to be locked up."

Contribution by Adults to the Delinquency Problem

The evidence indicates that an expanding system of social control and involuntary treatment can actually produce added amounts of deviance and sanctions. This reasonable inference poses a paradoxical problem for social policy. For instead of just one delinquency problem, we are likely to be faced with two: one presented by youth and one created by adults. In practice this means that when we read that the official delinquency rate in Oakland, Califorinia, is ten times the rate of Albany, New York, we doubt that the entire difference is due to youth behavior.[28] Or when we read that the California rates of detention have risen by nearly 50 percent since the infusion of massive subsidies, we doubt that the entire increase is due to youth behavior. These areas of doubt present independent contributions—by adults—to the delinquency problem.

High rates of order offenses or sanctions are not necessarily indicative of a community's youth behaviors. Instead, the rates may reflect the relative propensity of adults to utilize the police to deal with "disorderly" behavior *and* the relative receptivity by the po-

[27] Paul Lerman, *Community Treatment and Social Control* (Chicago: University of Chicago Press, 1975), p. 46.
[28] Wilson, *Varieties of Police Behavior.*

lice to citizen-initiated complaints. Each source can contribute to the rate of order arrests and sanctions, regardless of the actual output of juvenile deviant behavior.

Citizens are directly involved in deviance production because they are the primary agents that actually mobilize the gatekeepers of the social control system—the police. Reiss, one of our most knowledgeable students of the American police system, summarizes their role as follows: "Despite the existence of a youth division in many large police departments, its role in the production of juvenile offenders is generally negligible. Again, that function, for the most part, depends on citizen mobilization of the patrol division to respond to offenses committed by juveniles" [29]

Citizens, however, tend to classify as criminal matters many incidents that the police consider to be noncriminal. For example, a study of Chicago police found that in one month citizens classified as "criminal" about 58 percent of their complaints, but the police only considered about 17 percent of the total complaints criminal. The majority of incidents perceived by adults as criminal involved "disputes or breaches of the peace." In about one-half of these dispute incidents, the alleged offender was a juvenile. While the police made formal arrests in only about 6 percent of these disturbance complaints, the actual figures reveal that more arrests arose out of a "disturbance" than occurred because of all "criminal" incidents combined—1,892 to 1,787.[30] This outcome occurred because the police responded to many more order offense requests than incidents involving crimes.

It is evident that a lower rate of mobilization of the police for order offenses could have resulted in fewer arrests for this type of complaint. Correlatively, the proportion of arrests that were due to criminal complaints could have risen. Both outcomes could have occurred if *adults* had not perceived many incidents as criminal. In this sense adults can contribute to the raising or lowering of the final production of rates of delinquency. They can contribute by initiating a formal complaint and by exercising discretion in pressing the police to make a formal arrest out of their complaint.

The police can contribute to the production of delinquency in

---

[29] Reiss, *The Police and the Public*, p. 109.     [30] Ibid., pp. 71–75.

the areas of policing that are largely under *their* control. A good deal of policework is reactive, rather than proactive. Areas of policing that are dependent on proactive police behavior relate to drugs, vice, and morals, as will motoring behavior. Arrests for gambling, prostitution, homosexuality, sex in parked cars, or drug usage usually occur because of proactive police initiatives. Arrests for any of these "victimless crimes" can fluctuate dramatically, depending on police organization, resources, and discretionary standards.[31]

Police also have discretion regarding how they perceive and use their authority as law enforcement agents when mobilized to react to complaints. Many decisions to arrest are *not* made because of the incident per se, or because of the strength of the citizen complaint. Police possess enormous discretion to evaluate incidents—both criminal and order complaints. Many decisions are made because of police concern about *their* authority. Reiss summarizes the findings of thousands of observations of citizen-police interactions as follows: "Observation of police and citizen transactions show that an officer is more likely to arrest a juvenile or an adult offender when deference is withheld than when it is granted. Whether or not a complainant is present in citizen initiated encounters, the citizens who behave antagonistically toward the officer are more likely to be arrested than those who are civil or very deferential." [32]

While antagonism by the juvenile is certainly not directly under police control, behavior toward the initial incident and reaction to the lack of deference is under police control. Not all police-juvenile encounters are handled in a calm, dispassionate manner; nor are all displays of youth behavior perceived in a similar manner by all responding officers. Police exercise discretion in initiating interactions after being mobilized, perceiving, and interpreting youth responses, and in deciding whether to react to the "crime incident" or to the "demeanor and behavior" of the juveniles.[33] In all of these respects police can make an independent contribution whether to arrest and whether to hold a youth in custody.

[31] Wilson, *Varieties of Police Behavior.*  [32] Ibid., p. 136.
[33] Pilliavin and Briar, "Police Encounters with Juveniles."

Besides citizens and police there are other adults who can influence juvenile rates of arrest and detention. The previous section noted that probation and parole agents can utilize their positions of authority to suspend probation or parole for a variety of non-criminal reasons. Unlike the police, probation and parole personnel can rationalize their authoritative responses to youth by describing their activities as example of "therapeutic detention." As a task force in California noted: "The Youth Authority is not the first agency to use detention as a tool in the rehabilitative process. Other jurisdictions also have encountered a need for applying negative sanctions in the form of temporary detention. For many years, probation officers, parole agents, and other treaters have attempted to use detention in a therapeutic manner." [34]

While the police may claim that they are arresting and detaining youth for the "good of society," the newest group of social-control agents—probation and parole officers—can argue that their actions are guided by the "best interests of the child." Regardless of the rationale, it is evident that each official occupational group can make an independent contribution to a community's rate of delinquency and detention. Using this perspective, it is possible to suggest that a community can help produce a portion of its own delinquency. Since order offenses loom so large in many areas, the bulk of delinquency can be adult-produced.

### Summary and Conclusion

The best available evidence indicates that real crime is only a small part of America's delinquency problem. This aspect of the juvenile problem is usually minimized, or ignored, in many criminological discussions. If order offenses were dealt with in a trivial manner or if the proportion of arrests that arose from criminal behaviors were increasing, then it might be permissible to continue to set aside analytically the majority of arrested delinquents. The evidence indicates that a juvenile arrest can have potent consequences, whether or not a formal charge is entered in court. The

[34] Lerman, *Community Treatment,* p. 43.

facts indicate, too, that current reform efforts can maintain high rates of order arrests and even expand detention rates at a local level.

The dominance of local detention as the primary postarrest response of the juvenile social-control system has also received minimal attention. Instead, many discussions of correction focus on judicial dispositions and treatment programs. The evidence that more youth experience a detention or jail lockup than receive *all* of the formal correctional programs combined is rarely noted. This fact, first noted with the aid of 1960 data, does not appear to have changed in the 1970s.

The evidence indicates that American citizens and their enforcement agencies are willing to utilize the police power of the state when youth are perceived as symbolic or actual threats to morality, social order, and adult authority. While these threats are rarely deemed criminal by police, an authoritative response to youth has a long historical tradition. The continuance of this tradition appears to rely heavily on a concern about deference to authority, rather than operational concerns about prevention or reformation.

The American approach to order offenses offers insights into the way the social-control system actually operates. The American approach also indicates that a good deal of our delinquency problem is produced by adults. When we begin to understand more fully how adults have been making independent contributions to the problem, then it may be possible to pose some related questions:

1. What behaviors should constitute a restricted definition of delinquency?

2. Should we recognize degrees of harm in our delinquency definition, as we do in everyday life and in the criminal law?

3. Should there be some reasonable relationship between the type, degree, and duration of our actual sanctions and the degree of harm presented by the offender?

4. Does the handling of traffic offenses, zoning violations, health regulations, and building code violations provide any analogues for handling many juvenile order offenses?

5. What alternative societal arrangements can we use or devise

to handle developmental problems, or victimless crimes, that we do not deem appropriate to be handled by a juvenile social-control system?

These questions are concerned about the substantive operation of juvenile law. They do not require grand theories of delinquency as a prerequisite to formulating answers. Instead, tackling the questions requires a consideration of the societal justifications for denying liberty in a fair and just manner. A concern about only court procedures appears to be too limited. Any serious discussion about order offenses must at some point deal with these values. Since the emergence of the first reformatory, we have tended to minimize the significance of these conceptions for juvenile policy.

The fact that we can address basic questions of juvenile policy without reaching agreement on the causes of *youth* behavior does not mean that theory is unimportant. Rather, this reasonable inference means that an empirically based theory of social control as applied to juveniles will probably be most useful. Four lines of inquiry would probably be useful for future theoretical development. One line of inquiry would be historical, focusing on understanding the variability, over time, in the rates of arrests and coercive handling of order-type offenses. There are hints in the literature, for example, that New York City may have experienced a sharp drop in the rates of juvenile arrests in the 1870s.[35] How and why such drops occurred, and when and why the increases occurred, can be very instructive in understanding social-control systems. This research is particularly likely to be fruitful if attention is focused on order offenses, since these rates are heavily influenced by adult responses.

A second line of inquiry, also historical, would inquire why certain states, at about the same time, evolved different legislative and resource-allocation policies. It appears that Massachusetts, for example, did not evolve a detention capability—or interest—to the extent that occurred in Illinois or California. National data tend to obscure interstate differences that may not be fortuitous. Understanding how different jurisdictions cope with similar problems,

[35] Bremner et al., *Children and Youth in America*, vol. 2.

without being overrun by "disorders," may provide insights for both theory and social policy.

A third line of inquiry would focus on intrastate variability. There are many examples, within a state, of communities operating with different policies and systems in regard to the handling of juveniles. Understanding the existence, origins, and maintenance mechanisms of differing systems could also prove useful to a broad theory of social control.

A fourth line of inquiry is intersocietal. There are a number of European societies that rarely arrest and detain youth for order offenses. Understanding how these societies cope with comparable youth behaviors would, of course, be instructive.

All of these lines of inquiry would focus on adults and adult-sponsored institutions, rather than on youth behaviors. These lines of inquiry differ from many other studies in one other significant respect—they are unconcerned with the technical effectiveness of reducing "recidivism" or "preventing" delinquency. Instead, more fruitful lines of inquiry will probably be guided by a renewed interest in how communities and societies express their valuation of liberty, fairness, and justice.

# Part III
## Prescription for Reform

# Reconstructing Delinquency: Evolution and Implications of Twentieth-Century Theory

Travis Hirschi

THIS paper attempts to trace the evolution of academic theories of delinquency through the first three quarters of the twentieth century and to show their changing implications for social policy. There is an ironic timeliness about such an exercise: academic social scientists of all sorts have recently begun to express unusual interest in the policy implications of their work. The constriction of the academic market has apparently legitimized what were once miguided demands for "relevance" and has thereby produced an emphasis on the pragmatic or useful among those who only yesterday were defending the autonomous and disinterested character of the university.

Delinquency would seem to provide an excellent opportunity to explore the connections between social science and social policy. From the beginning this field has been considered too narrow and applied for full intellectual respectability. Now that the social sciences as a whole are being driven in the same direction, a field that has "been there" for some time should have valuable lessons to offer. Three-quarters of a century of continuous research and theorizing in the context of a clearly defined practical goal (the reduction of delinquency) should have produced solid information on the uses and limitations of policy-oriented research.

A quick look at the nature of delinquency theories and the social context in which they are constructed provides further grounds for optimism. In principle, a theory of delinquency does two things: it tells us what delinquency is, and it tells us the antecedents or causes of delinquency. In principle, then, a theory of delinquency should tell us how to *predict* delinquency and how to *prevent* or *control* its occurrence. Given possession of a theory capable of performing these tasks, all that is required to reduce the amount of delinquency is the power, and the will, to do what the theory tells us must be done.

Theories of delinquency are thus marvelously practical things. They tell us where to locate and how to identify potential delinquents (or even the potential parents of potential delinquents), at what age intervention will be most profitable, and even the form and content of intervention efforts likely to be effective.

Although theories of delinquency may be no different in form or possible utility from other social science theories, they appear especially easy to construct. Most people can come up with at least part of one in the time it takes a neighbor or a pollster to ask, and editors, columnists, and politicians seem to have little trouble devising sometimes complicated explanations of the "recent upsurge" in youthful misbehavior. In fact, it seems, theories of delinquency are hard to avoid: those sophisticated social scientists who argue that theories of delinquency are impossible or silly usually end up constructing one of their own during the course of their argument.

Delinquency itself differs from many other social problems in at least two ways relevant to the construction and use of theory. For one thing, there is broad agreement among responsible citizens that something should be done about delinquency. For another, legal institutions with the power to deal with delinquents, and, for that matter, even potential delinquents, are already in place. Widespread concern among the citizenry should facilitate theory construction by providing urgency, purpose, and money to the enterprise. Institutions designed to use social science knowledge should also encourage theorizing by providing the power and the facilities necessary to put theories to test.

So we have much to learn and an ideal setting in which to learn it. Before proceeding on our journey through this best of all possible worlds, it might be worthwhile to consider what is waiting for us at the end of it. Few fields of social science are currently less relevant to social policy than the field of delinquency. The academic response to demands for practical assistance in this area is largely negative. It is now said, in all seriousness, that nobody even knows what delinquency is, let alone its antecedents or causes; it is now repeatedly asserted that knowledge of the causes of delinquency is worthless, impossible, or even positively pernicious. It is routinely claimed (despite the considerable evidence to the contrary) that there is, in American society, little consensus about the gravity of the problem, and that in fact, from the informed point of view of social scientists trained in these matters, delinquency is not really worth the fuss anyway.

This outcome will not be obvious in the history traced here. The reason is simply that as long as scholars are creating positive theories of delinquency, they take for granted the worthiness of the subject, the possibility of studying it in a rational way, and even the hope of being able to do something about it. Still, since we know that delinquency theory is eventually going to come to a bad end, we should be able to see signs of trouble along the way that we might otherwise have missed. One such sign, in my view, is the modern tendency to dismiss the theoretical work of the Progressive era as inadequate and naive.

## Theory in the Progressive Era

The nearest one can come to a widely accepted "theory" of delinquency in the Progressive era is in the presupposition of science that *delinquency is caused.* Evidence of causation was assumed to come from correlation or from differences between delinquents and nondelinquents. In short, early American studies of delinquency were based on the assumption that if some kids are delinquent and others are not, there must be prior differences between them that explain the differences in delinquency. The task was thus simply to find these prior differences and to suggest ways of removing them.

Being relatively free of allegiance to a particular academic discipline and absolutely secure in the belief that nondelinquency is preferable to delinquency, these early students were free to look anywhere and everywhere for "causes" of delinquency. As might be expected, they found a good many. (Given the logic of the approach, the greater the number of causes the investigator could enumerate, the better the evidence that his search had been thorough.)

The multiple-factor "theory" and the individual-case emphasis that emerged from such efforts are now generally considered defective. Early studies *were*, on the whole, atheoretical and pragmatic. They *were* often based on defective research designs such that their "facts" did not necessarily mean what they appeared to mean. Their more abstract concepts *were* often vague and ambiguous. But the general logic of procedure was identical to that which now dominates those social sciences that pretend to empirical and statistical sophistication.[1] For that matter, the case study approach also remains an important, much defended strategy of sociological research, and its marvelous formula for the transmutation of science into mercy ("To know is to understand; to understand is to forgive") is still used as part of this defense.[2]

Academicians today tend to see the first two decades of the century as dominated by theories stressing the hereditary physical and mental defects of delinquents. It is true that early students of delinquency were not afraid of heredity and that they tended to see heredity where the modern student would see environment — for example, in the "alcoholism" of the father. If they found, or thought they had found, hereditary differences, they were per-

---

[1] The Healy diagram of the causal structure of delinquency that David Rothman (this volume) finds absurd differs mainly from diagrams in current issues of the *American Sociological Review* (on topics other than crime) in that these modern diagrams have numbers attached to the arrows.

[2] See George Herbert Mead, "The Psychology of Punitive Justice," *American Journal of Sociology* 23 (1918):586–92; David Matza, *Delinquency and Drift* (New York: Wiley, 1964), pp. 121 ff.; and Ernest van den Haag, "No Excuse for Crime," *Annals of the American Academy of Political and Social Science* 423 (1976):133–41 for discussions of the relation between knowledge of causes and the sentiment of mercy. In suggesting that Progressive era criminology differs little from modern social science in terms of general assumptions and strategies, I intend to suggest that modern criminology is out of step with modern social science. One could argue that criminology has progressed faster than social science as a whole, but I do not find this argument persuasive.

fectly willing to mention them. But it is not accurate to suggest that they emphasized hereditary or biological differences to the exclusion of other differences. It would be more accurate to say that they emphasized any "difference" they could find.

Compared to recent theorizing, the tendency was to emphasize the family over the school or the community.[3] Breckinridge and Abbott devote much of their work to the limited ability of foreign and poor parents to control their children; to the degradation of the delinquent's home (indexed by "brutality, drunkenness, immorality, or crime, paralysis and insanity following vice, imbecile and weak-minded children, and the misery of overcrowded rooms") and to the effects of these things on delinquents' adjustment to school and community. For example: "The point of view of the parents with regard to much that is considered essential to the proper bringing up of the child often remains singularly un-American. For example, the immigrant child frequently suffers from the fact that the parents do not understand that the community has a right to say that children under a certain age must be kept in school."[4] Parental control was weakened by the fact that the child often became superior to the parent in knowledge of English and of American ways. All in all, it was hard for the immigrant parent to win: "Even the old simple virtues seem to lead to disaster; thrift often means sacrificing the children's education, and parental discipline after the European fashion alienates the affection of the Americanized child."[5]

And then there was poverty. Early students of delinquency such as Breckinridge and Abbott had few of the current qualms about ascribing to poverty an important place in the causation of delinquency. Delinquency was defined by contact with the juvenile

[3] The historical progression of emphasis has been home, community, school, with the school dominant in current theorizing (and data). This progression in part reflects changing social conditions, in part changing ideology. Early childhood and the family have not been taken seriously by sociological students of delinquency for some time. See Karen Wilkinson, "The Broken Family and Juvenile Delinquency: Scientific Explanation or Ideology?" *Social Problems* 21 (1974):726–39.

[4] Sophonisba Breckinridge and Edith Abbott, *The Delinquent Child and the Home* (New York: Sage Foundation, 1912), pp. 105, 66.

[5] Ibid., p. 69.

court. Therefore, although it might well be true that children of all "social grades" do wrong, the children of the poor were the constituency of the court, and squabbling about whether they were really more delinquent than the children of the rich would not alter that fact.

The various ways in which poverty produced delinquency were laboriously cataloged: the mother was forced to work and thereby lost control of the family; the sons and daughters were forced at too early an age to assume "pecuniary responsibility" and often ended up in degrading jobs. (The "downfall" of the girls as a consequence of inappropriate work was frequently recounted.) [6] Poor parents sending their children on illegal errands (such as gathering coal at the railroad tracks) was especially noted in this as in many subsequent accounts of the place of poverty (and ignorance) in the causation of delinquency.

Yet in all this there was hope. The policy implications were clear. The child of the immigrant should be kept in school long enough for Americanization to take; counseling of parent and child could lead to an understanding of the value of education and the laws requiring school attendance. For the poor family it was necessary to "secure relief, find work, alter conditions of employment, or in some other way succeed in putting the family on its feet." Such things could be reasonably well accomplished by the probation officer, working alone.[7]

These Progressive era "explanations" have shown remarkable resiliency. Even such causes of delinquency as the avariciousness of immigrant parents resemble modern (and persuasive) accounts of ethnic differences in rates of delinquency—the other side of the coin being parental willingness to sacrifice for the child's education.[8] And the deprivation of poverty and the culture of the immigrant ghetto survived, until recently, as dominant themes in American theory.

The two elements of early explanations of delinquency that quickly dropped out of academic theorizing were the emphasis on individual heredity and the notion of unusual intrapsychic or

[6] Ibid., pp. 76–80.     [7] Ibid., pp. 69, 90.

[8] Jackson Toby, "Hoodlum or Businessman: An American Dilemma," in *The Jews,* ed. Marshall Sklare (New York: Free Press, 1958), pp. 542–50.

"mental" abnormalities among delinquents. Emphasis on the latter (which persists in the rhetoric and logic of casework) [9] is most evident in the work of William Healy, *The Individual Delinquent*.[10] Healy considered "mental abnormalities and peculiarities" and "mental conflict" as the main factor in over 60 percent of the 823 cases of "backsliding" he studied. This in contrast to the less than 20 percent of these cases he attributed to "defective home conditions, including alcoholism." (And the 5 percent he attributed to "bad companions.") Healy's emphasis on the mental condition of the delinquent did *not* stem so much from disagreement with the hereditarians or the environmentalists about the "facts" as from his rather straightforward assumption that psychological causes are "closer" to delinquency than are causes in the other categories. This assumption, too, survives to the present day.

Considerably stylized, the general causal model employed in the Progressive era went something like this: The first, or ultimate, causes of delinquency were biological. These biological causes (such as "weaknesses of mind and body") could produce delinquency directly, as in the case of the feebleminded child who was "unable to foresee and appreciate the consequences of his acts," or, as was more commonly assumed, by affecting family relations, and educational and occupational performance. These social variables, which were partly caused by biology, were in turn causes of psychological states such as "mental conflict," which in their turn "caused" delinquency.[11] If we distinguish two classes of social variables, the structural and the cultural, and interpose a set of "situational" variables between psychology and delinquent behavior, we have all of the general classes of causes required for subsequent discussion. (The distinction between "structure" and

[9] Lewis Diana, "What Is Probation?" *Journal of Criminal Law, Criminology and Police Science* 51 (1960):189–204.

[10] William Healy, *The Individual Delinquent* (Boston: Little, Brown, 1915).

[11] I do not mean to suggest that social scientists in the Progressive era employed this causal model in a systematic or consistent way. Rather, merely that there was an implicit tendency in this direction, which tendency has survived.

"culture" is basically a distinction between objective conditions and subjective states—beliefs, values, attitudes. Situational factors are those operating at the moment of the delinquent act—such as opportunity, fear.) In graphic form, the model might have looked like this:

Biology → Social Structure → Culture → Psychology →
Situation → Delinquency [12]

## Social Disorganization and the Gang

The concentration on social factors (both structural and cultural) that marks the next stage in academic theorizing was at first also seen merely as a shift in emphasis that would supplement rather than oppose previous work. Eventually, however, new concepts were introduced that had profound implications for previous work. In fact, as we shall see, these new concepts soon possessed such explanatory power that biological and psychological factors seemed unnecessary.

The major concept of this second stage of theorizing, *social disorganization*, may be traced to the work of W. I. Thomas, one of the founders of what came to be known as the "Chicago School"—the most important intellectual force in the American study of delinquency. This concept referred to a breakdown of customs, traditions, and institutions. Its major causes were migration or mobility. Its many effects included "personal disorganization," crime, and delinquency, the last coming about because in a state of social disorganization, the ordinary institutions of a stable society, the family and the community, were no longer able to satisfy the needs of children and were therefore no longer able to control their behavior.

---

[12] It is now recognized that debate about the relative importance of variables or sets of variables in such causal chains is unlikely to be productive. The closer a variable is to the final effect, the larger its correlation with the effect and the farther it is from the ultimate cause. So the model, even if true, cannot tell us *where* intervention should occur. This decision will have to be based on considerations other than the statistical facts.

Social disorganization theorists added little to the list of specific ills that beset the immigrant or slum community. These remained such things as "inadequate family life, poverty, deteriorating neighborhoods; ineffective religion, education, and recreation." [13] They did, however, introduce a broader conception of how these ills operate to produce delinquency, and they introduced the gang as an element of slum social structure with important implications for delinquency.

Two views of the place of the gang in the commission of delinquent acts eventually emerged. Adhering closely to earlier conceptions, Frederic Thrasher held that both delinquency and the gang were direct products of social disorganization. The child least under the control of conventional institutions was most likely to belong to a gang, and was most likely to become delinquent *whether or not* he belonged to a gang. The gang member might indeed be slightly more likely than the nongang member to commit delinquent acts, but the explanation had to do with such things as "mob psychology" or "safety in numbers." The gang was not organized around, or for, delinquent behavior. Gang membership was not a necessary condition for delinquency.

The second view, represented by the work of Clifford R. Shaw and Henry D. McKay, eventually led to a marked departure from earlier conceptions of the causal path leading to delinquency. [14] In their view delinquency is a *tradition* in the slum community. The child free from institutional controls takes up with the gang, learns this tradition, and becomes, as a consequence, delinquent. The gang, then, represents, or preserves, the delinquent culture. It competes with conventional institutions. In some cases membership in a gang is virtually a necessary and sufficient cause of delinquency.

Shaw and McKay were impressed by differences in rates of delinquency across *areas* of cities that were both large and stable

[13] Frederic M. Thrasher, *The Gang* (1927; reprint ed., Chicago: University of Chicago Press, 1963, p. 339.
[14] Clifford R. Shaw and Henry D. McKay, *Report on the Causes of Crime: Social Factors in Juvenile Delinquency* 2, National Commission on Law Observance and Enforcement (Washington, D.C.: U.S. Government Printing Office, 1931).

over time. These differences remained even though the ethnic composition of any given area might have shifted during the period of observation. Thus, Shaw and McKay concluded, there must be something about the *culture* of particular areas that is conducive to delinquency.

Rate differences in delinquency, they concluded, must reflect "the differential probability of a boy's having contact with other delinquent boys in the same area or of observing their activities." In high rate areas "the traditions of delinquency . . . are transmitted down through successive generations of boys, in much the same way that language and other social forms are transmitted." The gang in high rate areas is not simply available to boys who might find it attractive, it is an active force in perpetuating the traditions of delinquency—boys are actively and sometimes forcefully recruited, they are taught techniques for specific offenses, and their delinquency is "supported and sustained by the delinquent group" to which they belong.[15]

As long as delinquency was a direct consequence of the failure of the family, the school, and the community to control the behavior of adolescents, it remained reasonable to assume that those adolescents most likely to become delinquent were also most likely to suffer from various social, intellectual, mental, and moral deficiencies. The introduction of the gang as an intervening social organization and, finally, of an intervening system of beliefs and values undercut the assumption of individual "inferiority." At first it tended merely to deny the relevance of "individual" characteristics. Eventually, however, it led directly to the view that the delinquent was not simply equal to his nondelinquent peers but was, if anything, actually superior to them.

The policy implications of this stage of delinquency theorizing do not require guesswork. Both Thrasher and Shaw and McKay devote attention to this question. While Thrasher was willing to consider doing something about family deficiencies, ineffective religion, inadequate schooling, and unguided recreation, there is

[15] Clifford R. Shaw and Henry D. McKay, *Juvenile Delinquency and Urban Areas* (Chicago: University of Chicago Press, 1969), pp. 53, 174, 183.

a clear note of pessimism in his discussion.[16] These factors, he concludes, usually interact, and "it seems impossible to control one without dealing with the others."[17] While waiting (as we must) for the "disorderly life of a frontier" to become the orderly life of an advancing civilization, the gang represents the best line of approach to the problem of delinquency.

At this point we see introduced the idea of the delinquent as a *person*. A person, in the eyes of the Chicago School, is an *individual* with a *role* in a *social group*.[18] To understand the delinquent, it was assumed, one must take into account his group memberships. So, too, these memberships must be taken into account if he is to be dealt with effectively. Thrasher thus found another reason for neglecting family, religion, and school (a reason similar to Healy's concentration on "mental conflict"): for many boys, the gang becomes the most important source of satisfaction in life; it is then too late to do anything about previous group memberships.[19] If the gang is the source of the boy's satisfaction, there are two approaches open to those who would reform him: "he must be removed completely from the gang and the social world it represents, or his gang must be reformed." In Thrasher's view, attempts to remove the boy from the gang were likely to be repressive and unlikely to succeed. So there was little choice: the gang itself must be dealt with as a unit. Thus was born the concept of a detached, or area, worker, a person (?) sent into high rate delinquency areas with a mandate to contact delinquent gangs, establish relations with them, and work to modify the behavior of their members.[20] That Thrasher retained the optimism of the Pro-

[16] Recreation, as such, was not considered a serious problem by Thrasher. In fact, if anything, the problem was that the boys in disorganized areas had too much of it: "gangland provides a realm of adventure with which no playground can compete" (*The Gang*, p. 34).

[17] Ibid., p. 339.

[18] The subsequent theoretical issue might then be phrased thus: Is the delinquent an individual or a person? The "mistake" of the Chicago School was the automatic assumption that all individuals are fully and equally persons.

[19] Thrasher, *The Gang*, pp. 344–47.

[20] Walter B. Miller, "The Impact of a Total-Community Delinquency Control Project," *Social Problems* 10 (1962):168–91.

gressive era could not be better illustrated than by the set of "before" and "after" pictures he uses to show the transformation of a "destructive gang" into a Boy Scout troop.

The treatment implications of the Shaw-McKay theory were embodied in the Chicago Area Project, founded in the early thirties. This project appears to have relied more heavily on notions of social disorganization and lack of social control than on the competing-culture portions of the Shaw-McKay theory. In any event, the idea was to strengthen the local community. Solomon Kobrin outlines the assumptions upon which the program was founded and its major "procedural principles": "a delinquency prevention program could hardly hope to be effective unless and until the aims of such a program became the aims of the local populations. . . . An indispensible . . . task of delinquency prevention is to discover effective methods of inducing residents of disadvantaged city areas to take up the cause of [delinquency] prevention in a serious manner." The procedural principles: "development of youth welfare organizations among residents of delinquency areas; employment of so-called indigenous workers wherever possible; and the fostering and preservation of the independence of these groups."

As Kobrin notes, the founders of the Chicago Area Project were optimistic about the long-term prospects of bringing delinquency under control by organizing the local community to this end. Many of their ideas were to appear again in the social programs of the sixties. Social disorganization, even if conceptually distant from the commission of delinquent acts, was not a source of despair to those who would do something about delinquency.[21]

## Differential Association and Definitions Favorable to the Violation of Law

In emphasizing the place of the gang and the community in the causation of delinquency, Thrasher and Shaw and McKay shifted attention from the characteristics of individual delinquents toward

[21] Solomon Kobrin, "The Chicago Area Project—A Twenty-five Year Assessment," *Annals of the American Academy of Political and Social Science* 322 (1959):20–29.

their group memberships. The break with previous theory was by no means decisive. The slum community remained disordered or pathogenic. There was no reason to believe that delinquents did not retain characteristics traditionally attributed to them: defects of mind and body that inadequate institutions create. (Thrasher and Shaw and McKay could still refer approvingly to the work of Breckinridge and Abbott and Healy and suggest that they were simply adding a new dimension to their work.)

The stage for a complete break with notions of individual pathology was, however, set. It was to come with the theory of differential association of Edwin Sutherland. This theory stated: "Criminal behavior is learned . . . in interaction with other persons in a process of communication. . . . The principal part of the learning of criminal behavior occurs within intimate personal groups. A person becomes delinquent because of an excess of definitions favorable to violation of law over definitions unfavorable to violation of law." [22]

In one fell swoop Sutherland eliminated both *individual* and *social* pathology from the armamentarium of the delinquency theorist (and those who would treat him). Although "definitions favorable to violation of law" could have been located at the same point in the causal chain leading to delinquency occupied by Healy's "mental abnormalities and peculiarities," Sutherland was not interested in preserving the contributions of earlier theory and research. Rather, his intent (and, whatever his intent, the effect of his theory) was to suggest that earlier theories were simply wrong.[23] The objective conditions of the slum, the pathologies of its institutions and people, might indeed be correlated with criminality, but these correlations had been misinterpreted:

In an area where the delinquency rate is high, a boy who is sociable, gregarious, active and athletic is very likely to come in contact with the other boys in the neighborhood, learn delinquent behavior from

[22] Edwin H. Sutherland and Donald R. Cressey, *Principles of Criminology* (Philadelphia: Lippincott, 1970), p. 75.

[23] According to Sutherland, a general theory of delinquency "does not, or should not, neglect or eliminate any factors that are included in the multiple-factor theory" (ibid., p. 88). Unfortunately, Sutherland rarely follows this principle, preferring instead to discount elements of the multiple-factor theory, one at a time.

them, and become a gangster; in the same neighborhood the psychopathic boy who is isolated, introverted, and inert may remain at home,
not become acquainted with the other boys in the neighborhood, and
not become delinquent. . . . A child is ordinarily reared in a family;
the place of residence of the family is determined largely by family
income; and the delinquency rate is in many respects related to the
rental value of the houses.[24]

So, for the first time, the delinquent's family became just another
family forced by poverty to remain in a "delinquency area," to expose its children to definitions favorable to violation of law. The
family's poverty or even its inability or unwillingness to control its
children was no longer of direct moral significance. By the same
token, the many differences between delinquents and nondelinquents reported in the past were either no longer present (such
as intelligence) or no longer directly conducive to delinquency:
"the person who is not already trained in crime does not invent
criminal behavior." [25]

Sutherland's theory was a radical departure from previous
views. If the "delinquent" simply learns "delinquent" definitions
in the same way a Boy Scout learns Boy Scout attitudes and beliefs, there is no reason to think that the "delinquent" differs from
the Boy Scout. One was born and raised in a "delinquent" culture;
the other was not. One learns to tie knots; the other to rob old
ladies. Science cannot say that tying knots is "better than" robbing old ladies; it can only say that the process of learning the two
skills is identical. Who *can* say that one set of behavior should be
rewarded and the other punished? Those with the power to get
their definitions embodied in the criminal law (those without the
detachment of the scientist). The powerful classes or groups strive
to extend their values to all cultural segments of the society. They
therefore "criminalize" the natural behavior of those groups and
cultures with insufficient power to oppose them.[26]

Offhand, one might expect those who accept Sutherland's
theory to argue for a "live and let live" policy toward delinquents,
at least insofar as they and their victims share the same culture.

---

[24] Ibid., p. 77.       [25] Ibid., p. 75.

[26] This, then, is the origin of "conflict theory," one of the sources of labeling theory and radical criminology, and an important modern theory in its
own right, but one I neglect here.

The right of the reformer to intervene in the culture of a group that does not share his values and standards is, at best, questionable. Despite the explicit relativism of cultural theories, they have been the basis for suggestions for treatment and have been embodied in the design of treatment programs.

These programs resemble those of the earlier theoretical period in that they emphasize *group* rather than *individual* change. One point of difference, however, stems from the notion that crime results from crime-specific attitudes and beliefs. It is not enough, then, to redirect a group toward noncriminal *activities* be they recreational or vocational; instead, the new *attitudes* and *beliefs* fostered in the treatment group must be *anticriminal.*[27] Given the lack of specificity about just *what* the criminal believes, users of cultural theories must wait until criminal acts have been committed before they can know that the person holds beliefs favorable to the violation of law.[28] Thus the theory has not, to my knowledge, been as important in prevention as in recommendations for the treatment of convicted and preferably incarcerated criminals.

In any event, the "cultural transmission" theory radically altered the nature of delinquency; severely eroded the plausibility and persuasiveness of individual therapy; undercut efforts to better the conditions of the slum (insofar as crime prevention was the goal); and led directly, if not immediately, to the view that "crime control" is an unwarranted interference in the natural workings of a culture at least equal and in fact in many ways superior to that of the bourgeois culture from which "the law" emanates.

## Structural Theory Returns

Previously described theorizing represents a continuous chain of straight-line evolution from the individual through the social

[27] Donald R. Cressey, "Changing Criminals: The Application of the Theory of Differential Assertion," *American Journal of Sociology* 61 (1955): 116–20.

[28] Given current sentiments, theories incapable of predicting delinquency in the absence of delinquent acts are ideal since they protect the child from unwarranted interference by the state.

group to culture as the source of delinquent behavior. All of this work may be traced to a single academic tradition, almost to a single city, Chicago.[29] The Chicago tradition was rooted in observation of immigrants and their children. As a consequence it eventually stressed differences in or conflicts of values, beliefs, attitudes —in a word, culture. A major task facing those who would prevent or control delinquency was to promote assimilation of "foreign" elements into mainstream American culture.

Another intellectual tradition, whose roots were more academic-theoretical and less practical-empirical, started from the assumption that assimilation of foreign elements had been accomplished. The most influential document in this competing tradition was published by Robert K. Merton in 1938. It was titled "Social Structure and Anomie."[30]

The French sociologist Emile Durkheim had used the term *anomie* to describe a condition of deregulation he held to be typical of modern Western societies. In Durkheim's view a precondition of happiness it that the individual's wants or desires be limited. By himself the individual is incapable of limiting his wants. Such control must come from objective restrictions or from others, from society. In the event that the individual is stripped of connections with others, his natural wants expand until he "aspires to everything, and is satisfied with nothing." (Durkheim thus shared with the early Chicago School the idea that deviant behavior is a consequence of the absence of social control.)

Merton begins his discussion by rejecting the notion (shared by Durkheim) that certain impulses are given in the organism, in human nature. In the more purely sociological view, according to Merton, such impulses or desires are themselves socially induced. In fact, according to Merton, American society is especially desire-inducing, placing great emphasis on "success," particularly material or monetary success. At the same time, it does not provide equally to all the means of attaining such success. For large seg-

[29] Sutherland was also influenced by Thorsten Sellin, whose *Culture, Conflict, and Crime* (New York: Social Science Research Council, 1938) provided an additional source of support to cultural theories in general.

[30] Robert K. Merton, "Social Structure and Anomie," *American Sociological Review* 3 (1938):672–82.

ments of the population, opportunities to reach the "culturally induced" goal are simply not available. For such people there is little choice: they must either give up the chase (which solution is itself taken as a sign of moral defect) or they must turn to illegal behavior as an alternative (and not too heavily despised) means of continuing it. Delinquency is thus a consequence of discrepancy between culturally induced aspirations and socially conditioned expectations.

The major concept used to describe variation in accessibility to "legitimate means" was *social class,* and it was, of course, the *lower class* that was most likely to be forced to turn to delinquency. "Anomie" or "opportunity" theory thus agrees with earlier theories that high rates of delinquency are found in the "lower" classes. But this concentration is not due to the fact the lower classes are populated by people who barely speak English, who brutalize or ignore their untalented children, and who squander their wages on alcohol; instead, the lower class is populated by poor but honest folk doing their best to encourage their children to rise above their unhappy origins, to seek the American Dream, and to obey the law up to the point that it becomes no longer reasonable or sensible to do so.

Once again, the clear tendency of theory is to deny the relevance of individual "pathology" and even the inadequacy of institutions such as the family. Once again, too, this tendency to assert equality easily spills over into an assertion that those persons most likely to become delinquent are in fact superior to nondelinquents by the very criteria *traditionally used to explain delinquency.* (In other words, the delinquent is *more* ambitious and able; he is more likely to have learned the mandates of the culture or to have come from a striving family.)

In Sutherland's theory the delinquent learns in intimate association with others a set of crime-specific attitudes and beliefs. To the extent that these beliefs favor crime, the person holding them will commit criminal acts. In Merton's theory the delinquent learns the general or common attitudes and beliefs of American society; the relevant attitudes and beliefs are not crime-specific but tend if anything in the anticriminal direction. Still, these attitudes and beliefs foster an active approach to the satisfaction of needs, and when these needs cannot be satisfied within the law, the beliefs that foster them become an important element in the explanation of behavior outside the law.

The next step in American theory was to combine the cultural tradition of Sutherland with the structural tradition of Merton. This task was accomplished by Albert K. Cohen and by Robert A. Cloward and Lloyd E. Ohlin.[31]

The general logic of Cohen's and Cloward and Ohlin's approaches was identical: the strains that Merton describes were used to populate the delinquent gangs or subcultures described by Shaw and McKay and Sutherland. The theories start with the lower-class boy who desires something—something quite legitimate and conventional—respect, love, or money; they then show the difficulties he faces in achieving these things, the obstacles that stand in his way: discrimination, faulty preparation, lack of seed money. (Since education was considered central to achievement in American society, the lower-class boy's difficulties in school were emphasized.) The discrepancy between what the lower-class boy would like and his realistic chances of attaining it is productive of intense frustration, such that he must somehow find a way to relieve the strain. At this point the delinquent gang enters the picture, providing solace, protection, technical training, and a new set of values.

It is probably true that structural and cultural theories are basically incompatible, that they cannot be put together without inconsistency.[32] Still, Cohen's and Cloward and Ohlin's efforts to combine them were extremely persuasive to many sociologists, and their work may serve to remind us that the requirements of theory and those of social policy differ. The pragmatic implications of a theory are richer the greater the variety of things that, according to the theory, matter. For policy purposes, it isn't all that important that a theory be internally consistent, or even that it be

[31] Albert K. Cohen, *Delinquent Boys: The Culture of the Gang* (New York: Macmillan, 1955); Richard Cloward and Lloyd E. Ohlin, *Delinquency and Opportunity* (New York: Macmillan, 1960).

[32] Travis Hirschi, *Causes of Delinquency* (Berkeley: University of California Press, 1969); Ruth Kornhauser, "Social Sources of Delinquency: An Appraisal of Analytic Models" (Ph.D. Diss. Chicago 1975).

true. A theory, a positive theory of delinquency, is motive for action, for doing something; it is also a justification for seeking financial assistance. Once action is underway, strict adherence to "the theory" is both impractical and impossible anyway. Finally, the thing that matters most in terms of social action is the moral or political aura of the theory.

Of the theories thus far considered, none seems to have produced greater enthusiasm for social action than that summarized in the title of Cloward and Ohlin's book: *Delinquency and Opportunity*. This book justified and partially structured a massive program for delinquency prevention in New York's lower east side called Mobilization for Youth. This program had considerable impact on the social programs of the 1960s, including the War on Poverty (Mobilization for Youth itself quickly focused on poverty rather than directly on delinquency).

Cloward and Ohlin conclude their extensive theorizing with the rather bland statment that "the target for preventive action . . . [is] not the individual or group that exhibits the delinquent pattern, but . . . the social setting that gives rise to delinquency. It is our view . . . that the major effort of those who wish to eliminate delinquency should be directed to the reorganization of slum communities." [33]

But Mobilization for Youth was not a New York version of the Chicago Area Project. In Cloward and Ohlin's theory, lower-class people are not responsible for their failures. They are not inadequately socialized, demoralized, or disorganized. They are, rather, victims of injustice, prejudice, and discrimination, of more or less systematic efforts to keep them in their place. Given a population systematically oppressed (or, at best, misunderstood), the key to delinquency prevention is not somehow to teach them to control their own children, it is rather somehow to end oppression, to provide power to the powerless.

Mobilization for Youth, then, was directed toward the structure of oppression. Adjustment of the slum dweller to his circumstances was not to be encouraged. Greater "community" interest in delinquency nowhere appears in the literature of the program. The

[33] Cloward and Ohlin, *Delinquency and Opportunity*, p. 211.

program instead promoted social protest, subversion of conventional institutions, militancy, activism and advocacy, all in the name of the poor (and chuckled that it was occasionally accused of doing so). The line between "partisan political action" and "social action" was often thin indeed.[34]

More important for present purposes, Mobilization for Youth was consistently promoted as "an alliance of social reform with social science. . . . A scientific body of knowledge is now available to draw from and *reshape* for practical purposes. More important, social-science knowledge put to the service of social reform offers strength and sanction for change attempts. . . . We are convinced . . . that the MFY experience . . . constitutes a step toward the ultimate maturity of the collaboration [between social reform and social science]."[35]

There is a lesson here somewhere. The link between social reform and social science is often tenuous at best. Yet the failure of social reform is easily interpreted as a failure of social science, as a refutation of the specific theory on which reform was ostensibly based. Carefully controlled, scientifically adequate experiments rarely have as much to say about the adequacy of theory. Little wonder, then, that Mobilization for Youth is not now seen as an example of mature collaboration between science and social policy but as the last hurrah of Progressive era optimism about the place of scientific knowledge in the fight against crime.

Symbolic Interaction, Again

Meanwhile, a radically different (but equally radical) conception of the whole problem of deviance (and with it, delinquency) was growing. With the exception of Sutherland, previous theories of "delinquency" did not dwell on the meaning or definition of delinquency. Delinquency was merely the commission of acts in violation of the law. Delinquents were persons identified as such

[34] George A. Brager and Francis P. Purcell, *Community Action against Poverty* (New Haven: College and University Press, 1967), p. 335.

[35] Ibid., p. 338.

by neighbors, businessmen, parents, the police, or the courts. (The impetus for Mobilization for Youth is reported to have been a precipitous rise in the official rate of juvenile delinquency.) Most academic theorists were willing to admit that official counts may misrepresent the distribution of law-violating acts in the juvenile population, but (it was assumed) official statistics do a better job of representing acts that people care about than would any attempt to include those that do not come to the attention of officials. (Note, however, that Sutherland had introduced the idea that the definition of behavior as delinquent is a definition *imposed by outsiders* on behavior that is considered noncriminal by persons inside the culture that promotes or requires the behavior.)

As early as 1938 Frank Tannenbaum had argued that the act of defining or punishing delinquent behavior was implicated in the perpetuation of the behavior itself: "The process of making the criminal . . . is a process of tagging, defining, identifying, segregating, describing, emphasizing, making conscious and self-conscious; it becomes a way of stimulating . . . and evoking the very traits that are complained of. . . . The person becomes the thing he is described as being." [36] This view, characteristic of a theoretical perspective called "symbolic interaction," holds that meaning is not given in events or actions themselves but that they become meaningful as they are defined or interpreted. In the case of delinquency, it assumes that *acts* that could be defined as delinquent are frequently committed by all or almost all adolescents; that the major or only difference between delinquents and nondelinquents is that delinquents have been labeled by persons with sufficient power to make the label "stick."

The symbolic interactionist or labeling theorist is especially leery of the notion that any category of "deviants" is homogeneous with respect to the rule-breaking behavior implied by the label. Since "definitions of the situation" are not given in situations themselves but are to some extent creative acts, the view that officials merely record the delinquent behavior of adolescents is considered so obviously ludicrous that it is not worthy of serious investigation.

[36] Frank Tannenbaum, *Crime and the Community* (Boston: Ginn, 1938), pp. 19–20.

During the sixties the symbolic interactionist perspective dominated the sociological study of deviant behavior. It was at no time systematically applied as an explanation of delinquency, but it was implied that the same processes work with all forms of "deviant" behavior, and occasional specific references to crime and delinquency were enough to confirm the idea that a new theory of delinquency had appeared. The most widely quoted statement of this perspective was provided by Howard S. Becker: *"social groups create deviance by making the rules whose infraction constitutes deviance,* and by applying those rules to particular people and labeling them as outsiders. From this point of view, deviance is *not* a quality of the act the person commits, but rather a consequence of the application by others of rules and sanctions to an 'offender.' The deviant is one to whom the label has successfully been applied; deviant behavior is behavior that people so label." [37]

According to another proponent of this view, "The critical variable" in the sociological study of deviance "is the social *audience* . . . since . . . the audience . . . decides whether or not any given action or actions will become a visible case of deviation." [38]

This new perspective drew strength from the fact that its logic was similar to that underlying formation of the juvenile court: it is better to treat adolescent offenders as "delinquents" than as "criminals" because the stigmatizing effects of the criminal label are thereby avoided. It drew strength from the more general view widely held among educated citizens that to change the name *is* to change the game. (Although labeling theorists stoutly deny the allegation that they favor the euphemistic approach to the solution of social problems,[39] consumers of the theory apparently believe that if it is possible for policemen and juvenile court judges to "create" delinquency from neutral behavioral material, it should also be possible to "create"

---

[37] Howard S. Becker, *Outsiders* (New York: Macmillan, 1963), p. 9.

[38] Kai T. Erikson, "Notes on the Sociology of Deviance," *Social Problems* 9 (1962):307–14.

[39] Edwin M. Schur, *Radical Nonintervention* (Englewood Cliffs, N.J.: Prentice-Hall, 1973), pp. 126–30.

a *better* world by similar processes of definition and redefinition.) Labeling theory also drew support, especially among sociologists, from its explicit assertion that the juvenile justice system responds to its own definition of the situation rather than to the behavior of the child, that it is therefore by its very nature unfair, unjust, and discriminatory.

The specific implications of labeling theory for policy are clear: First, "correction" or treatment of the individual is misguided and pointless:

The point of view here developed rejects all assumptions that would impute crime to the individual in the sense that a personal shortcoming of the offender is the cause of the unsocial behavior. The assumption that crime is caused by any sort of inferiority, physiological or psychological, is here completely and unequivocally repudiated.[40]

. . . the treatment outlook [implies] that persons with certain characteristics . . . will be relatively *predisposed* to engage in delinquent behavior. . . . [The labeling approach, in contrast, would] repudiate the prevailing assumption that the delinquent is basically different. The "internal" types of individual difference do not provide a basis for explanation or a target for policy.[41]

Second, community action or reform is not going to do the job either. "What [delinquents] suffer from, more than either problems of the psyche or socioeconomic distress, is *contingencies.* . . . According to [the labeling] outlook, a complete and accurate depiction of delinquency (processed *and* unprocessed) would reveal that most types of youthful misconduct are common within all socioeconomic strata in our society." [42]

So "the basic injunction for public policy becomes: leave kids alone wherever possible." [43]

There can be little doubt that labeling theory *has* influenced public policy, both in its critique of traditional methods of treatment and prevention and in its positive advocacy of what Lemert

[40] Tannenbaum, *Crime and the Community,* p. 22.
[41] Schur, *Radical Nonintervention,* pp. 31, 153–54.
[42] Ibid., p. 154 (emphasis in original).    [43] Ibid., p. 155.

has called "judicious nonintervention."[44] Programs of diversion from the juvenile system, renewed interest in separate treatment of "status offenders" from those who have broken the criminal law, and indeed much of the movement toward decriminalization of marginal offenses (such as the use of marihuana), all draw much of their vitality from the persuasiveness of labeling theory, whether or not it is "properly" understood.[45]

## The Current Scene

A major trend in twentieth-century theory has been the shift in attention from the individual delinquent to the broader social forces creating him. The first step in this process, as we have seen, was to locate the delinquent in a social group, the gang. In succession, the gang was located in a community, and the community located in a society. The logical next step was to locate this *delinquency-creating society* in an even larger scheme of things, in a set of economic or political systems.

A related trend has been the progressive normalization of the delinquent. His defects or blemishes gradually disappeared until he became, if not always a hero, at least the innocent victim of internal colonialism, of unjust discrimination, a creation of meddling busybodies and uptight squares.

[44] Edwin M. Lemert, "The Juvenile Court—Quest and Realities," in President's Commission on Law Enforcement and Administration of Justice, Task Force Report: *Juvenile Delinquency and Youth Crime* (Washington, D.C.: U.S. Government Printing Office, 1967), pp. 96–97.

[45] My understanding of labeling theory is the understanding of a positivist. Labeling theorists frequently assert that their theory does not address the question of the causes of delinquency (that, in fact, they do not accept the idea of causation as it is commonly understood). They also frequently assert that they do not recognize their own theory in positivistic renderings of it. Apparently, this misunderstanding may be explained something like this: The consumer of delinquency theories is usually interested in the question, Why do they do it? The labeling theorist routinely attacks conventional theories of delinquency and goes on to talk about his own perspective on this question. The consumer hears this and therefore assumes that the labeling perspective must be somehow relevant to the question of the causation of delinquency. He therefore misconstrues the labeling perspective in the direction of relevance to this question.

A third and partially independent trend has been the progressive acceptance of the view that the field of delinquency is somehow exempt from the ordinary rules of scientific logic and procedure.

These trends and reactions to them have produced a politicized and troubled field. One faction, explicitly political, has followed to its logical conclusion the tendency to find the causes of delinquency in the basic structure of American society.

Radical Criminology

According to the radical criminologist, "reform is the adaptive mechanism of advanced capitalism." In his view advanced capitalism uses "criminology" to control the dangerous classes, to oppress blacks, women, and children, and thereby to "further enhance the hegemony of the privileged." It follows as a matter of simple logic that criminologists committed to "a new life," to "the struggle of creating a socialist society," would not wish to aid the capitalist masters in their efforts to control their slaves and preserve the present system of domination. It is therefore no accident that, from the point of view of the radical, critical, or humane criminologist, "criminology has very little to offer by way of explanations and less still with regard to solutions [of crime.]" [46]

The task of radical criminology is not to explain or to offer solutions to the problem of crime (thus it is more than just convenient that nothing is now known), it is rather to "unmask" and "demystify" current arrangements, to show how the law, criminology, and even crime itself function to preserve a system of repression. The task of demystification is fairly easily accomplished. The Progressive era "was designed to strengthen the existing social structure through the introduction of rational and scientific means of controlling the 'dangerous classes.' " "The

[46] Richard Quinney, *Critique of Legal Order* (Boston: Little, Brown, 1974), p. 169; Barry Krisberg, *Crime and Privilege* (Englewood Cliffs, N.J.: Prentice-Hall, 1975), p. 62; Quinney, *Critique of Legal Order*, p. vi; Clayton Hartjen, *Crime and Criminalization* (New York: Praeger, 1974), p. 187.

concept of crime, as usually presented, serves to deflect attention from the violence and social damage that those with power inflict upon the mass of people in order to keep them subordinate and oppressed." "Laws that protect the sanctity of private property primarily benefit those who have the most property. Laws that condemn individual violence are primarily designed to support the monopoly on violence that is claimed by the state." "Crime functions to further enhance the hegemony of the privileged through the creation of a criminal stereotype." [47]

Another tactic of the radical criminologist is to expose the fact that government agencies, such as LEAA and NIMH, provide "substantial grants to graduate departments that design training programs in some aspects of crime and corrections," and that "social scientists receive funds from a number of government agencies to conduct research on the crime problem." [48]

As of now, then, radical criminology is largely a description of the criminal justice system in the United States from a radical point of view. The description itself appears to be reasonably accurate or objective. Criminologists of all political persuasions would agree that the criminal justice system functions to preserve current arrangements, to protect people and their property. [49] And no one could reasonably dispute the detailed evidence Quinney has assembled to show that public monies are available for training and research in the crime and delinquency area.

If radical criminology is treated with careful respect by criminologists, the reason is not far to seek: just plain criminology is so widely held to be useless, impossible, or both, that no line of defense seems tenable.

## Sophisticated Criminology

The decision by radical criminologists to study things other than crime and their attack on the political bias of conventional criminology are less damaging to delinquency theory and research than the widely held notions that (1) the quest for causes of

[47] Krisberg, *Crime and Privilege*, pp. 15, 20, 62.
[48] Quinney, *Critique of Legal Order*, pp. 35, 37.
[49] Van den Haag, "No Excuse for Crime."

delinquency is futile and that (2), even if causes could be located, knowledge of them would add nothing to questions of social policy. Important recent spokesmen for this point of view include Norval Morris and Gordon Hawkins and James Q. Wilson. Wilson's confusion on the logic of causation and its implications for social policy is absolute: "Causal analysis attempts to find the source of human activity in those factors which themselves are not caused—which are, in the language of sociologists, 'independent variables.' Obviously nothing can be a cause if it is in turn caused by something else; it would then only be an 'intervening variable.' But ultimate causes cannot be the object of policy efforts precisely because, being ultimate, they cannot be changed." Wilson of course cannot discuss crime and delinquency in any reasonable way and remain faithful to this view. He mentions "independent variables" that are subject to change and "intervening variables" that act as causes. For example, he offers a traditional explanation of the increase in heroin addiction during the 1960s: "the continued disintegration of the lower-income, especially black, family living in the central city may have heightened the importance of street peer groups to the individual, and thus . . . placed him in a social environment highly conducive to heroin experimentation." He also concludes "that [heroin] addiction produces a significant increase in criminality of two kinds—stealing from innocent victims and selling heroin illegally to willing consumers." By Wilson's own logic, nothing can be done about the disintegration of the lower-income black family because *in his model* this variable is the ultimate cause (which "cannot be changed"), and efforts to deal with peer groups or with heroin addiction as a means of reducing crime must be pointless because *in his model* these are "only 'intervening variables.' " [50]

[50] Norval Morris and Gordon Hawkins, *The Honest Politician's Guide to Crime Control* (Chicago: University of Chicago Press, 1969); James Q. Wilson. *Thinking about Crime* (New York: Vintage, 1975), quotations on pp. 55, 145, 157. If unemployment were introduced as the "ultimate" cause in this model, it could then not be changed. The disintegration of the black family would then no longer be the ultimate cause but would be caused by something else, thus eliminating it once again from policy considerations. So, by Wilson's logic, all causes of delinquency are irrelevant to public policy.

The significant point here is not that Wilson is wrong; it is the offhand way in which he feels free to dismiss traditional criminological research and theorizing as though anyone familiar with elementary logic could see through the enterprise in a moment. This license to say *anything* (no matter how absurd and ridiculous) that suggests that traditional criminology is nonsense is the hallmark of contemporary thought.[51] Witness Morris and Hawkins: "the search for the causes of crime is illusory. . . . The assumption that youth can be discretely divided into the delinquent and nondelinquent is a mistake which has had unfortunate consequences. . . . But the basic error is the idea that juvenile delinquency is a pathological phenomenon which requires explanation." These same authors, like Wilson, of course go on to tell us what really causes crime. For example, they say: "The *evidence* suggests, we believe, that a great deal of juvenile crime does not arise from deep psychogenic or sociogenic causes but is situational—an immediate response to temptation and opportunity." Once again, then, it appears that the critic of traditional criminology would have it both ways: previous theory is pointless, silly—based on obviously defective assumptions. One's own theory, based presumably on the same research and founded on the same assumptions, is miraculously "consistent with the evidence." [52]

[51] A recent textbook asserts that "all empirical studies of delinquent and criminal behavior involving the error [of assuming that delinquent and nondelinquent groups are homogeneous and can therefore be compared on a given trait] *must be discounted as having any scientific validity*" (Sue Titus Reid, *Crime and Criminology* [Hinsdale, Ill.: Dryden, 1976], p. 97, emphasis added). The author continues: "There is no theory of crime that meets the most elementary demands of scientific theory. With the exception of labeling . . . theory, all of the theories presume the existence of a phenomenon called 'crime,' which does not exist and which therefore cannot be distinguished from noncrime" (p. 240). The book devoted to this nonexistent phenomenon covers 740 pages.

[52] Morris and Hawkins, *Honest Politician's Guide*, pp. 154–55, 171. Morris and Hawkins report on the "effectiveness" of various treatment programs in reducing "delinquency." If it is impossible to separate delinquents from nondelinquents and if the search for the causes of crime is illusory, there can be no place for words like "effectiveness" and "delinquency."

Libertarian Criminology

Ironically, a major factor working against construction of theories of delinquency is the fear among criminologists-sociologists that their theories might influence public policy.[53] A good, clear, reasonably specific theory of delinquency will often suggest the possibility of "intervention" before a crime has been committed. Such theories are therefore in the eyes of many nonradical criminologists potentially dangerous tools of repression: "Conclusive results, if ever forthcoming, may lead to behavior modification and subsequently thought control. Criminologists are dealing . . . with information about respondents, which, if improperly used, could mean their demise. . . . We . . . owe our disciplines and our subjects the responsibility to evaluate our role as data gatherers and the potential actions our knowledge can bring. It is not unlike the social and moral responsibility facing the physical scientist who works in the area of bacterial war or atomic physics." [54]

Group differences in crime rates, notions like "predelinquency," correlations between innocent behavior (truancy) and serious criminal acts (auto theft) or between individual characteristics (XYY chromosome) and subsequent criminality—in short, all of the ingredients of possible theories of delinquency are of potential value to those who would use social science to justify evil policies in the name of crime control.

With such considerations at the forefront, ignorance, obscurantism, and dissimulation become higher virtues than the free exercises of theoretical imagination. From the Progressive-era injunction to find any and all differences between delinquents and nondelinquents of possible value for public policy, criminology has thus come to the modern injunction to find nothing of possible use to anyone.

[53] "Theories of Crime in a Free Society," The Pinkerton Lecture. State University of New York at Albany, March 12, 1975.

[54] Paul C. Friday, "Problems in Comparative Criminology: Comments on the Visibility and Implications of Research," *International Journal of Criminology and Penology* 1 (1973):151–60.

If we put these trends together and exaggerate just a little, it begins to appear that delinquency, like smallpox, has been conquered by modern science, leaving those who study and those who fear it with nothing but their own illusions. The smashed window and the missing cash, the knife at the throat, and the kick in the face seem to have vanished with such phrases as "no act is inherently deviant" and "crime is normal." The burglar, the rapist, and the mugger presumably hold no terror for those who realize these are merely labels attached to boys next door by people with their own problems working in effect for the DuPonts and Rockefellers. And of course the search for the causes of crime and the study of the backgrounds of criminals become obviously silly once it is established that "everybody does it," that "no one knows what delinquency is," or that "crime does not exist."

As is usual in such cases, some do not realize the war is over. They go on collecting, analyzing, and attempting to make sense of data on crime and delinquency. Ironically, these data suggest that *everyone* (except criminologists) knows what delinquency is and that *few* do it to any degree (these few do quite a bit of it). They also show that delinquency *is* caused by factors beyond the immediate situation and that it is not simply a creation of the juvenile justice system. Further, they provide no convincing evidence that empirical studies or theoretical explanations of delinquency are the handmaidens of illegitimate authority.

So we are left with a choice between illusions. Perhaps it is time for those who see to point out that our victorious emperor is naked as a jaybird, and to help the poor fellow find his clothes. He started out, in the Progressive era, resplendent in the robes of reason and research. He is now, after all, despite his posturing, pretty damn ridiculous.

# Prescriptions for Reform: Doing What We Set Out to Do?

Justine Wise Polier

> It is no evil for things to undergo change, and no good for things to subsist in consequence of change.
>
> *Meditations* of Marcus Aurelius

AMERICAN "populism," a bad word in the current political vocabulary, is described by C. Vann Woodward as a movement that was too advanced to be accepted by a complacent gilded age but an effort that deserved a serious hearing from posterity.[1]

At its inception the juvenile court movement was, likewise, daringly innovative. Child welfare and the first White House Conference were still a decade away. Social work had not become a recognized profession. Freud had not yet loomed on the horizon. The use of psychological tests and psychiatric treatment was unknown. It was not until over thirty years later, in depression days, that this country began to accept responsibility for providing aid to children in their own homes.

Like populism, the juvenile court movement was too advanced both in the complacent Gilded Age and in the materialistic ages that have followed. While the aspirations and mistakes of both movements have much to teach, there is one vast difference. The

---

[1] "[Populism was] . . . a mass movement that earned the contempt and hostility . . . of most intellectuals. . . . On the eve of the consolidation of the corporate state . . . [it was] too advanced to be accepted by a complacent Gilded Age. . . . Granted the Populist effort was a failure and its aspirations probably impossible from the start, it would seem to have earned enough for its boldness and nobility of purpose to get a serious hearing from posterity" "The Promise of Populism," *The New York Review,* October 28, 1976, p. 28.

juvenile court movement succeeded in securing state laws that created a new judicial institution, so that consequences can be measured against the original concepts.[2]

A serious "hearing" of the juvenile justice movement demands questions about its unfinished agenda as well as about its short-comings or failures, and of how new prescriptions for reform deal with this agenda: What do new and old prescriptions have in common? Where does the sharpest cleavage arise and what are the reasons for such cleavage? Are there values in past prescriptions that should be incorporated in new reforms? To what extent are new prescriptions overlooking or discarding what has been learned from medicine, from mental health, from knowledge about child development, and from the juvenile court movement? Are today's reformers, intent on criticism of old dogmas, avoiding reexamination of dogmas of more recent vintage, including their own? To what extent are today's reform prescriptions a response to widespread disillusionment during the past decade about governmental failures and abuses in regard to human needs? Finally, how ready is America now to take new and positive steps to change attitudes toward children, to provide needed resources for their well-being, and begin a hard upward climb to provide justice for children in its broadest meaning?

Child savers of an earlier period sought to save children from the cruelty and harms of the criminal justice system, from contamination by being placed with adult offenders in jails and prisons. Now they are held up to criticism, if not contempt, by the modern child savers who seek to save children from the ineptitude of juvenile courts and from the cruelty and barren alienation characteristic of juvenile institutions.

Both groups share the virtue of seeking better ways of meeting the problem of deviant youth. Both share the error of selecting too narrow targets for their efforts. The pioneers of the juvenile court system did not realize that no single institution

[2] While all states eventually enacted laws authorizing the creation of juvenile courts, special courts with specialized personnel have generally been established in only large metropolitan areas.

could successfully rise above the level of the social conditions which society imposed on children. Nor did they face the reality that in an acquisitive society, where wealth was equated with special rights and privileges, a court dealing with the problems of the poor would, together with other institutions developed for the poor, become a poor and denigrated institution. Today's reformers have in similar fashion also selected too narrow targets for basic reforms as they concentrate on the juvenile court as "the enemy" instead of the larger social and economic conditions that provide child fodder for inadequate public schools, health services, mental hospitals, and child-caring facilities which primarily serve poor children.

Within the juvenile court system, a still narrower target, the status offender, has been selected as a prime beneficiary of many new efforts. In doing so, today's reformers consciously or unconsciously overlook the fact that the original juvenile court proponents had attempted to have all children brought before the courts treated as status offenders—noncriminals—whose problems rather than whose acts were to be the center of concern.

In the need to distinguish present reformers from past reformers, the Progressives who established the juvenile courts are treated with condescension for having believed that the welfare of individual children coincided with the well-being of the state and that of the juvenile court. That they were overly optimistic about the ability of any one institution to achieve such unity cannot be denied. But I would submit that this goal is and will continue to be the lodestar for present and future reformers, including today's critics of the juvenile court and the future critics of today's critics in any democratic society.

## Historic Concepts and Tasks

The initial concept of juvenile justice is ofttimes described as romantic, simplistic, elitist, and even as the brainchild or device of club women and settlement-house workers. It is asserted that the purpose of the originators was to transform poor, illiterate, nonconforming children of immigrants into good, god-fearing, and, therefore, assimilated upright Americans.[3]

The pioneers of the juvenile court movement included some few persons of distinction and wealth, as have all revolutionary and reform movements of the past centuries. Far more relevant is the fact that they were living in this country at a time when hordes of immigrants were pouring into or being brought to American shores as cheap labor to build railroads and industry. There were no restraints on the exploitation of laborers or their children. There was no protective legislation to require safety devices or compensation for accidents. Minimum wages and maximum hours were not yet a matter for serious consideration. Unionization was a criminal offense. Children were regarded as the property of parents and there were no protections against cruelty to children. Poverty of parents led to placement of children in almshouses and asylums or removing them from their families to work with farmers as free boarders and unpaid hands. Children charged with misconduct or violations of law were treated as adult criminals, tried without counsel and sentenced to adult jails and prisons.

More significant than the economic or social background of individual supporters of the juvenile court movement is the fact that they were among a comparatively small group who opposed exploitation of adults and children by the robber barons of their day. They supported the right of workers to organize and were among the first to support legislation to protect women and children in industry. This was true of Julian W. Mack, the first juvenile court judge in Cook County, Illinois. Even more dramatically it was true of Judge Ben Lindsay, who, in addition to his participation in the battle for unpopular social legislation, anticipated the idea of trial marriages for persons without children and was subsequently removed from office.

So much for the dramatis personae apart from the concepts that

---

[3] It is true that the reformers in the juvenile court movement, as other persons in America, became enamored of the melting pot theory. But this was not special to the juvenile court supporters. It is to be found in any discussion of education, religion, politics, or general welfare of that period.

lay behind the juvenile court movement. There were three basic concepts:

1. A child is not a miniature adult and should be treated as a changing, growing human being, more responsive to guidance than an adult.

2. A child, whether brought before a court as dependent, neglected, or delinquent, should be studied and seen as a whole human being with unique strengths, weaknesses, and a potential for growth and given appropriate help.

3. As the needs of children before the court were made known to the larger community, it would provide care, support and rehabilitative services as needed.

True, the early reformers did not foresee that juvenile courts would be relegated to an inferior status by bench, bar, and politicians, as property rights were assigned a place far superior to that of human rights under law. They did not foresee the woefully inadequate concern for the welfare of children at local, state, and federal levels of government. They did not foresee the urbanization of America or the extent to which racism would be institutionalized in every area of life that affected the growth and well-being of children. They did not foresee that the development of new knowledge and skills concerning child development would not be made available to the children of the poor (the court population). Finally, they did not foresee that their faith in the will and ability of America to create a brave new world would be replaced by widespread disillusionment and doubts about government and its capacity to do more good than harm when it intervened in the lives of children. Their work may be seen as "part of an historic aspiration in its innocent and necessary striving." [4]

It is now over a decade since varied spotlights have been played on the juvenile justice system by many critics. The lights have varied in color according to those who managed the display: from white with promise to red with anger, and on to the now fashionable black of despair. It is right that the faults and failures of juvenile justice should be exposed. Even some distortions are more

[4] Foreword, by Lincoln Kirstein, *The Hampton Album* (New York: Museum of Modern Art, 1966), p. 11.

encouraging than the decades of indifference that characterized the attitude of bench, bar, community, and even academe toward the juvenile justice system until recently. Whether the interest will be sustained is hard to guess. Policies in regard to child welfare and juvenile justice, like American policy toward the Indians, have been subjected to ad hoc decisions and an on-again, off-again interest that makes for uncertainty, as well as confusion.

It is unfortunate that in most of this volume juvenile justice is seen as primarily dealing with juvenile delinquents, who violate criminal laws, and the status offender. Too little attention is paid to the significant proportion of juvenile court work that deals with protection of children from neglect or abuse, the releasing of children from harmful or woefully inadequate parental ties, the freeing of children for adoption, and with custody battles. Yet these are among the most difficult areas where the court plays a significant role in modifying traditional values about the rights of biological parents and the rights of children as persons.[5] How far such issues involving the rights of children, parents, and substitute parents can or should be delegated to administrative agencies raises serious questions, including how to safeguard slowly won rights to due process and other constitutional rights for children.

### Old Failures: Inadequate Prescriptions

The purpose of this chapter is to examine recent prescriptions for reform of the juvenile justice system. No one familiar with the failures, the limitations, and the shortcomings of the juvenile court, as it has evolved or staggered along, can fail to welcome prescriptions for reform. The need is rather to examine recent prescriptions to discover how far they correct old wrongs to children and offer better ways of achieving benefits. It is time to examine some of the fragmented prescriptions and try to discover what

[5] The comptroller for New York State recently reported that delays in moving mentally retarded persons from Willowbrook State Hospital had resulted from the federal court requirement for parental consent and due process as well as community resistance to establishing community residences (*New York Times*, May 25, 1977.)

kind of mosaic they make. Another question is whether worthwhile knowledge or skills have been overlooked or cast aside and whether there are some glaring omissions in present prescriptions.

The acceptance of this assignment in no way contradicts appreciation of the great good that has been accomplished by recent interest in juvenile justice and the earnest efforts to develop prescriptions for reform. Significant accomplishments of these efforts include the challenge to old, harmful, and unfair procedures and attacks on institutions and agencies that violate the constitutional rights of children. But beyond these they have increased wider understanding that banishment from home and community are not the right answer for juveniles whether troubled or troubling by reason of their behavior, their mental disabilities, their membership in minority groups, or their poverty. And this understanding has, in turn, led to some, but not nearly enough, constructive community programs as demonstrations of what diversion can mean if it is to be of value to either children or the community.

By the 1930s observers of and participants in the juvenile courts had become increasingly aware of many of its shortcomings. There was growing concern about insensitivity to children of other cultures, about moralistic hypocrisy, about overt and covert religious and racial prejudice, about the limited capacity of the courts to render services to children and families, and about vast gaps between rhetoric and performance. A little later, personal reaching out to children or their families became labeled as "overinvolvement." In addition, concern for their hierarchical position among judges, and for their professional status among social workers, probation officers, and psychologists, joined with heavy caseloads, added to the depersonalization of court functioning.

Judges of the juvenile court, long treated as inferior because they were involved in "social work" rather than "real law" (commercial law), saw withdrawal from involvement in "social work" problems as adding to their judicial status.[6] Probation officers were

[6] "Abdicating its judicial role in the community by placing too great an emphasis on the social aspect of its function at the expense of accepted legal procedures and rights could spell death for the juvenile court experiment and deprive the community of its only authoritative resource" "The Handbook for New Juvenile Court Judges," *Juvenile Court Journal* 23 [Winter 1972]:5).

ordered to make shorter reports and even these were often not read. Social work and clinic reports fattened folders, but were all too rarely used to provide the nourishment of children. Later, as greater emphasis was placed on due process and more attorneys appeared for children, judges and probation officers seemed to feel ever more relieved of the responsibility for understanding individual children or seeking dispositions to meet the needs of each child.

Without defending past or present abuses of judicial power or other shortcomings of the juvenile courts, it remains necessary to examine to what extent new prescriptions for reform are targeted to restrict or overcome either serious malfeasance or nonfeasance that prevents justice to children. It is now acknowledged that the juvenile court system serves as a coarse filter and that only a small proportion of delinquent children ever reach the court: of 500 possible juvenile arrests only 2 or 3 are sent to a correctional institution.[7] It is hard to square such figures with the conclusion that "The whole [juvenile justice] system embodies a continuous use of the state's coercive power—with the juvenile court as a last resort—to force a disposition on a child and parents." Thus, the word *coercion* is applied regardless of how little the state does or does not use the juvenile court as a last resort. Decisions that are not reviewed by courts, when made at other stages of the filter, by police, intake, probation officers, are accepted as providing necessary flexibility. Lack of accountability as to results, including acceptance or rejection on referral for service, are not recognized as having a coercive effect.

Few questions are asked about coercion when administrative agencies or those from whom services are purchased move in to fill a vacuum or about the extent to which due process is denied children trapped in administrative or voluntary agencies.

Thus far, the prescriptions have too largely focused on abuses of judicial discretion. They have concentrated on malfeasance in the courts rather than on nonfeasance by the courts or other governmental agencies. Therefore, they have failed to reach some of

[7] Paul Nejelski, "Diversion: The Promise and the Danger," *Crime and Delinquency* 22 (1976): 394.

the most basic barriers to justice for juveniles. For example: Although harms done to children through nonfeasance are more widespread than those due to willful misfeasance, prescriptions for reform rarely confront the results of nonfeasance.

While prescriptions for reform stress that little can be achieved through "coercive" intervention by the state, faith is placed in voluntary and administrative agencies without sufficient regard for their coercive power or the extent to which arbitrary exclusion from services may be the most severe form of coercion practiced.

While prescriptions for reform oppose discrimination in principle, they have not adequately confronted the discriminatory practices in social agencies on which courts are forced to rely for services. Juvenile courts have been justly criticized for discriminatory dispositions that disproportionately place white children in private residential treatment centers and nonwhite children in training schools. Yet the prescriptions which support purchase of services fail to challenge pervasive racial and religious discrimination in the private sector that determines which children will be accepted or rejected for service. Current prescriptions for reform fail to recognize that diversion from the court will not end such discriminatory selection of children. As overt discrimination is replaced by covert action, including the concealed use of quotas, new and more effective prescriptions are required.[8]

Prescriptions for reform have thus far failed to broaden their targets and challenge treating government largesse as a privilege rather than as an entitlement of children. While there has been general support of preventive services, the prescriptions for reform have not tackled the legislatures that continue to provide more generous support to voluntary, nonprofit, and proprietary agencies for care of children outside their homes than for children within the homes of their parents or relatives.[9]

[8] Juvenile courts have also been properly criticized for lending themselves to the enforcement of school segregation both in the South and the North.

[9] In most states AFDC does not allow foster care payments to grandparents, and it is reported that the projected welfare reforms will restrict even welfare assistance for children in the homes of relatives by requiring that the total family income not be above the welfare budget allowed (*New York Times*, June 2, 1977.)

## Prescription for Reform: From Opposite Poles

Juvenile courts are under attack both by what may loosely be categorized as the political right and "liberal" proponents for reform.

From the right, juvenile courts are attacked as too permissive toward juveniles and too unconcerned about protection of the community. The adult criminal justice system is applauded as aimed at achieving public protection, despite its dismal failures. The juvenile justice system is attacked because public protection is not its primary purpose. In the words of Lord Chief Justice Widgery of England, The public is less troubled by the threat to life, liberty, the pursuit of happiness, and by disregard of law in high places, than by the forces of evil in the streets where they live. He saw law and order "slipping away again through fingers which seem powerless to resist the slide." He concluded that the prescription for achieving law and order required above all that society should rid itself of "the canker inherent in an over-permissive society." [10]

In this country the current prescription from the right is to lock up and throw the key away for juveniles who commit serious offenses. Legislation, responsive to this prescription, authorizes the transfer or waiver of children to the criminal justice system in almost every state.[11] This prescription is also welcomed by those who see the juvenile court, with its requirements for services to juveniles, as one more costly extension of the welfare state. "Violent juveniles" are regarded as expendable and not entitled to services.

The new bottom line that capitalizes on community fear and hostility toward crime in the streets has strangely affected, if not infected, even some of the "liberal" reformers, although their mo-

---

[10] "The Rule of Law," *New York University Law Review* 51 (1976): 365–73.

[11] In some states authorization for transfer is limited to juveniles who are charged with serious felonies; in others it is extended to children charged with any felony. In still others the power is vested in the prosecutor. The age of children who may be transferred ranges from eighteen down to thirteen years.

tivation and rationale are far different. In seeking to reduce the jurisdiction of juvenile courts, the removal of status offenders, and the abandonment of the medical model, the supporters of these prescriptions for reform have largely given up on the "violent juvenile." Few prescriptions against waivers to the criminal courts have emerged. Requirements for ascertaining what happens to juveniles when incarcerated in adult jails or prisons are lacking in the prescriptions.[12] When challenged about joining with those who favor custodial care for serious offenders, one hears rationalizations about limited professional time, the need for husbanding its use for where it will do most good, and skepticism that professional skills are effective for multiproblem children. (Economy of effort has always been reserved for those most in need!)

In the steady march by "liberal" reformers toward due process for children, some lockstep movements are prescribed which seem to be at odds with the purpose of protecting children or respecting their sensibilities. Among these is the demand that juvenile courts shall be opened to the public and the media. It is argued that "the right to know" is essential to uncovering injustice and to the protection of children subject to the deprivation of freedom. This position is supported not only by those concerned with due process but by legislators who have found promises of swift punishment and exposure of permissiveness by courts the politicans' vote-getting dream. Sadly lacking is understanding of the juvenile brought before the court or of how judges will use the discretionary power to close or open their courts.

Judges have not always been known for heroic independence. Few can be expected to close their courts without anxiety that they will be subjected to media censure when they face reappointment or reelection. No judge has a crystal ball to warn how destructive evidence about a child or family will prove, if made public. Possibly even more significant for anyone who has observed children brought before a court is the effect of whether there is privacy in the courtroom. Even the coming or going of probation officers in a courtroom affects a child's response to questioning and how he speaks or explains his actions. Whether par-

[12] *Children in Adult Jails,* The Children's Defense Fund of the Washington Research Project, Inc. (December 1976).

ents appear when a child is on trial may seem a colorless, harmless "fact" to the media but has awesome significance to a child, deeply hurt by the lack of "family."

The safeguards proposed, apart from the limits of self-policing by the American press, raise constitutional questions, including protection against prepublication censorship.

### Prescriptions for Justice: Substantive and Procedural Rights

It is significant that *Brown* v. *Board of Education* preceded *In re Gault* by some thirteen years.[13] The Supreme Court in *Brown* rejected the segregation of school children by governmental action and the doctrine of "equal but separate" as violative of the substantive right of children to equal protection. It encouraged efforts to demand substantive rights of children under law. It required that government services be rendered so that they would not violate a child's right to equal services or diminish a child's sense of worth. *Brown* thus first laid the groundwork for subsequent federal actions that won the right to education, recreation, and treatment plans, and for federal actions to enjoin the abuse of children in archaic institutions by solitary confinement, the denial of reading material, and the denial of appropriate treatment in hospitals and institutions. It also laid the groundwork for prohibitions against state use of private facilities that rejected children on the basis of race.

*Gault* made a different contribution toward assuring justice for children by asserting the right to due process of children when charged with delinquency. And a series of steps had been taken by legislatures and courts to require due process protections for children. *Brown* and *Gault* together constitute the cornerstone for a new architecture designed to achieve justice for children.[14]

The progress made during the days of the Warren court is now

[13]*Brown* v. *Board of Education*, 347 U.S. 483 (1954), *In re Gault*, 387 U.S. 1 (1967).

[14] Yet prescriptions for reform too often emphasize Gault only. In a recent volume, *Pursuing Justice for the Child*, ed. Margaret K. Rosenheim (University of Chicago Press, 1976), one finds no reference to Brown.

endangered by the Burger court.[15] In addition to narrowing access to the federal courts to protect constitutional rights, the "paddling" decision in *Ingraham* v. *Wright* threatens the substantive rights of children. That 5 to 4 decision holds protection against cruel and unusual punishment is to be reserved only for offenders convicted of and incarcerated for violating the criminal law.

Juvenile justice was a latecomer to the area of constitutional rights accepted for Supreme Court scrutiny, so that the restrictions imposed on lower federal courts to hear and fashion appropriate remedies against violations of constitutional rights for children present a special threat. It is still too early to predict how far or how long the Supreme Court will seek to limit federal courts in protecting children against cruel and unusual punishment, coercive medical intrusions, the absence of educational opportunities, the denial of appropriate treatment for institutionalized children, or against the use of unnecessarily restrictive placements.

Due Process and Formality Confused

In the prescriptions for reform that have focused on procedure, there is a questionable assumption that increased formality assures greater justice. This prescription is based in part on fear that a judge will have too direct involvement with a child and may use what he learns from a child to engage in dispositional decisions for which he is not competent.

The old argument that a child's honesty was good for his soul has yielded to recognition that the lack of due process provided an all too easy way of securing confessions without a child being aware of its possible consequences. But the sound prescription for change has been encumbered by a newfound faith in formality. Raised benches that elevate the judges above child and family, judicial robes to add remoteness and dignity to the judge, are embraced both by those who prescribe reforms and by many judges. Such agreement raises questions as to whether the pre-

[15] See Statement, Board of Governors, Society of American Law Teachers (October 10, 1976).

scriptions are more appealing to the legal fraternity and judges than they are relevant to the promotion of justice for children. While there need be no relation between physical or visual proximity to a child and greater justice, there is surely no evidence that remote, detached postures generate greater understanding or wisdom to those ensconced in high places.

When prescriptions for formality are joined with prescriptions to restrict considerations of other than the offense by the juvenile court at dispositional hearings, two other questions arise: Will they together create one more wall to obscure the state's obligation when courts intervene in the lives of children? Will they further justify blindness or silence on the part of judges to the discrepancy between the rhetoric and realities of correctional services?

Prescription for Certainty

Endless efforts have been made throughout history to achieve justice or order through codes, regulations, or other prescriptions for the control of human behavior. Hammurabi, Justinian, Jeremy Bentham, and, more recently, Goldstein, Freud, and Solnit, as well as the National Standards Project, have sought to bring light and order to the handling of deviance. None provides certain or immutable answers to the questions raised by the endless variations in complex and ever-changing human relations that resist control by general answers or prescriptions for justice through scheduled punishment.

Abuses of judicial power, as exposed and condemned in *Gault*, led to adversarial procedures to protect due process rights. They also properly led to restricting the issues in a juvenile case to the facts as alleged in a petition. Paradoxically, this beneficial result for many children has also prevented benefits children received from earlier approaches. As an example, in 1941, when a probation investigation revealed a long history of past neglect of a child since her mother's death, the court vacated its finding of delinquency and made a finding of neglect, stating: "The trend of the times and the trend of the law is away from straight jacketed interpretation of the law, and rather in the direction of so interpreting the law as to mete out justice as the circumstances require and compel." [16]

That was 1941. It could not happen today under the prescription that a finding must be based solely on the offense.

In the search for certainty today, new prescriptions would substitute legislative codes fixing penalties to restrict discretion by judges in dispositions in juvenile as well as in adult courts. In doing so, the focus is placed on the offense. The child's past history, problems, and potential for change are largely removed as reasons for variations in dispositions. Too little attention has been paid to "the impact of living under conditions of social injustice," [17] and there has been far too little recognition that where this impact is lightened, a child may respond to a far greater extent than another child who has committed the same offense without having suffered from social injustice.

These prescriptions accept or go along with unproved assumptions by prosecutors, political figures, and the general public that fixed and sure punishments will provide general deterrents to juvenile delinquents and so protect the public. The one nod to repulsion against too harsh punishment of a juvenile is that the penal codes for adult crimes are to be reduced by subcodes that fix lesser penalties for children. This is, in sum, the new accountability prescription with its emphasis on certain punishment as *the* answer to deterrence of juvenile offenses.

A further claim for certainty through the new prescriptions for accountability is that fixed penalties based solely on the offense would allow identification and incapacitation of offenders who are likely to commit future serious crimes. It is contended that elaborate techniques have been devised to identify the dangerous offender and distinguish him from someone who has merely commited a dangerous offense. This promise of certainty is unfounded and contains an inherent contradiction. First, those who have studied prediction of future dangerousness acknowledge that prediction is in a primitive state and that attempts to use it show that

[16] *In the Matter of Modification of Finding in Case of* XYZ, Domestic Relations Court of New York City (January 7, 1941), Justice Jacob Panken.

[17] Leon W. Chestang, *The Current Status of the Black Family: Implications for the Juvenile Justice System* (June 1974), paper prepared for the Juvenile Justice Standards Project.

many nondangerous offenders would be incarcerated in order to identify one "dangerous" offender.[18] Also, there is a contradiction in the doctrine that punishments shall fit the crime while at the same time basing punishments on prediction concerning future acts of the offender so as to warrant longer incarceration.

Reduction of casual, haphazard, ad hoc decisions through limiting judicial discretion is too often offered as a means of also providing objective and certain standards for juvenile justice. The false promise that I.Q. tests would provide objective certainty for the classification of children should ring an alert to how "certain, objective standards" established by one generation are found flawed by succeeding generations. As Binet warned against the "brutal pessimism" of those who saw intelligence as a fixed quantity, there is reason to question the "brutal pessimism" of those who now propose that fixed punishments based on the offense committed will provide certain, objective standards, and so assure justice.

### Restrictive Prescriptions for Neglected and Abused Children

As previously noted, most of the prescriptions for reform have been focused on the delinquent and the status offender. However, in recent years (including the IJA-ABA proposed standards) child-abuse and neglect statutes have been criticized as vague and unfair in that they fail to specify the exact limits of permissible parental conduct. Some prescriptions would limit juvenile court jurisdiction to cases in which physical harm has been done or there is imminent danger of serious physical injury to a child.

Although the proponents of these prescriptions generally acknowledge the right of a child to a stable, nurturing relationship with a parent, little consideration is given to the erosive destruction wreaked on children by continuing emotional injury or depri-

[18] See Ernest A. Wenk and Robert L. Emrich, *Assaultive Youth: An Exploratory Study of Assaultive Experience and Assaultive Potential of California Youth Authority Wards* (Washington, D.C.: National Institute of Law Enforcement and Criminal Justice Law Enforcement Assistance Administration, 1972).

vation. Such a coarse net is akin to public fury when a specific case of brutality by a parent is reported in the press. It is all too reminiscent of the criticism by Jeremy Bentham of punishment meted out on an emotional basis: "If you hate much, punish much; if you hate little punish little; punish as you hate."

The restrictive prescription against intervention on behalf of neglected or abused children, combined with the prescription against the "medical model," would also exclude or drastically limit the use of clinical observations by physicians to identify children at risk. It has been contended that for a physician at a prenatal clinic or at the time of delivery to note reactions of a parent that indicate a child is at risk constitutes a wrongful invasion of privacy. Here, abstract theory would lead to denial of preventive services or action to protect the small percentage of children for whom removal from natural parents is essential to life or health. [19]

Without so intending, the prescription for reducing intervention in neglect and abuse cases plays into the apathy and indifference toward conditions in which children on welfare are left to survive. Three examples are illustrative: In the case of a child seriously abused by a parent, when study of the welfare record showed previous episodes of serious neglect, the worker was questioned as to why no earlier action had been taken to protect the child. In justification the worker replied, "This is the culture of poverty." On another occasion, a commissioner of welfare stated when he had no facilities for neglected children that the District Offices were notified not to report cases. In another geographical area, welfare workers were told not to bring neglect actions on behalf of minority children since no facilities were available.

Prescriptions for reducing jurisdiction in neglect and abuse cases have come largely from lawyers concerned with violations of human rights. Their stance is not inconsistent with the behavior of counsel assigned to neglect and abuse cases who show less ardor and involvement than when they represent a child charged

---

[19] As a result of twenty years of study and work, Dr. Henry Kempe reports that with service to parents, approximately 10 percent of children abused or at risk of abuse need to be removed from their biological family.

with delinquency. It may be that such assignments seem less ad-versarial and less a lawyer's meat. At times, it seems that counsel prefer to defend the parent charged with an offense rather than the child alleged to be in need of protection.

Despite such reservations about prescriptions that would nar-row neglect and abuse jurisdiction, it is only fair to note that they are not only based on noninterventionist abstract principles. They are also based on the tragic life experiences of children removed from their homes by reason of court findings or placed "voluntar-ily" by parents because of fear of court action. Woefully inade-quate care following removal, the endless limbo of foster care, and a failure to either work with the natural family or to secure a permanent substitute family have provided impetus for these pre-scriptions.

Yet the negative aspects of the prescriptions are also woefuly inadequate to meet pervasive nonfeasance concerning poor chil-dren. They reject the use of knowledge and preventive skills to protect children and limit the scope of concern to cases where severe "dangerousness" is involved.

### The Medical Model—Discarded by Prescription

After a short boom and grandiose expectations of what psychiatry could do to rehabilitate deviant children, present prescriptions would all but outlaw its use by the juvenile courts. The mental health professions, now often derisively held responsible for "the medical model" (as though there were one) have played many roles in the history of the juvenile court. Little recognition has been given to the birth of community psychiatry and its contribu-tions through attention to the social conditions that contribute to emotional disturbance, barriers to learning, and mental disabili-ties.

By turn, mental health services have been bitterly opposed as endangering sexual morality, leaned on all to heavily in disposi-tional orders, and used as a ceremonial sanction for whatever de-cisions courts render. The reasons for current prescriptions for rejection also vary greatly.

To some, the imposition of mental health services is only one more invasion of privacy without informed consent. No valid difference is recognized between ordering surgery without consent of a patient and requiring a diagnostic study of a child, or that a child attend counseling, vocational training, or therapy sessions either while in placement or as a condition of probation. All are grouped together under the rubric of "coercion by the state" if ordered by a court.

To others, the absence of good mental health diagnostic or treatment services warrants characterizing them largely as pretension, fraud, or cover-up to rationalize punishment. For them, opposition to the medical model and the use of psychiatry in treatment is based in part on the low level of such services available to children both in courts and in institutions. They point to evidence that mental health services have never been available or used by juvenile courts or agencies to which children have been committed in more than haphazard, fragmented, and minimal fashion. The few clinics that have been established within juvenile courts are regarded as the proverbial geraniums planted in front of houses of ill-repute and used to obscure dispositional actions that ultimately assign children to the dumping grounds of custodial institutions.

The mental health professions must also share responsibility for the hostility underlying present prescriptions that would outlaw or reduce their role in the juvenile justice system. Professionals have generally resisted working in the courts or child-caring agencies. They have preferred private practice or work in voluntary agencies where conditions of work and the choice of patients have been more to their liking or more promising from a professional point of view.

The scornful prescriptions of today may be the price for frauds practiced against the majority of children who continued to be placed in custodial, impersonal institutions, untouched by any knowledge, understanding, or use of mental health services. Even where diagnostic services in juvenile courts were provided, they were reduced all too often to a belt-line production of psychometrics to separate the retarded, the psychotic, and the "normal." Early efforts to identify problems of individual children diminished. Psychometrics to label children were required by treatment agencies so that they could reject "too difficult children." This procedure under which least was provided for the children who needed most help provided one more justification for discarding "the medical model."

"The medical model" is also under attack by a third group, which holds that since "the medical model" has been unable to affect criminal behavior through treatment and since it undermines the general deterrent effect of the criminal law, general deterrence through punishment should be the legitimate, if not first, concern of the juvenile court. It is also contended that retribution, condemnation, incapacitation, along with *general* deterrence, are appropriate functions of the juvenile court. For opposite reasons and with different verbiage, other supporters of prescriptions for doing away with the medical model claim it is used to justify or extend coercive punishment in the name of rehabilitation.

Apart from the general theory underlying prescriptions for reform through minimizing governmental intervention, there are, therefore, many reasons for current attacks on mental health services as part of a "failed" experiment. Whether past failed expectations justify such prescriptions for the future or how the elimination of the medical model will help rather than hurt juveniles is highly questionable. Confusion also arises from the conflict between the prescription to discard the medical model and the emerging concept that when a juvenile or adult is deprived of freedom in the name of treatment, the right to, and the duty to provide, appropriate treatment is created.

Not seeing problems, failing to identify neurological problems, is justified in today's reforms. Such justification is once more being questioned by those seriously working with children, with child development problems, and with both the extensive physical and mental disabilities of children brought before the court when rigorously assessed. Personal concern for individual children and their families by professionals in psychiatry and psychology is challenging the conclusion that depersonalized justice is all that is possible.[20] With this challenge, some of the best professionals are once more appearing in the field of juvenile justice.

[20] See Dorothy O. Lewis and David A. Balla, *Delinquency and Psychopathology* (New York: Grune and Stratton, 1976).

### The Three D's: Prescriptions at Risk

Among all the prescriptions for reform, the three D's have become most central to prescriptions for reform. These prescriptions have been hard to implement. Of the three, more has been accomplished in deinstitutionalization than in diversion, and far more than in reducing or improving detention. There is the added danger that while the public rhetoric approving the three D's continues, the process of recriminalization and more institutionalization of juveniles is outstripping achievements in accord with these prescriptions.

### Detention

The prescription for reducing detention was too narrowly focused. It failed to challenge the use of adult jails to hold children, regardless of the category to which they were assigned. The horrendous conditions in the jails were not made the center of attack. Instead, detention was described as a police/court processing for social control, and criticism was addressed largely to the higher use and the longer use of detention for status offenders. Those who prescribed reforms to remove the status offender from jails or their commingling with juvenile delinquents did not come to grips with the harsh reality that police, probation, and judges are not provided with alternative facilities, when parents cannot or will not cope with difficult juveniles, or when juveniles refuse to return to their parents.

After early positive legislative responses to the prescription, the realistic problems, including the lack of alternative facilities, cooled legislative efforts and led to the postponement of effective dates for change for both status offenders and juvenile delinquents. And the use of adult jails for children continues at the rate of some 500,000 admissions each year.

### Diversion

The central target for diversion has also too often been limited to the status offender. Since he is generally described as the child who is disobedient, stays out late at night or truants from school, the real problems between parents and children before court action are played down, as are the problems of the children.

Contrary to general misconceptions, in a high proportion of these children, as among juvenile delinquents, the case history, social investigation, and diagnostic studies reveal many serious problems. Behind the word *incorrigibility* as behind the word *delinquent* one finds the long history of a troubled child, left without help until he becomes so troubling that a crisis forces parental or community action. A high incidence of persistent truancy, failure in school, late hours, poor peer relationships, drug abuse, addiction, emotional disturbance, alcoholism, and, in some cases, mental retardation or mental illness is present in both categories. In addition, family relationships have often become so strained in the status offender group that there is less possibility of return to the family than where the child's delinquent act is against someone outside the family. In both groups there are a disproportionate number of children who are members of minority groups and come from the most deprived families and neighborhoods of the inner cities.

Characterizing parents as unloving, uncaring custodians who wish to rid themselves of incorrigible children fails to portray the problems of either parents or children, except in a small fraction of the cases. The parent who files a "status" petition is frequently frightened and even desperate about what is going to happen to a child. Feeling inadequate, unable to cope or secure help on a voluntary basis, the parent finally turns to the court. Concern about stealing, late hours, joyriding in borrowed cars, drinking, use of drugs is reduced to a complaint of late hours so as not to hurt the child, together with a plea for help. With the provision of counsel for the child, cross-examination lays bare parental inadequacies and faults. It also may again widen the breach between parent and child so that it becomes irremediable. This prescription is leading to more delinquency petitions and fewer status petitions in some areas, and one must question whether the new prescriptions are geared to meeting the complex problems for either the youths or their families.

Harder thinking is also needed about the prescriptions for excluding truancy from juvenile court jurisdiction. The correlation between school truancy and school failures, school suspensions, expulsions from school, and consequent delinquency had been shown over and over again. Whether a child is labeled by court action or not, absence from school and the inability to master basic skills cause the child to label himself, and causes society to pigeonhole the child for later failure.

Diversion has correctly been described as "the overture of the 'new correction.' "[21] The prescription calls for the creation of services and facilities to which a juvenile could be referred for help without being subjected to formal court action, labeling, and the risk of commitment to an institution. In some areas, local efforts have achieved a substantial decrease in the number of court petitions. However, a national survey reports that only 25 percent of the youths accepted by Youth Service Bureau programs were in immediate jeopardy of the juvenile justice system. As Nejelski notes, the "youth service bureaus may be following the established pattern of . . . increasingly turn[ing] their attention to more malleable children."[22] Communities have been slow to set up alternative services, and establishment agencies have been reluctant to accept difficult youths. Diversion of children from state hospitals has not been accompanied by reallocation of institutional funds for community-based services.

In addition, the federal government, which has endorsed the concept of diversion through legislation and some funding, has shown ambivalence toward its use for other than status or minor offenders. Thus, in one community funds were granted by LEAA to a local accountability board to which youths charged with minor or status offenses were referred by police and the juvenile court intake. Simultaneously, federal funds were granted by another division of LEAA to add more prosecutors in the juvenile court. The net result, found in a report from the prosecutor's office, showed an increase in the number of children prosecuted for delinquent acts, increased promptness of trials, and an increase in the number of juvenile delinquents committed to state institutions.

Three major questions about the present prescriptions for diversion remain.

1. It is not clear whether the singling-out of the status offender

[21] Nejelski, "Diversion," p. 394.    [22] Ibid., p. 397.

was based on what was regarded as a new concept about status offenders or seen as a pragmatic strategy toward reducing juvenile court jurisdiction. Those intent on reform could not have foreseen the present tendency to label status offenders as the "good" youths and the delinquents as the "bad" youths, incapable of rehabilitation and not entitled to services. Yet that is just how the prescription for reform is being increasingly used.

2. Without any real research, including follow-up, on juveniles for whom responsibility is assigned to schools, welfare departments, community-based facilities (public and private), and other voluntary agencies, there is the questions of how to secure effective monitoring of the consequences of diversion.

3. There is the question of the extent to which prescriptions for diversion are imposing new threats to due process for juveniles referred for supervision by the police or other agencies without benefit of counsel or court review.

Deinstitutionalization

Prescriptions for deinstitutionalization have given a significant push to the slow movement, begun some fifty years ago, to remove children from large custodial institutions. At variance with many other prescriptions for reform, these rely heavily on what has been learned from the mental health professions and students of early child development. They stress the importance to children of their sense of identity with a caring adult and of stability in a family with a sense of belonging. In contrast to prescriptions regarding neglect and abuse, the emotional needs of children are recognized.

These prescriptions for reform have achieved and continue to achieve direct benefits for more children than any other prescription.

"Deinstitutionalization" has become a rallying cry for those who with good reason have come to abhor institutions, for those disillusioned about the benefits from government intervention, for those who have suffered hurt and humiliation in institutions, and for well-intentioned reformers who have picked up the cry. Now, the word *deinstitutionalization* is used with too little differentiation to attack a range of institutions and programs, including jails, prisons, state hospitals for the mentally ill, clinic examinations, medication imposed without informed consent, probation, and the public schools. It has even been used in regard to foster home care for children removed from their families by reason of serious neglect or abuse.

In response to demands for deinstitutionalization, state institutions, voluntary agencies, and the courts discharge children prematurely and without sufficient regard to what will happen to the children after discharge. Where responsibility will be placed for continuity of care has not been made a mandatory part of the prescription for deinstitutionalization. As a result, another turnstile child has emerged. This is the child for whom deinstitutionalization has been ordered without assurance of a place to live which can provide appropriate care. The child may be dumped in a shelter, a detention home, returned to an unfit family setting, placed in foster care, or sent to an institution in another state far from home. When the child breaks again or acts out, hospitalization or custodial institutionalization of some other kind is ordered. Failure of the child in his natural family or in out-of-home placements, followed by reinstitutionalization, add up to misery upon misery for the child, but these failures are too rarely subtracted from the marked up victories for deinstitutionalization.[23]

There is one more deeply troubling deficit in the present prescriptions for deinstitutionalization. This is the omission of a clearly articulated and integral injunction against the recriminalization of juveniles. Recriminalization and more institutionalization of juveniles through the use of adult jails, waivers, and transfers to the criminal courts are proceeding on tracks parallel to those that support deinstitutionalization. Despite federal funding and private grants, neither LEAA nor independent researchers have studied what happens to adolescents who are recriminalized. The

[23] In New York the director of Special Services for Children recently reported: "We have 400 children placed all over the country. At least half of them are discharged from state mental hospitals. In the name of deinstitutionalization we took a child from one institution and placed him in another." *New York Coalition for Juvenile Justice and Youth Services Newsletter* ([May 1977], p. 5).

statutes have been summarized, but there are no studies on what happens to adolescents in jail awaiting criminal trials, how long they wait, what sentences are imposed, where they are incarcerated, to what extent they are mingled with adult offenders, what programs are provided, or what happens to them after parole or discharge.

### Purchase of Services: Dangerous Prescription

It is not clear why purchase of services has been tied to the reforms of diversion and deinstitutionalization, except as part of an assumption that anything government buys is better than what it is capable of doing. This prescription distances the state further from responsibility for the quality or quantity of services, indeed, from the quality of life for children, except as a bursar. Yet this prescription has not been modified even by the uncovering of curelty, abuse, and mistreatment of children sent to institutions in Texas by Illinois and Louisiana or by exposés concerning abuse in private day care programs purchased with public funds.

### Prescriptions for Reform and Child Advocacy

"It is extraordinarily difficult to love children in the abstract. . . . It is only through precise, attentive knowledge of particular children that we become as we must—informed advocates for the needs of children." [24] Prescriptions for reform have been supported by child advocacy on many fronts, and in turn have been strengthened and modified by the involvement of child advocates who learn from real life situations.

After *Brown* and *Gault* it was hoped that the Bill of Rights would no longer be regarded as for adults only. Child advocates began to present facts that had not previously confronted juvenile courts, state and federal courts, administrative agencies, voluntary agencies, or the public. Findings such as those about children suspended from school, expelled or not registered, about children

[24] Margaret Mead, *Blackberry Winter* (New York: William Morrow & Co., 1972), p. 282.

denied health services, about children incarcerated in adult jails raised the consciousness of those concerned with what was actually happening to children. More demands were heard for monitoring.

Child advocates at the community level became a source of political strength as they came to know what was happening to children. Aided by prescriptions for reform to restrict the use of detention, institutionalization, and other hurtful practices including discriminatory treatment of minority children, they brought a new impact to the support of prescriptions for reform. Child advocacy also raised questions about some prescriptions, such as nonintervention where children are at risk, as actual case histories about what actually happens to children caused revisions based on experience.

As advocates become more involved with children, there is growing concern about the need for adult-child relationships that were so important in the early days of the juvenile court. For a while discarded as sentimental or middle class, there is rerecognition that children who have suffered many deprivations desperately need a sense that some adult cares, has confidence in them, and stands ready to help. Whether achieved through professionals, paraprofessionals, or volunteers, the rediscovery of this reality needs to inform present prescriptions to a far greater degree.

Advocacy within communities must, then, include not only a challenge to systems that are hurtful to children but advocacy on behalf of individual children. Such comprehensive advocacy is needed to expand prescriptions to embrace the full entitlements of children and examine what local, state, and federal governments omit in programs for children. Such advocacy is needed to challenge inadequate services that result in children being lost in the limbo of foster care, subjected to racial discrimination, or being recriminalized.

### Limits of Prescriptions for Reform: Needed a Jurisprudence for Children

Fashions in what has been described as juvenile justice have come and gone swiftly during the past seventy-five years of this century.

During the first two decades, the focus was on the ideal of individualized justice. The juvenile court movement was unable to translate a jurisprudence based on the idea of the uniqueness of childhood into laws and procedures that safeguarded children from harm and enhanced their opportunities to develop and fulfill their potential. They were unable to secure the right of children not just to separate or different services but to something more than is accorded to adults. They did not recognize that such concepts could not succeed in one institution separate and apart from, yet dependent on, the other public and private institutions that dominated the lives of children: family, education, health, employment, or the emerging welfare world. They failed to confront the gaps between law on the books and the realities for children and youth that would undermine their insular structure.

Between World Wars I and II sociological and psychological explanations of deviant behavior and greater concern for human rights led to scrutiny of the discrepancies between what judges said and what they did. Sociological or experimental jurisprudence, the growth of legal realism, legal fact-finding as an essential tool of jurisprudence, the concept of law as an instrument of social action—these flourished in this period and into the 1950s. It was in the mid-1940s that a great legal scholar, Alexander Pekelis, described three main characteristics of jurisprudence as the outcome of modern schools of thought dealing with law and social sciences. "These are: an insistence on the gap between what the law appears to be in the books and what it is in reality; a feeling for the dissonance between the abstractness of general rules and the individuality of concrete cases; and an awareness of the creative nature of the judicial function." [25]

The description of and comments on these characteristics of welfare jurisprudence written some 40 years ago raise questions that are relevant to issues of juvenile jurisprudence and current prescriptions for reform: What are the gaps between the law on the books and the realities for children and their families? Is there sufficient concern for the dissonance between abstract generalities

[25] Alexander H. Pekelis, "The Case for a Jurisprudence of Welfare," *Social Research* 2 (1944):313.

and the concrete needs in individual cases? Is there awareness of or need for the creative nature of the judicial function? Are courts still needed to exercise intelligent lay control over experts and administrative decisions as "the best defense against the tyranny of experts"? It is worth noting that in this same paper Pekelis held that the balanced coexistence of legislative or administrative action and intelligent judicial review thereof are compatible and the essence of constitutional government. He saw welfare jurisprudence as an essential foundation for judicial review if it were not to perish from either atrophy or overexertion.[26]

Within ten years after the writings of Pekelis, the *Brown* decision of the Supreme Court, relying in part on social science findings, brought children within the horizon of the Bill of Rights and broadened the concept of justice for juveniles. Followed by *Gault* and other decisions of the Supreme Court and lower federal courts, juvenile jurisprudence was given promise of new meaning. But by the late 1960s the high expectations of unending progress in securing the constitutional rights of adults or children were dimmed. There was rising skepticism about the implementation of rights even when asserted by the courts, about abuses of judicial discretion, about the effectiveness of rehabilitation methods, as well as serious question as to whether governmental intervention could or would do more harm than good to children and families.

This skepticism led to acceptance of a dogma supporting abstention by government from intervention in the lives of children, although children in this country have been far more subject to denials of aid as a result of this doctrine than in other Western countries. Only recently Gilbert Steiner quoted words written by Grace Abbott in 1908: "All children are dependent but only a small number are dependent on the state." Some seventy years later he found that "that description of governmental reticence remains valid."[27]

Skepticism also led to a turning away from questions of philosophy or jurisprudence and toward concentration on pragmatic pre-

[26] Ibid., pp. 351–52, 330.
[27] Gilbert Y. Steiner, *The Children's Cause* (Washington, D.C.: Brookings Institute, 1976), p. 1.

scriptions for reducing specific wrongs inflicted on children within various systems, and especially within the jurisdiction of juvenile courts. As one reviews the series of prescriptions for reform of juvenile justice developed in this period, the sum total of these prescriptions falls short of what might be regarded as a new jurisprudence for juveniles. Ongoing adherence in this country to traditions that support rugged individualism, parental rights, and a pragmatic approach to the solution of social problems does not provide fertile soil for conceptual approaches to meeting the complex problems of children or families. In addition, widespread indifference and hostility toward those who are deviant and to those who are poor have created all but insuperable barriers to social change that challenges such attitudes.

Whatever the causes, the absence of an effective juvenile jurisprudence in this period has not only invited but made necessary prescriptions for overcoming specific wrongs done to children, one by one as they are recognized, with notable achievements to their credit. Despite these achievements, without a core philosophy that demands an ongoing commitment toward a larger goal, even effective efforts addressed to specific problems come and go, like staccato notes, with little holding power. Thus, addiction, child abuse, alcoholism, violent juveniles successively compete for interest and funding. Even the right of children to counsel, as established by the Supreme Court, is ignored or left without implementation in many areas. Segregation of and discrimination against children of minority groups continues. Separation of poor from nonpoor by programs and procedures with resulting denigration of the quality of services that affect many children in the juvenile justice system and more outside has not yet been challenged as a suspect classification.

In this perspective, efforts to correct wrongs by prescriptions must continue, but hopefully they can be joined with creative efforts to develop a philosophy of law that goes beyond the "don'ts." This is not to suggest that any juvenile justice concepts now developed will give final answers. They can, however, provide goals based on what has been learned from the law and the social sciences and what can be learned through ongoing awareness of the necessity for further fact-finding and further learning.

There are still some advocates for human rights who, despite full awareness of the limitations and failures of legal institutions and government during the past decade, present a positive role for law and legal institutions. Only recently Professor Thomas Emerson, described by Norman Dorsen as "the founder of civil rights law," challenged the tendency in law schools, universities, editorial offices, and courts to denigrate the capacity of law, legal institutions, and government to achieve social reforms in words that go to the essence of the future of juvenile justice:

The argument that government is not capable of solving our problems is based upon the premise that government is overextended, incompetent, bureaucratic, responsive only to vested interests, and corrupt. The solution urged is to withdraw government controls and leave much more to private economic forces. Again, there is of course some truth in the proposition. But the indictment against government is overdrawn, particularly in its blanket form, and the solution totally unacceptable. . . .

It is small wonder that people have become disillusioned. But the solution is not to abandon government. The solution is to make a government more like *government* instead of management, to make it represent the community rather than become an elitist system run by technological bureaucrats. . . .

The underlying issue, however, goes further. It is not whether or not we can change our institutions themselves. Can we develop institutions that will be able to learn instead of calcifying: that will have *human* relations with people rather than bureaucratic relations? . . . How can we make our institutions operate on behalf of the people they are supposed to serve? . . . How do we infuse into the structure a sense of moral responsibility for the lives and fortunes of our fellow citizens? [28]

The future of children in the juvenile justice system, as the future of far larger numbers of children, will be determined by how far the people of this country and its government ready themselves to assure the welfare of all children. The same forces that determine what is done for children through child welfare, public welfare, schools, hospitals, or community services will determine what

[28] Thomas I. Emerson, "Summary of Retirement Address by Prof. Emerson," *Yale Law Report*, fall 1976, pp. 22–23.

can be done for children and youth through the juvenile courts. The essential question for juvenile jurisprudence as for all governmental structures is then how fully it meets the needs and respects the rights and liberty of human beings within its jurisdiction. The same test must be applied to prescriptions for reform.

# Delinquency and Social Reform: A Radical Perspective

Herman Schwendinger
and Julia Schwendinger

## Introduction

THE approach in this article is representative of radical criminology. Consequently, by way of introduction, a few observations are in order. As an academic trend in the United States, radical criminology is wholly unprecedented, dating from the end of the 1960s. Similar trends, though based on decades-old traditions, exist among criminologists in Western Europe. Finally, among socialist countries criminological theory and research are developing vigorously. Representatives of these trends generally assume that crime and delinquency can be enormously reduced and eventually eliminated by socialist developments.[1]

Around the turn of the 1970s radical criminologists emphasized great harms perpetrated by American corporations and imperialism. They wrote about the suppression of political dissension, the brutality of prison life, and the degree to which criminal justice policies maintain class and racial privilege. At present, radical criminology is just beginning to enter the area of social policy formation. Simultaneously, it is rapidly consolidating its analytic identity around Marxist theory.

---

[1] The writings by representatives of these trends have increased considerably in recent years. Articles and bibliographies in *Crime and Social Justice,* a radical criminology journal, refer to writings by radicals in the United States. Routledge and Kegan Paul, and Pluto Press have published articles and books by radical criminologists in Great Britain. Finally, for an example of criminological writings from a socialist country, see Erich Buchholtz, Richard Hartmann, John Lekschas, and Gerhard Stiller, *Socialist Criminology: Theoretical and Methodological Foundations* (Lexington, Mass: Lexington Books, Heath and Co., 1974).

A short introduction cannot describe a Marxist theory of law systematically; however, certain aspects of this theory should be noted. First, Marxists contend that legal relations in the United States secure an economic infrastructure that centers around a capitalist mode of production. The infrastructure includes the *forces* of production: the labor force, knowledge, skills, tools, division of labor, and the like for producing commodities. It also includes the *relations* of production based on the exploitation of wage labor. The social classes created by such production relations are the bourgeoisie and the proletariat. By securing the capitalist mode of production, legal relations guard the reproduction of the class structure.

Second, legal relations in the United States maintain the family and the school to secure (among other things) the intergenerational reproduction of the labor force. Therefore, in addition to the mode of production, bourgeois laws secure still another level of institutional relations, which includes the family, school, and even the state itself. Criminal laws prohibiting such acts as killing, rape, and incest are interrelated with the protection of these institutions. In addition, civil and administrative laws also regulate the capitalist mode of production together with the social relations based on that mode of production.

Third, behind the mature capitalist state is a robust civil society, a sphere of private interests encompassing innumerable interest groups. But the basic structure underlying this sphere is a social class structure. The dominant member of this structure is the bourgeoisie. In early capitalist societies the bourgeoisie organized political relations in their own interest. As capitalism matures, however, this organization is challenged by antagonistic class formations, composed of rural and urban proletarians and their allies. As a result, the state itself becomes an arena within which class struggles and contradictions are expressed.

Fourth, the class interests that underlie the basic laws of the land (such as constitutional laws) are based on the conditions that reproduce the class system as a whole. Therefore, although at any given time the state supports special interest groups legally and illegally, it cannot for long maintain bourgeois domination without securing relations that underlie capitalism as a whole. To secure a ruling class, laws regulate even individual members of this class and, at times, override special ruling class interests. Therefore, laws are generally instruments of a ruling class and/or its fractionated groups, but the most important class interests that are fulfilled by legal relations cannot be defined by reference to the arbitrary will or special interests of ruling-class fractions. These class interests, therefore, are represented by the general interests of a ruling class, which transcend the particular interests of ruling individuals or groups.

Fifth, legal relations under capitalism secure compatible as well as incompatible class interests. On one hand, legal relations support exploitative and oppressive conditions that are extremely harmful to working people. On the other hand, the legal relations that guard one's person, property, and political rights may at any given time be in the interests of working people. For example, there are legally binding contracts that protect personal income obtained through wage labor; therefore, laws may safeguard working-class needs even though wage labor is institutionalized by capitalism. Other laws, recognizing the right to bargain collectively and to organize political parties, for example, may institutionalize economic and political conflicts within a capitalist framework. Nevertheless, they too may serve the interest of working people.

Finally, due to capitalism's inherently antagonistic characteristics, the practical application of legal relations inevitably contradicts their generally stated aim, the establishment of a harmonious and just society. By securing the capitalist mode of production, legal relations maintain the patterns of individualism and selfishness and the conflicts between individual and society that undermine social harmony and social justice. Thus, although the bourgeoisie introduced comprehensive systems of criminal justice, that class personifies a social system characterized by anarchy, oppression, and crime.

But capitalism has also introduced the social formations that will eventually eliminate this contradiction in legal practice. Capitalism has raised the level of productive forces throughout the world and it has propelled humankind along the path of evolutionary development. Simultaneously, it has generated class struggles everywhere that are now eventuating in socialism. In a very short period almost half of the world's population has become incorporated into socialist societies.

Radical criminologists argue among themselves about the directions and merits of socialist developments. By and large, however, they agree that socialist societies have enormously reduced ordinary crimes, including robbery, rape, delinquency, organized crime, heroin use, and prostitution. In some countries, such as Cuba, the reduction is startling because it includes organized crime. (Cuba, in the prerevolutionary period, was the main center of organized crime in the Caribbean.) In other countries, such as the German Democratic Republic, the long-term decline in ordinary crime is also impressive, because such a reduction has not taken place in the Federal Republic of Germany. In China prostitution, which existed for generations, is substantially eradicated. For radical criminologists such reductions are due mainly to the development of economic security for working people and to the state planning that is genuinely regulated by social needs. Doubtless, such reductions are also due to the stable collective relations at the workplace and in the community that support social solidarity and moral obligations.

Although some of the ideas expressed above will appear in the sections to come, the control of crime and delinquency in capitalist societies is the concern of this article. We begin with a discussion of causal relations that generate delinquency under capitalism, especially among proletarian youth. Social policy formulation certainly requires more than a causal theory; nevertheless, causal assumptions constrain the most important recommendations regarding delinquency prevention and control. Even James Q. Wilson's call for virtual abandonment of social theories of crime (because theorizing about root causes allegedly cannot "supply a plausible basis for the advocacy of social policy") is founded in a theory of criminal behavior. He recommends that swift and certain punishments are effective deterrents; yet such a recommendation is partly based on the utilitarianism of Bentham and Beccaria. Ironically, without assumptions about root causes, Wilson's policy recommendations would hardly be "plausible." [2]

Thus, causal theories implicitly or explicitly underlie important recommendations for crime control. With regard to delinquency, radical causal theory is being presented in published writings by the authors.[3] Although this theory also deals with social formations among middle-class youth (that is, petty bourgeois and bourgeois youth) who exhibit high rates of unofficial delinquency, space limitations preclude a full discussion of these formations.[4] In any case, as we shall see, the juvenile justice system converges mainly on marginal youth. Consequently, restricting the theory here to marginalization and youth is not unjustified.

## Marginalization and Youth

Historically, marginal youth emerged along with bourgeois youth in the earliest centuries of capitalism. Historians have documented the gradual demise during these centuries of the main forms of feudal servitude. Although a class of independent peasants appeared alongside the independent artisans in the fourteenth and fifteenth centuries, the subsequent rise of the great landowners and merchant-capitalists transformed the social structure. This early bourgeoisie relied on the state and its armed might to protect their claims to the ownership of the

[2] James Q. Wilson, *Thinking about Crime* (New York: Basic Books, 1976).

[3] Herman Schwendinger and Julia Schwendinger, "Collective Varieties of Youth," *Crime and Social Justice* 5 (Spring–Summer 1976):7–25; "Marginal Youth and Social Policy," *Social Problems* 24 (1976):184–191; "Penal Trends in the United States: Standards of Life in Penal Institutions (Part I)," *La Questione Criminale,* trans. Dario Mellosi (Bologna), in press; "Social Class and the Definition of Crime," *Crime and Social Justice* 7 (Spring–Summer 1977), in press.

[4] For a discussion of middle-class delinquency, see Schwendinger and Schwendinger, "Collective Varieties of Youth," pp. 17–25. In addition, no attempt is made in this article to present aspects of the theory that deal with delinquency and ideological relationships (e.g., ethics, morality, etc.).

most productive property. Equally important was the role of the state in securing every conceivable species of labor power for expanding large industrial enterprise. People from many walks of life were cast out of their traditional modes of existence by the dissolution of the older modes of production. They became marginal members of the labor force and were denied consistent participation in self-sustaining economic relationships. This process of marginalization was expressed by the expansion of youthful criminality, by the emergence of social types such as the Wilde Rogues, Wilde Dells, Kynchen Coes, Kynchen Morts, and Black Guard.[5]

The prolongation of youth and the creation of delinquency are inventions of capitalism. In its most vigorous periods capitalism accelerates the trend toward the replacement of living labor by machines, and it thereby underwrites the creation of a relative surplus labor force by long-term declines in the rate of capital accumulation. The labor of youth in this process becomes redundant, and youth are gradually but not completely eliminated from the labor market. In this process the dependent status of youth is prolonged, elevating the theoretical importance of certain socialization agencies, which include the family but center on the modern school. Certain characteristics of these agencies, as we will see, uniquely recreate the process of marginalization *within* the socialization agencies themselves.

Marginalization processes within socialization agencies are serially related to industry. Most socialization agencies concentrate on youth who will generally become proletarians and who, therefore, require certain types of services for the production of their labor power. These services are largely provided by parents and teachers, whose efforts are exerted in the family and the school. With regard to reproduction of their labor power, both socialization agencies appear to operate separately while, in fact, they are quite interdependent.

This interdependence emerges because the reproductive re-

[5] For the relationship between these social types and delinquency, see ibid., pp. 8–11.

lations in the school are largely dominated by industrial relations.[6] The standards used to reward and punish a student's behavior within the school, for instance, correspond to the standards that are used by managers to control workers. The reproductive relations within the family are also dominated by industry, but this form of domination is partly mediated by the school. As indicated, the school, in spite of appearances, essentially organizes its educational productivity around industrially related standards. By dominating production relations within the family, the school as well as industry imposes these standards upon parents and children.

At least two general consequences flow from these serial relations of domination. First, the reproductive relations within socialization agencies are synchronized with the alienated social relations that generally characterize commodity production. These alienated relations are not confined to the youngsters; they include both the parents and the teachers, who are involved in the long-term production of labor power.

Second, the domination of socialization relations by industrial standards is expressed in the same general laws of investment and profit maximization that culminate in the uneven development of various groups and nations.[7] This means that investments in the development of the labor force are allocated unevenly. Such investments concentrate on those groups of persons considered to have a greater potentiality for meeting the meritocratic criteria prevailing in educational institutions. Conversely, unless political struggles broaden educational policies, the investments of private or public resources—calculable in terms of

[6] For the meaning of the word *domination*, see Maurice Godelier, *Rationality and Irrationality in Economics* (London: New Left Books, 1972). For the concept of "correspondence" as it relates to the schools and industry, see Samuel Bowles and Herbert Gintis, *Schooling in Capitalist America* (New York: Basic Books, 1976) and Martin Carnoy, ed., *Schooling in a Corporate Society: The Political Economy of Education in America*, 2d ed. (New York: David McKay, 1975).

[7] Barry Bluestone, "Capitalism and Poverty in America: A Discussion," *Monthly Review* 2 (June 1972):64–71.

money, equipment, facilities, faculties, and even in the teacher's time, attention, and expectations—will be minimal for the development of these groups of persons who do not appear to meet these criteria.

Consequently, the allocation of educational resources favors the youth who have already been the recipients of superior resources. Simultaneously, the competitive position of the least favored students deteriorates, and the process analogous to marginalization within the economy occurs in the context of the school and the family. This inherently contradictory trend results in anarchic behavior patterns, created by students who are not strongly motivated to achieve and who do not make any disciplined effort to achieve. These are also the students who actually do not achieve the cognitive and noncognitive traits that generally favor sustained labor force participation in the future. Although their chances for future employment are somewhat independent of their status in socialization agencies, these children manifest early in life the adaptive characteristics that evolve in capitalism among numerous owners of the least valuable forms of labor power.

Thus, the relations that favor the uneven development of labor power generate early in life a youthful population of *prototypic* marginals, whose status is not actually determined directly by economic institutions. The members of this population are not usually counted among "the employed" or "the unemployed." Instead they are generally regarded as students, and during most of their adolescent years the workaday life is very far from their minds.

Within communities across the United States adolescents speak among themselves about these prototypic marginals. Such names as Greasers, Vato, Dude, Honcho, Hodad, and Hood appear whenever they are mentioned in conversations. These metaphors refer to individual marginals and groups and, among other social regularities in personal behavior, to their conduct, carriage, attitudes, gestures, grooming, argot, clothing, and delinquent acts. Marginal youth perform a variety of offenses, and generally their offenses are of a more serious nature than those of other youth.

## Juvenile Justice and Penal Practices

Paradoxically, although juvenile justice policies are aimed at delinquency prevention and control, they cannot be understood by limiting our observations to delinquent conduct alone. A conceptual connection between policy formation and delinquency exists, but intervening between the two are the functions of crime control in a *class* society.

Radicals for some time have analyzed the class forces determining the nature of juvenile justice policies. Anthony Platt's *The Child Savers,* for instance, is a pioneering work on the juvenile justice system.[8] When that work was published in 1969, it analyzed the social movements that supported the introduction of the juvenile court during the so-called Progressive era. It debunked conventional historical reviews of these reforms, suggesting instead that the child-saving movement was led by middle-class women and that it was not simply a humanitarian effort on behalf of the lower classes against the established order.

In 1974 Platt incorporated his specific analysis of the child-saving movement into a more general theory about the impact of monopoly capitalism on governmental relationships. The impetus for the juvenile court, he declared, "came primarily from the middle and upper classes who were instrumental in devising forms of social control to protect their privileged positions in American society. The child saving movement was not an isolated phenomenon but rather reflected the massive changes in productive relationships, from Laissez-faire to monopoly capitalism, and in strategies of social control, from inefficient repression to welfare state benevolence."[9] Platt based this later analysis of the introduction of the juvenile court on changes in the political economy.

[8] Anthony Platt, *The Child Savers: The Invention of Juvenile Delinquency* (Chicago: University of Chicago Press, 1969), with new Introduction to New Enlarged Edition (University of Chicago Press, 1977).

[9] Anthony Platt, "The Triumph of Benevolence: The Origins of the Juvenile Justice System in the United States," in *Criminal Justice in America,* ed. Richard Quinney (New York: Little Brown, 1974), p. 369.

The juvenile court established a general system of juvenile social control, and it extended state sovereignty over juveniles and their families in civil society. The court authorities, more-over, assumed the roles of prosecutor, judge, and jury, thereby discarding the due process requirements formalized in criminal law procedure. Usurping the traditional rights of parents and the formal legal rights of individuals, this court identified the population of official delinquents as well as other youth whose legal status was ambiguous but who were considered in need of guidance and control.

In other words, the court performed the minimum integrative functions that are preconditions for a general system of social control. For example, it selectively allocated these youth to a number of private and public agencies, including vocational training, family service, child guidance, probationary, and reformatory institutions. The legitimation and operation of the other agencies within this weakly regulated system of social control required some accommodation to juridical authority.

Such an integrated juvenile system did not exist earlier; in fact, the forerunners of modern delinquency treatment and control programs emerged quite haphazardly. Yet since such programs are viewed by many as innovative today, their manifestation as early as the sixteenth and seventeenth centuries is startling. In precapitalist and early capitalist England, one finds halfway houses for boys and girls released from prisons, workhouses for dealing with juvenile gangs in London, and laws about apprentices and destitute youth, aimed at the control and prevention of delinquency.[10] Furthermore, within the United States, from the colonial period onward, we find laws buttressing patriarchal authority over disobedient youth and various juvenile programs involving industrial training and foster homes. From 1838 onward juridical precedents considered parental rights natural but not inalienable. (Such rights could be superseded by the doctrine of *parens patriae*, that is, by the state, the common

[10] For examples of delinquency control during early capitalism, see Wily B. Sanders, ed., *Juvenile Offenders for a Thousand Years* (Chapel Hill: University of North Carolina Press, 1970).

guardian of the community.) [11] Rather than being new and innovative, such laws, precedents, and programs are antiquated and conventional.

This conclusion is supported by Alexander Liazos, who analyzed the strategies used in delinquency programs from the nineteenth century onward. In the first half of the century, work in houses of refuge and reform schools emphasized unskilled labor, and work-training was for the lowest status occupations. After comparing such work activities with contemporary job-training and placement programs, Liazos concludes, "Present programs and trends, though they differ in tone, language, and form, resemble past ones in most essentials. They still try to fit the children of the poorer classes into the bottom of society and dead-end jobs. The changes are in style, not in function. Capitalism, which demands the existence of the disciplined, exploited working force, is not questioned." [12]

Mobilization for Youth, which received massive funding in the 1960s, illustrates Liazos's conclusion. This program simulated ten work situations, such as a gasoline station, an auto repair shop, a shoe factory, a luncheonette, that emphasized regularity, punctuality, neatness, and demeanor toward employers. "But most youths," according to Liazos, "did not go on to get similar jobs as those they had been trained for, or any jobs. Of 46 gasoline station trainees, only one got a gas station job." Overall, jobs were found for only 25 percent of 1,700 youths in 1962–63, and most of them were in "marginal occupations at relatively low wages." [13]

In the early 1960s the President's Committee on Juvenile Delinquency recommended policies oriented toward changing social conditions rather than treating individual delinquents directly. Although this may sound like a radical recommenda-

[11] For a good historical account of juvenile justice policies and programs, see Barry Krisberg and James Austen, *Children of Ishmael: Critical Perspectives on Juvenile Justice* (Palo Alto, Calif.: Mayfield Press, 1978).

[12] Alexander Liazos, "Class Oppression: The Functions of Juvenile Justice," *Insurgent Sociologist* 1 (Fall 1974):2–23.

[13] Ibid., p. 14, and Peter Morris and Martin Rein, *Dilemmas of Social Reform*, 2d ed., (New York: Aldine, 1973), p. 88.

tion, Morris and Rein investigated the implementation of these policies by the Office of Economic Opportunities and concluded that the community action programs were not at all radical because few social changes were actually attempted. Ninety percent of these programs were still based on individual treatment strategies.[14]

Liazos indicates that such strategies have failed to control delinquency. The failure of individual treatement strategies has also been observed by many rigorous studies of counseling, job development, community resource, and recreational programs. But conventional surveys of these evaluation studies provide no general rationale for the failures, because such a rationale would focus on the capitalist state.

### State, Crime Control, and Class Reproduction

The capitalist state fails to prevent and control delinquency because, while ruling class interests enable it to utilize a variety of methods for controlling individual conduct, these methods cannot conflict with dominant bourgeois priorities. Thus, on one hand this domination favors policies that support the reproduction of class relations; on the other, it precludes policies that threaten the conditions for reproducing the capitalist mode of production and its exploitative relations. Among these conditions are the laws of investment and profit maximization and the marginalization processes, mentioned in the first section of this article as contributing to delinquency. To curb delinquency, therefore, the state should restrict or eliminate these economic arrangements; it should at least ameliorate their effects on the family, school, and labor market. But the state is a *capitalist* state, and its crime-control policies are characterized by conflicting political priorities. The state secures the class conditions that cause delinquency, even though it simultaneously prohibits delinquent conduct. The same logic applies to the state control of crime in general. There, too, the state maintains the capitalist relationships that reproduce legally prohibited behavior.

[14] Morris and Rein, *Dilemmas of Social Reform,* pp. 258–59.

Obviously, then, the constraints on crime-control policies are *primarily* due to objective relations rather than ideological relations involving, for instance, the effect of liberal theories on delinquency policy formation. In the 1960s opportunity-structure theories justified job creation as well as job training programs. But the state emphasized the latter instead of the former because, up to a certain point, unemployment is useful to capital both at home and in the world economy. Unemployment depresses wage rates and forces employed workers to increase their labor discipline and productivity. It also slows down the rate of inflation. Capital, therefore, supports job-creation programs only when unemployment threatens political stability. Even then such programs tend to be temporary, and they directly or indirectly feed the private sector, usually channeling youth and adults into the secondary labor market. Consequently, regardless of theory, the weight of job-related programs has been toward highly restricted solutions to unemployment problems.

The small number of federal job-creation programs, from the 1960s onward, further demonstrates the powerful forces constraining social policy. The federal government funded the youth corps and other types of job programs for young people, but these programs were extremely limited. In addition, the impact of the programs was inconsequential because they were geared to satisfying secondary labor market requirements. Even the fairly recent federal job program, which was funded in 1973 by the Comprehensive Employment Training Act (CETA) at a cost of three-quarters of a billion dollars, is not really designed to counter sustained high level unemployment or to guarantee decent jobs for youth.

## Penal Convergence on Marginals

There are no issues more central to criminology than those involving the political and economic conditions whose dual effect contributes to crime while prohibiting genuine alternatives to crime control. The kernel of a theory of such conditions has just been offered to explain the glaring discrepancy between what we know and what is being done about delinquency. Our theory has thus far focused on class constraints that restrict crime control and penal policies to individual punishment and treatment strategies. Now we will briefly consider the class differentials in criminal justice practices that direct these official policies primarily toward marginals of all ages. Clearly, social policies regarding official delinquency require knowledge of what these class differentials are all about.

Granted that penal practices protect legal rights to life, property, and so on, but placing the sole emphasis on these obvious functions of penal practices overlooks certain primary class differentials that are not obvious. The primary differentials which illuminate class justice have to do (1) with the selection of the types of social harms that are actually defined and punished as crimes by the state (as opposed to those that are not) and (2) with the variation in sanctions that are prescribed for these different harms.

Generally, class factors differentiate social harms and punishments in the following way. First, because of their relation to state power and capital accumulation, many serious harms committed by members of the American bourgeoisie, such as the promulgation of the Indo-Chinese War and the forcible overthrow of the Chilean (Allende) democratic government, are not regulated by law. Second, bourgeois harms regulated by law are usually controlled by civil laws; hence, they are subject to the milder restitutive sanctions rather than the harsher penal sanctions. Third, the remaining bourgeois harms that are defined as crimes receive relatively less punishment than is provided for the types of harms committed frequently by proletarians. Thus, while it cannot be justifiably claimed that proletarians generally commit more economic crimes than the bourgeoisie, it can be maintained that under capitalism certain types of economic activities, more than others, are sanctioned. The primary types of crimes receiving penal sanctions are committed, in the main, by proletarians. Penal sanctions are also applied universally, but, for obvious reasons, they are applied especially to marginal proletarians.

On the other hand class differentials in the types of punishable harms and penal sanctions still do not fully demonstrate the class nature of justice in the United States. Penal law in bourgeois democracies remains class law essentially because it safeguards the exploitation of free wage labor. However, since this form of exploitation is mystified by an ideology based on the fetishism of the wage transaction, the essential class functions of bourgeois laws are also unobservable. Under these mystified conditions, the state does not appear to reproduce class relations when it protects economic rights, especially the rights of wage earners. Yet by safeguarding these rights, penal practices secure the economic relationships that operate behind the backs of individuals and that reproduce the class structure on the basis of exploitation.[15]

In other words, penal practices protect the invisible processes of exploitation that reproduce the basic structure of capitalist societies. But the unique function that underlies the predominance of marginals in criminal courts or among the inmates of prisons involves the rate of exploitation rather than exploitation itself. The key point here is that penal practices, by generally deterring marginal proletarians from reproducing themselves illegally, maximize the numbers of persons who are in the labor market regardless of the demand for their labor. This maximization constitutes one of the many preconditions for the surplus labor force. Penal practices thereby indirectly affect rates of exploitation, because the surplus labor force is used by capitalists to depress wage rates and to heighten labor discipline and productivity.

In sum, penal practices protect the entire system of legal relations in society; thereto, and among other things, they secure the monopoly of violence for the state as well as the hegemony of bourgeois morality, politics, and property. But, as indicated,

---

[15] This point is fundamental to the Marxist interpretation of the relation between legal systems and economic exploitation in mature capitalist societies. However, because of its complexity, commodity fetishism, the mechanism that regulates this relation, cannot be described within the limits of this paper. For clarification of this mechanism see Karl Marx's opening chapters in the first volume of *Capital*. Norman Geras, "Essence and Appearance: Aspects of Fetishism in Marx's *Capital*," *New Left Review* 65 (January–February 1971):69–85, is helpful here.

the types of sanctions that *converge* on the marginal members of the labor force underwrite higher rates of exploitation. Penal practices maximize the supply of living labor at the disposal of capital by deterring proletarians from reproducing themselves illegally. They insure that labor power remains competitive regardless of the level of labor-market demand; they guarantee that it is available when wage rates are low and that it renews itself through exploitation despite work alienation.

Under these conditions the traditional bourgeois practice of punishment acquires its brutal parameters. Since it is assumed that marginals would not be deterred from crime if prison conditions were superior to conditions on the outside, this practice of punishment tacitly ignores the distinctions between deterrence based on the deprivation of liberty through incarceration as opposed to deterrence based on punishing people by subjecting them to material, social, political, and cultural deprivations greater than those suffered by social groups outside of prisons. Because penal sanctions converge on marginals, the standards of life within prisons are generally set below the levels for these members of the labor force.[16]

The convergence on marginals reproduces social relations in prisons that are similar to the most brutal features of life among marginals outside of prisons. Such relations as materially, deficient living standards, institutionalized racism and sexism, savage repression of political dissension, exploitative criminal networks, and the virtual disregard for the personal dignity and medical needs of prisoners exist within American prisons. These kinds of relations may, for bourgeois social scientists, appear to develop spontaneously or by diffusion, or because of such bureaucratic priorities as the necessity to maintain institutional security. But they are actually special instances of broader relations that determine similar features of life outside as well as inside prisons.

[16] For the historical development of this bourgeois practice of punishment, see Georg Rausche and Otto Kirchheimer, *Punishment and Social Structure* (New York: Russel and Russel, 1968), p. 108. In addition, see Schwendinger and Schwendinger, "Marginal Youth and Social Policy," *Social Problems* 24 (1976):184–91, for an expanded analysis of this practice.

The Convergence on Marginal Youth

Juvenile justice in certain fundamental respects mirrors the aforementioned penal tendencies. During the first decade of its existence, 80 percent of the children referred to the Chicago juvenile court were from poor and working-class families. This socioeconomic bias has not changed in Chicago or elsewhere. In Massachusetts, for instance, 88 percent of the youth committed by the courts to the Department of Youth Services (the correctional arm of the juvenile system) in 1972 were from families at, or near, the poverty level. The closing down of traditional custodial institutions in that state has not changed the convergence on marginals as a central feature of juvenile justice. In addition, despite reforms across the nation, many youth detention and correctional facilities continue to be substandard and brutal; hence, such conditions are by no means confined to adult institutions.

In fact, juvenile justice policies are *special* instances of penal trends because they place constraints on the social relations that reproduce the labor force intergenerationally. To locate this in context, let us take the family as one of these social relationships. Capital has all but eliminated the domestic economy organized around self-sufficient families. As a result, the working-class and petty bourgeois family is now perceived as a socialization agency with narrowly restricted functions, limited to reproduction of labor power. Furthermore, capital-intensive industries require a knowledgeable, skilled, disciplined, and indoctrinated labor force, to be employed under exploitative conditions. To meet this need, education has become compulsory throughout most of the adolescent period. Consequently, juvenile laws, building upon older legal traditions, guard both the school and the family. Such laws single out youth from adults. They prohibit status offenses, such as truancy, running away from home, and incorrigibility, that would not be criminal if they were committed by adults.

Thus, there is a continued accommodation between juvenile justice and socioeconomic change. Deference to parents and other types of adults still requires legal supports, particularly in the face of labor market restrictions and the unnatural prolongation of youth. Furthermore, public schools teach and enforce habits of punctuality, regularity, obedience to school authority, and political conformity, but, because of the alienation that characterizes the schools, legal sanctions as well as external rewards remain necessary for maintaining social order.

Legal codes accordingly circumscribe the social relations of modern youth. Additional constraints exist regarding such consumption patterns as drinking and drug use, late night leisure activities, and the extent of tolerance toward sexual behavior. Such constraints are also deemed necessary in a society that subjects youth, on the one hand, to commercial forces that sell everything for a price and, on the other, to the requirements for an industrially disciplined proletariat.

Regardless of their apparent universality, such codes hardly apply to wealthy bourgeois youth. First of all, such youth are only incidentally subjected to juvenile laws that have essentially been established to control the behavior of young proletarians. Wealthy youth may (if they choose) take their family's place in industry, but they will hardly reproduce the exploitable labor force. Furthermore, if such youth are disobedient or perform badly in public schools, they can be sent to a private school, to a psychiatric counselor, or on an "educational trip" abroad. Private tutors can even be hired to meet compulsory educational standards. Thus, the requirements for punctuality and regularity that are imposed by bureaucratic authorities can be avoided. The same point can be made regarding the legal restrictions on the social space allocated for leisure-time pursuits. Legal restrictions are sharper in the ghettos, where the available social space contrasts with the private pools, playrooms, and exclusive resorts of the bourgeoise. Status offenses under the latter conditions are not even visible.

Consequently, while it can be seen that marginal youth, more frequently than other types of youth, violate juvenile justice codes that protect life and property, this frequency is not great enough alone to explain the extreme convergence on marginal proletarian youth exhibited by the juvenile justice system. Furthermore, less serious offenses, such as status offenses, petty theft, and vandalism, are given considerable emphasis by the system. The distribution of these types of offenses suggests differences between marginal and nonmarginal youth that are largely quantitative, but too many youth from other classes or strata relations commit these offenses with impunity every day to allow for a simple explanation. Hence, there must be additional reasons why marginal youth are the prime recipients of juvenile justice sanctions.

Several factors account for the extreme convergence on proletarian marginal youth. An obvious factor is that these youth spend considerable time on the streets under scrutiny of neighbors and police, who activate sanctions readily. In addition, low status families have less political influence; therefore, justice officials are less accommodative in relation to such families. But other, less obvious factors than visibility and discrimination also determine the convergence. Families of marginal adolescents are disproportionately drawn from poorer families. Consequently, under American capitalist conditions, these families are more disturbed by fluctuations in the health of their members, by labor market instabilities and other characteristics, and by internal conflicts and separations. Family disturbances critically diminish the ability of parents and school officials to discipline marginal youth, because no adult-controlled arrangements other than commercial entertainment industries provide any alternative source of positive satisfaction. Such youth are generally less successful in school; hence, negative sanctions remain the only means for securing their punctuality, attendance, and performance. Their lives are further diminished by the impact of school demands on family relations and by the restricted youth job market. Is there any wonder, then, that they grow less obedient to adult authority when, by contrast to youth in other classes, that authority sustains the conditions that offer so little yet demand so much?

Consequently, as one moves down the class ladder, favorable conditions for avoiding sanctions directed at status offenders diminish. The least favorable conditions exist for young marginal proletarians. Furthermore, these youth are most frequently sanctioned by the juvenile justice system because, when faced with the destructive impact of the political economy on their lives, too few resources can be marshaled by their families to systematically secure orderly socialization.

## Delinquency Prevention and Control

This final section discusses guidelines for prevention and delinquency control. At the outset, however, it should be stated that viable policies for delinquency prevention in this country do not exist. Historically, social policies for eliminating the causes of delinquency have never been developed here. The full-employment provisions of the Humphrey-Hawkins bill might have established a precedent because they transcended the inconsequential job-training and job-creation proposals still being justified in the name of delinquency prevention. These provisions, however, were eliminated from the bill in congressional hearings. The bill now does not guarantee anyone the right to employment. Thus, the terrain on which delinquency *prevention* policies can be formulated remains conspicuously devoid of realistic options.

On the other hand, with regard to control there has been a meaningful expansion of the terrain on which conflicts can be waged over *juvenile justice* reforms. We previously mentioned the loosely integrated system organized around the juvenile court for sanctioning and treating individuals. Policy formations continue to focus on this system, but now they reflect a variety of political persuasions. The persuasions from the right are represented by updated conservative proposals. On the left the anarchism and populism of the late 1960s, which espoused the complete elimination of jails and prisons, has been supplanted by newer radical standpoints.[17] Among these is a call for consistent efforts to enforce the law regarding certain crimes. Such enforcement includes imprisonment.

[17] "The Politics of Street Crimes," *Crime and Social Justice* 5 (Spring–Summer 1976):1–4.

To avoid any misunderstanding, it should be emphasized that radicals do not call for wholesale incarceration. A great many people imprisoned in the United States should not be confined at all. (The United States rates of imprisonment outstrip all other Western bourgeois democracies.) This opinion applies especially to juvenile offenders, since tens of thousands of these delinquents do not fit the primary-objective criterion for social harm.[18] In addition, there are numerous adults who, for example, are incarcerated for committing victimless crimes. These offenders have neither violated elementary rules of social life nor harmed the interests of the working class and its allies.

Working-class individuals and the petty bourgeoisie are primary victims of street crimes, including rape, robbery, and thievery. Other harmful acts, which may not even be defined legally as crimes because they are committed by people who manipulate the law in their own interest, also affect this class and stratum. However, the elimination of this array of crimes will not occur until advanced socialist developments have taken place. Until then, legal sanctions, including imprisonment, remain necessary.

Since incarceration remains a necessity, the recommendations for closing down substandard juvenile correctional agencies should also provide for high-standard juvenile correctional care. Without this provision youth will be diverted to adult prisons and the subordination of youth correctional systems to adult prison authorities will be encouraged. In either of the latter cases, such a change would be retrogressive.

Consequently, the most retrogressive view in recent years is that prisons and punishments can substantially reduce crime of both juveniles and adults.[19] There are several reasons why this is objectionable. With depressed economic conditions, this trend might readjust downward the standards involved in the imple-

---

[18] The primary criterion refers to social relations that objectively harm the interests of the working class and its allies. For a discussion of this criterion, see Schwendinger and Schwendinger, "Social Class and the Definition of Crime," *Crime and Social Justice* 7 (Spring–Summer 1977):4–13.

[19] For example, see James Q. Wilson, *Thinking about Crime* (New York: McGraw-Hill, 1970).

mentation of traditional bourgeois punishment. If adopted, the
key policies that exemplify the trend would expand the imprisoned population, and, in light of the fiscal crises in government, prison standards of life would become even more brutal.

In addition, the "swift and certain punishment" trend undermines prison reform movements. It had become traditional to
label as rehabilitative virtually every humane policy as long as
it improves the well-being of offenders. The wholesale discredit-
ing of the rehabilitative ideal, under present conditions, has left
"law and order" conservatives free to support forms of government intervention that make matters worse. This contrasts with
prison reform movements that are working toward the individual's "right against debilitation." [20] The reliance on punishment
and incarceration by this movement is against prison reform developments that are interested in expanding services for inmates
and in diverting individuals of all ages from brutal and substandard custodial institutions. [21]

Furthermore, by providing "law and order" conservatives with
added justification for enacting politically repressive legislation,
the professional exponents of this trend reinforce the waves of
political repression that periodically engulf the United States.
During the 1960s and early 1970s, such repression encompassed

[20] The phrase "right against debilitation" refers to a multiple class-action-
suit decision by Judge Frank M. Johnson in 1976. This decision found the
lack of meaningful rehabilitation programs and the inhumane living conditions in Alabama's state prisons sufficient reason to order the prisons closed
if the court's guidelines were not followed. Judge Johnson indicated that
this prison environment "not only makes it impossible for inmates to rehabilitate themselves, but also makes debilitation inevitable." His was the
first order listing constitutional standards for state prison operations.

[21] Donald McNamara, "The Medical Model in Corrections," *Criminology*
14 (1977):439–47, notes, for example, that "Norval Morris, James Q. Wilson, Andrew von Hirsch, Robert Martinson, David Fogel, and Ernst van
den Haag, now reject equally the 'tear down the walls' war cry of those
who would abolish prisons . . . and *the prison reform movement* which
campaigns . . . for smaller, treatment-oriented institutions, court-mandated
inmate rights, expansion of community corrections, decriminalization of
victimless offenses, and diversion from the criminal justice system for many
now subject to its sanctions" (our emphasis).

adolescents as well as adults who demonstrated against racism and imperialism.

The exponents of this retrogressive trend are called "new penologists," but this label is misleading.[22] Analytically, the label *neo-idealists* is more precise, because these exponents derive their basic assumption from very traditional idealist theories of law, deterrence, and retribution, established by eighteenth- and nineteenth-century utilitarians (Bentham) and German idealists (Kant.) The neo-idealists claim that their proposals will reduce crime, but these claims should be regarded with great reservation. Barry Schwartz in 1968 indicated that legislation prescribing more severe penalties for rapists had no long-term effects on the incidence of rape in Philadelphia.[23] Just a short while ago newspapers reported that the Draconian laws against narcotics users and dealers in New York State had failed. The most dramatic effect (and the only consequence of these laws, apart from the misery they caused) was a substantial increase in the number of police informants. Thus, the repressive laws did not deter crime; they may, in fact, have contributed to it.[24]

With regard to delinquency, moreover, there are added considerations. Our research indicates, for example, that more than

[22] The idealistic foundations of this retrogressive trend are described in Schwendinger and Schwendinger, "Standards of Living in Penal Institutions, Part II—Social Policy Trends," forthcoming.

[23] Barry Schwartz, "The Effect in Philadelphia of Pennsylvania's Increased Penalties for Rape and Attempted Rape," *The Journal of Criminal Law, Ciminology and Police Science* 59 (1968).

[24] Alan Kalmanoff, *Criminal Justice* (New York: Little, Brown, 1976), p. 102, states, for instance, "A recent New York statute . . . enacted severe penalties for anyone convicted of narcotics involvement, making the 'cost' of such activity even greater. Many lowly marijuana and heroin dealers are now known to carry guns to protect themselves more completely against informants and undercover agents" (New York penal law §220, amended 1973, effective Sept 1, 1973). For additional findings that contradict retributionist expectations, see Dorothy Miller, Ann Rosenthan, Don Miller, and Sheryl Ruzek, "Deterrent Effects of Criminal Sanctions," Progress Report of the California Assembly Committee on Criminal Procedure, Sacramento, California (1968):10–18; and Patrick Tornudd, "The Preventive Effect of Fines for Drunkenness," *Scandinavian Studies in Criminology* 2 (1968):109–24.

95 percent of the boys in our study were never detected by police, or, if detected, never referred to the juvenile court. Regardless of whether the court actually sentenced those who were referred, the amount of crime that is not detected by the law is astounding. Even if *solely for the sake of argument* we granted that the neo-idealist proposals would significantly deter delinquency, one still has to ask how many youth must be incarcerated to produce this effect. The possibilities here are astronomical, and the juvenile justice system would have to be increased more than a thousandfold in order to conform to neo-idealist expectations.

To avoid misunderstanding: we are *not* proposing the desirability of warehousing delinquent youth in correctional institutions. We simply want to suggest that in addition to our political objections, the new neo-idealists are unrealistic and insufficiently acquainted with the characteristics of delinquent and criminal behavior.

Our opinions about the neo-idealists are reinforced by other research findings. Many serious forms of delinquency—especially victim offenses—are based on the development of illegal commodity markets having both supply and demand crowds. But although the extensiveness and level of complexity of such markets are sensitive to police operations, the elementary forms of these markets are fairly impervious. The disintegration of a market by the removal of some of its members through arrest and incarceration, as a rule, eventuates simply in the reformation of irregular activities to meet ongoing demand.

This conclusion is not idle speculation. We have actually witnessed the disintegration and reformation of such markets during four and a half years of participant observation with delinquent groups and during three years of field operations while administering a delinquency research project. During these seven and a half years we observed that the demand crowds in the illegal markets were always available even though the suppliers were occasionally destabilized because of official sanctions. However, since the demand generally guaranteed the creation of new suppliers, the frequency of sanctions imposed by officials had virtually no long-term effects on the existence of the market itself.

Fluctuations in sanctions only affected the turnover rate of suppliers.

Massive propaganda from the politicians, press, and television make punitive proposals for sure and certain punishment seem to be effective and simple solutions to crime and delinquency. But knowledge about the characteristics as well as the basic causes of these phenomena leads in a different direction. Aside from the personality characteristics that often make utilitarian guides to punishment especially useless for deterring short-sighted marginal youth, we have the problem of administering sanctions that will fit the punishment to the crime. In illegal markets it is a constellation of delinquent activities that must be prevented. Each individual contributes to a configuration of acts and not merely to an individual event. How can punishment deter an irregular commodity market? If the supplier receives punishment, then the structure may be disrupted for a short time, but it will re-form. If the innumerable buyers are pursued relentlessly, then thousands will protest this unjust harrassment. If both the supplier and the buyer are punished, then to accommodate all these offenders the juvenile justice system will have to be increased astronomically. And even if both are punished, there are younger adolescents who will spontaneously take their places as suppliers and buyers. In short, the empirical nature of crime and punishment in our society reveals that the punitive proposals will help no one—neither the delinquent nor society.

## Status Offenders and Class Priorities

Civil libertarians have proposed more constructive reforms for the juvenile justice system. Youth are not treated equally before the law, since they are prosecuted for offenses that would not be criminal if committed by adults. Hence, libertarians advocate either decriminalization or legalization of status offenses. Further suggestions for extending individual liberties are made in relation to youth accused of criminal offenses, such as rape, robbery, and theft. Here recommendations include the right to bail, counsel, and appeal, and other rights that curb arbitrary and repressive juvenile justice practices. The jurisdiction of the juvenile court and detention, adjudication, and disposition of juvenile offenders are all being scrutinized to establish legal rights for children and parents.

The reaction of radicals to such reforms is favorable yet critical. Radicals across the board are favorable to due process guarantees for juveniles and parents. At the same time, however, they are acutely conscious of the limitations of these procedural reforms. For example, it is pointed out that due process guarantees are less influential than one would infer from media depictions of the courts. About 90 percent of all prosecutions are resolved by guilty pleas, in part through plea bargaining, which is antithetical to due process procedure. In actuality, adjudication that is subject to adversary procedures and jury trials is only honored in the breach.[25] Thus parents and children should be accorded due process, but such guarantees cannot be expected to resolve the many inequities in juvenile courts.

Such a critical reaction is due chiefly to radical sensitivity toward social class and racial inequities. Granted, procedural safeguards are fully justified because they broaden the possibilities of democratic rights for individuals. However, such safeguards tend to be implemented by the criminal justice system only when an individual can mobilize private resources (such as expensive lawyers) or collective aid (such as civil liberties organizations). Ordinarily, poor people can, at best, count on such publicly provided legal services as public defenders and "own recognizance in lieu of bail" programs. Such services in the justice system have not substantially eliminated class and racial discrimination. Once again, despite justifiable improvements, such services would not make the juvenile system radically different in this regard from other parts of the criminal justice system.

As indicated, civil libertarians recommend legalization or decriminalization of status offenses. Our opinions of these recom-

[25] Robert Lefcourt, ed., *Law against the People* (New York: Vintage Books, 1971).

mendations, however, may differ from those of other radicals who have no class criterion or evaluating criminal justice practices. Some status offenses, such as prohibitions against late hours, are fairly minor matters; in addition, there are appropriate (if ambiguous) laws for disorderly conduct on the books. Legalization here will force police to focus on social harms and it will thereby somewhat reduce the harrassment of working-class youth. However, laws that support family and school relationships are more serious. For instance many attempts to undermine working-class educational standards are now taking place. In some states, such as Nevada, proposals are being made for lowering the age limit of compulsory education to sixteen years of age. Such a change would withdraw important legal supports from working-class families and public schools where the issues go beyond education alone. Schools, unfortunately, are also holding operations because no other means for integrating working-class youth into society are available. There are no jobs for these youth, especially for black youth, for whom official estimates indicate around a 40 percent unemployment rate and unofficial estimates, a 65 percent rate.

Working-class families have a difficult enough time controlling their children in the face of poor public schools and meager community resources. The need for greater resources should not be met by legalizing truancy and creating added pressures for working-class parents. There is no question of the serious inequities in the ways these laws are implemented; however, without the development of alternative policies, their removal would only make matters worse. Therefore, we strongly oppose incarceration for status offenders, but we do not believe that all status offenses should be eliminated.

Our opinions about status offenses are different from those who feel that the best radical policy is to "leave the kids alone whenever possible" [26] In this approach, for instance, it is suggested that offenders be diverted from juvenile courts; however,

---

[26] Edwin Schur, *Radical Non-Intervention: Rethinking the Delinquency Problem* (Englewood Cliffs, N.J.: Prentice Hall, 1973).

intervention by social-control and socialization agencies is also opposed.[27] Consequently, such recommendations are essentially laissez-faire; they leave youth altogether at the mercy of class-related conditions. In the face of laissez-faire policies, the lives of working-class youth, especially marginals, will continue to be determined by the same general forces that create the delinquency problem in the first place.

Laissez-faire radicals and liberals are distinguished by a humanistic focus on the individual offender and by commendable desires to alleviate social harms inflicted by the justice system on individuals who may not be guilty of crimes. But too many unknowns are associated with the impact of laws about truancy and incorrigibility, for example, on working-class families and youth in general. At the very least, policy formation requires scientific, class-conscious evaluations of the possible consequences of laissez-faire reforms in order to deal adequately with these status offenses.

Thus, as far as decriminalization of status offenders is concerned, research is necessary to determine the potential impact on working-class families of nonoffenders as well as offenders if existing sanctions for status offenses are removed. Critical points of reference for this research would be as follows. How many working-class youth will *begin* to avoid school if truancy laws are decriminalized? What alternative activities are likely to fill their time? What alternative supports for continued schooling and/or jobs are available for these youth as well as for youth who avoid school when truancy laws *are* in effect?

Furthermore, if status offenses are decriminalized, it might be necessary to develop policies that mitigate penal sanctions for juveniles who would previously have been treated as status offenders. Our research findings indicate that many status offenders also commit criminal offenses. For instance, let us consider the case of the eleventh-grade Mexican-American boy in

[27] Some laissez-faire theorists encompass certain minimal intervention, based on labeling theory, or on "deschooling" and other so-called radical changes in culture (e.g., Schur, *Radical Non-Intervention*, pp. 153 ff.). But such interventions are not based on any Marxist analysis of delinquency.

our study who was referred to the court by the police for incorrigibility. The parents of this status offender had turned to the police in desperation for help in controlling their son's narcotics abuse. The police classified the boy as incorrigible rather than as a narcotics user because the latter offense category would, then or later, have created serious difficulties for the boy. To what extent do status offenses lessen court reliance on penal sanctions and provide discretion to deal with the offender more humanely? Such questions should be answered before status offenses are decriminalized across the board.

Community Treatment Programs

Many reformers are conscious of the need to provide positive concrete social services for offenders. Particularly with regard to status offenders, the Hon. Justine Polier observes: "Behind the formal parental petition alleging truancy or late hours, we have found the drug abuse, hard drug use, stealing from the home, periods of disappearance, promiscuity, excessive drinking, or gang involvement emerge in many cases. One sees parents at the end of their wits, fearful of what next may happen to their child. One also finds a higher proportion of emotionally disturbed children in need of residential treatment among these children and youth than among those children who have committed a criminal act and who are therefore found to be delinquent." [28] Our research, as indicated, reinforces this conclusion.

The need for social services has been dramatically highlighted in recent years by the radical correctional reform introduced by Jerome Miller, who was commissioner of the Massachusetts Department of Youth Services. After two years of very limited success, Miller decided that there could be no significant changes in juvenile correctional practice unless the traditional custodial institutions were closed down. These custodial institutions have since been replaced by a developing "network of community

[28] Justice Polier, "Myths and Reality in the Search for Juvenile Justice," *Harvard Educational Review* 14 (February 1974):115.

services including residential and non-residential placements for individuals and small groups; some centralized services for the institutional treatment of dangerous and disturbed offenders; ways to monitor the development of programs to reassign, retrain, or discharge former staff members in ways minimizing personal hardship and injustice." [29]

Such changes represent a massive shift in individual treatment from traditional incarceration and punishment to community custodial care and human service orientations. Regardless of its limitations, the shift represents a departure from the classical bourgeois principle of punishment. Hence, it is, in general, a progressive development although it has limitations that will be discussed later.

Miller's dramatic move, closing down the traditional custodial institutions, occurred in the winter of 1971–72. Since that time it appears that the worst fears of reformers have not been realized. One concern has been that a greater number of commitments would result. Although a more suitable and potentially larger network of social agencies is now available for delinquency control, this development has not increased the numbers of youth committed by the juvenile court in Massachusetts. Furthermore, though the traditional juvenile institutions have been closed down, the courts have not responded negatively by sentencing youth to state prisons for adults. Forthcoming publication of research on the changes in the Massachusetts system will undoubtedly clarify the positive features as well as the limitations of these reforms.

The constriction of traditional custodial treatment and the expansion of the loose network of

alternative individual treatment agencies, has posed new problems of organizational integration. For many decades the juvenile court and probation department have allocated youth among private and public agencies, but, aside from cursory review and reallocation procedures, they only loosely coordinated the relations with the agencies. The court itself did not develop the discretion to perform systematic moni-

[29] Lloyd Ohlin, Robert Coates, and Alden Miller, "Radical Correctional Reform: A Case Study of the Massachusetts Correctional System," *Harvard Educational Review* 14 (February 1974):95.

toring and control of the agencies. Now, however, such discretionary power is being developed, especially where the system pays for services by public or private agencies. In such cases, when treatment services are found inadequate, juvenile justice officials can either request changes within an agency or cease purchasing services from that agency altogether.

The necessity for such financial controls is a natural outcome of present developments. The state does not have the resources to create a full complement of diversion programs. Hence it is forced to rely largely on existing community-based agencies. And even if it did have the funds, contracting of services might still be an effective method for insuring accountability.

On the other hand there are questions about the scope of these controls. Diversion to service agencies is being introduced upon first contact between police and juveniles and hence before these youth are referred to court. Such diversion increases the numbers of youth being sent to agencies by the criminal justice system. This type of diversion seems desirable because necessary services, if available, could be provided youth and their families. But it also implies that juvenile justice monitoring and control over social agencies can be justified before as well as after adjudication. As a result, a new concern emerges. Every possible social service available to youth and parents might, to some degree, become oriented toward and controlled by the juvenile justice system.

Yet despite this possibility there are several reasons for expecting fairly restricted developments. Despite public speeches by officials and politicians about the necessity of controlling crime, reforming the justice system has far less priority than subsidizing local and national business interests. The fiscal crisis in government translates this low priority into token expenditures. The number of diversion programs that are subordinated to the criminal justice system, such as halfway houses and community correctional agencies, is restricted. Furthermore, most of these programs are financed by "soft money" and they are not assured long-term stability. Consequently, the impact of these programs on community life as well as individual delinquents is extremely limited.

Fiscal restrictions on diversionary developments are emphasized in Andrew T. Scull's radical analysis of the decarceration movement. He maintains that the state markedly expanded social services in the 1960s and 1970s.[30] Coincident with this expansion, the incentives to accelerate deinstitutionalization intensified because these alternative community services (though insufficient) had become available. Also by the late 1960s the fiscal crisis of the state precipitated and underwrote the success of the decarceration movement.[31] Scull indicates that the rapid expansion of diversion programs occurred after the state became less able to meet the costs of new programs, of relief for the poor, and of other services. As cost benefits of community approaches are being documented, the diversion programs continue to be adopted.

The decarceration movement, in Scull's opinion, is realizing success because fiscal conservatives interested in cost savings have joined the liberals devoted to rehabilitation. This coalition of conservatives and liberals "has helped to render decarceration politically irresistible, since it has reduced the possibility of the movement's central premises being subjected to political scrutiny, and has lent the whole enterprise the character of self-evidence."[32]

Scull also contends that the *outcome* of the decarceration movement is determined by structural pressures to curtail costs and that rehabilitative priorities have been reduced to rhetoric. Thus, in actuality, Scull observes, decarceration has, in practice, little correspondence to liberal rehabilitative aims. Indeed, the primary value of the liberal "rhetoric (though far from its authors' intent) seems to have been its usefulness as ideological camouflage, allowing economy to masquerade as benevolence and neglect as tolerance."

Scull maintains that the decarceration movement is producing

[30] Andrew Scull, *Community Treatment and the Deviant—A Radical View* (Englewood Cliffs, N.J.: Prentice Hall, 1977), p. 140.

[31] James O'Connor, *The Fiscal Crisis of the State* (New York: St. Martin's Press, 1973).

[32] Scull, *Community Treatment*, p. 147.

"deviant ghettos." [33] Some persons are being diverted to communities where they blend unobtrusively with residents. Others, however, get dumped where they are unwanted but where the communities are too disorganized to exclude them. These persons drift among the down and out or prey upon the poor and unwary. In short, the decarceration movement ends up where the reformers of the Progressive era left us. By creating "deviant ghettos" rather than "therapeutic communities," the movement maintains a tradition of unfulfilled hopes begun decades ago. Now, however, the ghettos created by the reformers are located in the intersticial areas of the city rather than in secluded custodial institutions.

## Further Problems with Diversion

The fiscal crisis thus encourages decarceration of offenders because of cost benefits; this same crisis, however, restricts the development of adequate community services. Yet would diversion better control or prevent delinquency if adequate funds were available? An affirmative answer to this question is by no means certain. The infusion of additional funding can lead to agency expansionism and the preoccupation of bureaucracies with their own survival. For example, in addition to administrative sleight of hand which minimized actual costs of new probation programs,[34] California's progress toward diversion is marked by the expansion of the probation department. Here, the adaptation of the system to changing priorities is determined by the interests of the bureaucracy.

Another author found control by the courts being expanded. A study of diversion by Thomas Blomberg indicated that after juveniles were diverted to family service agencies, their families

---

[33] Ibid., pp. 152–53.
[34] Paul Lerman, *Community Treatment, Social Control and Juvenile Delinquency: Issues in Correctional Policy* (Chicago: University of Chicago Press, 1975).

were unable to cope with the agencies' family-intervention and control methods.[35] Family noncooperation led to court action in the placement of juveniles and/or their siblings out of their homes. In the end, however, after a year of agency referrals, rather than decreasing the number of youth controlled by the courts, the diversion program actually increased this number by one-third. In addition, the programs extended the court control of juveniles to include control over their families, which were, in turn, powerless to contest the consequent family disruptions in independent court proceedings.

This expansion of social-control functions is attributed to organizational imperatives, which insure bureaucratic stability and power. Yet scrutiny of the control functions being performed also suggests the inevitability of this expansionism if the job is to be done *within the limits* of the family-intervention treatment strategy. As an example of family disruption created by the diversion strategy, Blomberg cites a "not atypical" case concerning a fourteen-year-old runaway boy.[36]

In this case the father (age 43), stepmother (age 18), and two brothers (age 16 and 10) agreed to participate in family intervention counseling if the boy was released from juvenile hall. The counselor, on becoming acquainted with the family and learning that each of the boys was leaving the home for short periods, diagnosed "a general sibling rivalry for the stepmother with sexual overtones in the case of the 16 year old." The parents refused to go into a permanent therapy program following the mandatory five counseling sessions. The boys subsequently "went wild" and were referred back to the court. All three were then given out-of-the-home placement orders (foster care or institutional) following the family-intervention counselor's determination of the unfitness of the home.

The case above is used to illustrate the extension of control

[35] Thomas Blomberg, "County Juvenile Probation and the Client Concern: A Case Study" (Ph.D. Diss. Berkeley 1973); idem, "Diversion: Family Control in Juvenile Justice," paper presented at the Annual Meetings of the Society for the Prevention of Social Problems, San Francisco, California (1975).

[36] Blomberg, "County Juvenile Probation," pp. 215–16.

by diversion over families. But at issue is the reason for this extension. How realistic is the expectation that any family service in our sexist culture will enable an eighteen-year-old wife to discipline rowdy boys almost her equal in age? Is it organizational (probation, family service) survival alone that regulates the discretion of the family-intervention counselor? Or, given this kind of family situation, is it an inevitable consequence of the limits of the family-intervention strategy for treating juvenile offenders?

Granted, in the case above, the parents could have been given "vouchers" to choose case workers or family service agencies that may have provided superior services. Perhaps legal appeal procedures would have prevented the dissolution of the family after the boys were referred to court for "running wild." But there still remains the problem of an effective strategy for intervening in family relationships. Negative coercive effects of the institutions also may be minimized by vouchers and the like; nevertheless, such measures themselves give us no inkling of how to deal with family difficulties and the delinquent conduct illustrated above. Would quality family service programs do the job? Again, the question cannot be answered with certainty. The limitations of family service agencies have been emphasized by innumerable social scientists and professional social workers.

For more than sixty years additional alternative approaches to the prevention and control of delinquency have been considered. Sociologists such as Frederick Thrasher have urged the development of recreational programs for gang youth. During the 1950s the government established numerous detached-worker programs to service delinquent groups in the street. Despite the serious shortcomings in these programs, the federal government's current interest in diversion projects has led to arguments for positive youth service approaches that recreate the group-work delinquency-control rhetoric of the 1950s.

There is a twist to the recent proposals for youth services, however, that hearken back to the 1920s, when recreational agencies were considered effective for controlling delinquents. The proposals suggest that cost-benefits accrue if services are purchased from existing youth service agencies rather than funding new delinquency programs (such as independent detached services for gangs).[37] On the surface one might expect that agency response to such a proposal would depend simply upon the actual amount of money available for such services and the degree to which private and public social agencies are in need of funds. But stable (and usually superior) community agencies have other priorities besides servicing delinquents. In fact, the largest community service programs for youth service primarily nondelinquents. Such programs include recreational agencies (parks and recreation programs), group work agencies (sectarian and nonsectarian community centers with programs for adolescents), and other after-school programs (scouts, football leagues). Our research experience and our experience as trained social workers who have worked with delinquent gangs in the streets and have administered highly professional youth service agencies suggest that these programs will not provide significant services for delinquent youth. These agencies cannot influence a delinquent youth's peer relations despite the central importance of peer relations to any diversion strategy.

Furthermore, for such agencies a major shift toward programs for delinquents would drive out the nondelinquent youth already receiving services, thereby threatening the social base of the agencies. It is hard to see such agencies preserving their ties to a significant proportion of families in their communities and, at the same time, making substantial accommodations to extensive juvenile diversion requirements.

The final solution offered by the diversion treatment strategy is to identify a suitable type of treatment, preferably in the community, for each type of offender. Numerous demonstration programs—monitored by research evaluators—have been funded and will continue to be funded for this purpose. Out of these endless modifications of treatment methods and out of the discovery of a few unrecognized possibilities, some small positive results may be obtained. But in our opinion no fundamentally effective preventive methods are likely to be found in this process.

[37] For example, see *Programs to Prevent Delinquency*, Appendix 4, Office of Juvenile Justice and Prevention, Law Enforcement Assistance Administration, U.S. Department of Justice, Washington, D.C. (November 1976), pp. 1–11.

What, then, can be expected or recommended from all of this? First, a substantial gain may be made by diverting thousands of youths from traditional custodial institutions. Second, some of these youth and their families will receive needed services within the limits of prevailing welfare-state policies. Third, research should be undertaken to evaluate possible effects of decriminalization of status offenses, the prosecution of which provides support for families and schools. Fourth, greater effort should be made to understand and deal with family problems that are beyond the capacity of family-intervention strategies. Fifth, such efforts should be generalized to include all problems that trigger coercive and disruptive pressures on individuals and families by the juvenile justice system. Finally, these efforts should be less concerned with recidivism and bureaucratic expansionism than with identifying and understanding the systematic limits inherent in treatment strategies that inevitably trigger justice sanctions. With regard to the administration of such sanctions, there are justifiable reforms connected with the establishment of individual rights and due process guarantees.

There are equally, if not more, important reforms that would modify the power relations between the working class and the state. Such a reform is represented by the creation of popular justice councils, composed of people living in working-class communities who are active in working-class organizations. Such councils would oversee juvenile justice policies that affect community relations within a particular state, county, or municipality. With appropriate powers and resources, such as a research arm and right of access to information, these councils would be enabled to monitor juvenile justice programs so that they do not threaten community life. The councils would also help formulate justice policies that are in the interests of working-class families and children. Certainly such councils could have advisory committees composed of professionals representing justice agencies as well as social service agencies receiving justice funding; however, because of conflicts of interest, these professionals should not be council members.

Furthermore, the councils should also monitor the juvenile halls and other juvenile custodial institutions, because they will now house the more frequent and serious offenders who will be largely from minority groups and who will have greater needs. Despite the rhetoric of diversion, these institutions will continue to have serious problems. Since the custodial institutions may not be located in the countryside, they should also be monitored by state-wide popular justice councils that are composed of representatives from the local councils.

Popular councils would represent a structural reform. Such reforms affect the distribution of power that determines the balance of class forces under given conditions. The councils thus would counter the class constraints on justice policies, broadening possibilities for progressive developments. In the absence of such councils, the quality of diversion programs will certainly remain frozen along traditional lines.

That the diversion programs are traditional is indicated by historical evaluations of their antecedents. Although the aggregative effect of the programs may significantly reduce the rate of incarceration, Liazos's observations are still correct. Qualitatively, the social services and job programs being planned for delinquents favor inculcation of bourgeois morality and conformity to class conditions. They emphasize personal adjustment and not working-class struggles for liberation. Since they are confined within treatment modalities that do not threaten capital, these services and programs (in relation to delinquency prevention and control) produce very slim results.

### Long-term Strategies for Delinquency Prevention and Control

The limitations of diversion programs bring us back to the societal relations that encourage official delinquency and block effective delinquency prevention. To deal with these relations, we have to keep the implications of a Marxian perspective in mind. From this perspective long-range strategies for delinquency prevention and control are aimed at strengthening family life, especially in working-class communities; at the attainment of stable employment and nonalienating work; and at the development of economic planning that forces production to meet social needs.

Consequently, such strategies are concerned with the importance of recognizing capitalist contradictions, the need to foster class consciousness, and the movement toward socialist alternatives stressing the eventual elimination of classes.

Generally, long-range strategies are not primarily concerned with the conduct of individual youth who are already delinquent. However, certain organizations, which are directly oriented to delinquency control, can also broaden possibilities for social change. For instance, popular justice councils backed by class-conscious worker's movements might direct attention to policies for preventing massive criminalization of marginals of all ages. Toward this end, such policies would curb the laws of investment and profit maximization that undermine working-class family life and community life. They would recommend a massive shift in social investment away from monopoly capital toward working-class families and communities. Public education, transportation, recreation, housing, dietary, and social services are priority areas for such investments. Here the investments should be directed at altering the market forces that generate the urban slums and ghettos which consolidate marginal families in areas with the worst urban conditions. In these areas there exist sizable domains of marginal groups. Such domains are characterized by very stable, culturally elaborated delinquent modalities.

Especially important, too, for the prevention of delinquency are social investments and social planning that would guarantee full employment while restricting uneven development and marginalization. Such investments and social plans cannot prevent crime and delinquency if they are designed according to opportunity-structure theories. With regard to schools, opportunity theory in the 1960s and early 1970s favored compensatory education programs. Although these have appeared plausible, we have indicated, elsewhere, the drastic limitations of these programs.[38] Among other things it has been noted that unless structural changes are made in schools, such programs will not eliminate marginalization. Various mechanisms (such as grading by the

[38] Schwendinger and Schwendinger, "Marginal Youth and Social Policy," pp. 189–90.

"thirds" or other standardized scores) would maintain the same competitive and hierarchical school relationships, despite the fluctuations in average levels of individual productivity. Hence, if the programs were successful, marginal youth would still be produced by the school, but with higher levels of productivity than before.[39]

To counter such results, massive investments must be made in educational services for children in poorer communities. Simultaneously, the effects of structural mechanisms based on competition have to be minimized so that equal opportunity to fail (as well as succeed) is undermined. Collective rewards and learning activities might be introduced to generate a new moral consciousness. Obviously, however, such developments can hardly take place unless there is a possibility of reinforcing school reforms with changes in economic relations. Yet this reinforcement itself cannot emerge unless class struggles in the economic sphere have begun to restrict the powers of capital by socializing the means of production. Such a change automatically means curbing anarchic market forces and expanding the public sector at the expense of monopoly capital.

These economic changes do not flow at all from the logic of opportunity-structure theories. With regard to economic policies, these theories have favored job-training programs that would ostensibly prevent delinquency by enabling individuals to overcome their disadvantages and to compete successfully for jobs. Actually, however, official delinquency and the disadvantages possessed by these individuals are both largely generated by the same laws of uneven development and the same marginalization processes. Thus, among marginal youth the inability to compete successfully is a concomitant and not a cause of delinquency.

Job-training policies, furthermore, have serious problems in the face of restricted job markets. Elsewhere we have cited evidence demonstrating that the numerous manpower training programs, which concentrated on black marginals, have failed to make any improvement in black communities.[40] The same dismal conclusion

[39] Carnoy, *Schooling in a Corporate Society*, pp. 369–70.

[40] Schwendinger and Schwendinger, "Marginal Youth and Social Policy," p. 189.

applies to job-creation programs that have been supported by opportunity-structure theory, because these programs are limited, impermanent, and attuned to secondary labor force requirements.

For whatever reasons, opportunity theories studiously avoid dealing with the economic mechanisms that prevent opportunities for marginals from being instituted on a wide scale in the schools and the economy. They are conspicuously silent about the relation between unemployment and cyclical crises, between delinquency and marginalization processes, and between high unemployment rates and the government's refusal to vigorously lower these rates. Their recommendations take no stock of the fact that full employment has only been achieved in our society during wartime, and that, to protect business interests, unemployment has been trade-off against inflation by the federal government. In place of a sophisticated analysis of economic realities, such theories recommend equal opportunity programs that directly or indirectly intensify socially induced competition for limited rewards in school and the economy. Their brand of theory and social planning, in our opinion, is unfortunately constrained by the same class forces that prevent the development of effective crime-control policies.

In the United States the class constraints on crime control are at present overwhelming. But continued high unemployment may yet tip the balance of political forces toward policies dealing with criminogenic economic conditions. Popular pressure for jobs has led to a revival of interest in employment legislation, and although the Humphrey-Hawkins bill has been stripped of its best features, the original provisions of the bill are important for crime control. Originally the bill was designed to facilitate social planning and to guarantee full employment. The right to employment on a decent job is vital to any long-term strategy for controlling crime. A crucial point is that the issues here do not involve jobs for youth alone. They also involve employment levels that sustain family stability and ameliorate the effects of marginalization processes on people of all ages. The Humphrey-Hawkins bill is therefore important because in its original form it justified *full* employment. Furthermore, certain original provisions would have acted against the basic economic causes of delinquency.

In the original bill full employment was pegged to goals that are in the interests of most people in society (but not necessarily in the interests of capital). The bill would have required the president to plan for the production of goods and services that meet individual and social needs in such areas as housing, child care, health care, other social services, construction of public facilities, and transportation. Such planning would estimate the kinds of employment needed for this production as well as the public and private investments required to sustain this employment.

The bill would also have required assessment of public expenditures and economic controls that might undermine uneven development and marginalization. Anticipating economic problems connected with full employment in a market economy, problems which are related, for instance, to competing priorities for funds and to inflationary pressures, the bill called for a review of necessary reductions and conversions in military and other industrial activities. In addition, it prescribed an analysis of price levels, capital export, monopoly practices, and the distribution of income and wealth.

The bill then stressed the establishment of reservoirs of public service and private employment projects to supplement existing employment opportunities. Importantly, the bill specified that wages for the public service jobs would be equal to prevailing regional pay levels—the minimum wage or existing collective-bargaining agreements, whichever was highest. Such a provision would undercut the dual wage systems in secondary labor markets.

Also minimizing secondary labor market activity was the provision for a Job Guarantee Office. This established job training and it also enforced the right to employment. Counseling, training, transportation, and migration assistance would be given to workers who had special problems or who were being discriminated against because of sex, age, and race. The physically and mentally handicapped and the technologically or otherwise displaced workers would also be aided. Finally, workers who felt that their rights were not being protected by the Job Guarantee Office could sue the government in federal court.

Congressional committee hearings have eliminated the job guarantee and full-employment provisions. They have also stripped the bill of most provisions that represented "a clear break with tradition in that it aimed to make the whole range and quality of employment in the United States a matter for public, rather that private, determination." [41] Of course, full employment has not been established anywhere in the capitalist economic system. (Full employment can only be guaranteed in certain types of socialist economies.) Nevertheless, the mere attempt to construct legislation in the United States with such provisions could be a harbinger of things to come.

In the last quarter of this century class-conscious working-class movements will undoubtedly become stronger in the United States. The persistence of economic stagnation and crisis in the face of socialist development in Europe and elsewhere will favor policy formulation that few criminologists today would think possible. As the capitalist economy continues to constrict and as socialist societies develop higher standards of living, the issues that are now considered beyond the ken of conventional criminology will come to the fore. At that time criminogenic social conditions will finally be brought under public scrutiny and social planning efforts will be made that override the private interests of capital.

[41] Elliot Currie, "The Politics of Jobs: Humphrey-Hawkins and the Dilemmas of Full Employment," *Socialist Revolution* 7 (March–April 1977): 106.

# Epilogue

# Epilogue

## LaMar T. Empey

A hurried recapitulation of the messages contained in this volume reveals the following.

### Disillusionment

The juvenile court was created in an era of great optimism. Child savers at the turn of this century firmly believed that a benevolent system of justice for juveniles would not only serve as a device for rehabilitating criminal children but of saving all children in danger of falling through the institutional and moral cracks of society. During the past twenty years, however, these optimistic beliefs have turned to ashes. Revisionist historians, criminologists, influential presidential commissions, liberal reformers, and ordinary citizens, for quite different reasons, have joined together to demand "reform."

### Prescriptions for Reform

The most popular prescriptions for reform have been constructed upon a body of beliefs that were first articulated by Edwin M. Lemert in 1967. Writing for the Task Force on Delinquency, of the President's Commission on Law Enforcement and Administration of Justice, Lemert argued that the grandiose hopes and professional contumely which have been associated with the juvenile court should be put into a more realistic perspective:

The aims of preventing delinquency and the expectations of definitively treating a profusion of child and parental problems have laid an impossible burden upon the juvenile court, and they may be seriously considered to have no proper part in its philosophy. *If there is a defensible philosophy for the juvenile court it is one of judicious nonintervention.* It is properly an agency of last resort for children, holding to a doctrine analogous to that of appeal courts which require that all other remedies be exhausted before a case will be considered.[1]

Lemert had much to support his argument, as we have seen. Neither experience nor scientific investigation had been able to provide support for the idea that the juvenile court was a panacea. Hence, Lemert's admonitions were taken to heart. The ground-work was laid for a series of reforms which can now be encapsulated into a list of alliterative, and familiar, catchwords:

1. *Decriminalization.* Reduce the number of legal rules by which juveniles can be defined as delinquent, particularly those covering status offenses. Juveniles should not be prosecuted and receive penal sanctions for behavior which, if exhibited by adults, would not be prosecuted.

2. *Diversion.* Divert more first-time and nonserious offenders from legal processing. The goal of any official action should be to normalize behavior. This is best accomplished by nonlegal rather than legal institutions.

3. *Due process.* Extend the constitutional protections of due process to juveniles, not only in cases involving charges of criminal conduct but in cases involving issues of dependency, neglect, or moral turpitude.

4. *Deinstitutionalization.* Remove correctional programs from places of confinement and locate them in open community settings. Their purpose should be to integrate the offender into the nondelinquent activities of the community, not into the routine of a reformatory.

Contumely versus Humility Today

But what of Lemert's call for humility rather than contumely? Does it not apply equally to *our* theories and to *our* fervent prescriptions for reform as well as to those of prior generations?

[1] Edwin M. Lemert, *Task Force on Delinquency,* President's Commission on Law Enforcement and Administration of Justice (Washington, D.C.: U.S. Government Printing Office, 1967), p. 96 (emphasis added).

Today we willingly acknowledge that the theories and reforms of the Progressive era did not turn out to be pure and unmistakable steps in the progress of humanity. But if that is the case, how should today's "reforms"—the four D's—be regarded?

Based on his insightful historical analysis *The Discovery of the Asylum*, David Rothman provides a warning for all generations of reformers. Let me paraphrase that warning: If we are to describe any, or all, of the four D's as "reforms," we will be taking for granted precisely what ought to be the focus of investigation. We should be asking not only whether the four D's will represent improvements over existing conditions but whether they are superior to *other possible alternatives.*[2]

Some of the essayists in this volume have suggested that, in light of society's prior failure to grant the juvenile court the resources necessary to fulfill its mandate, current reforms may turn out to be nothing more than an officially sanctioned form of benign neglect. Disillusioned with the grand hopes of yesterday, the injunction tomorrow will be to "think small." There is no assurance, for example, that turning status offenders or abused children over to administrative, rather than legal, agencies will solve their problems. These agencies are no more capable of redressing the effects of poverty and discrimination than was the juvenile court, nor of overcoming the ambiguous status of the young in modern society and giving them a stake in conformity. Perhaps worse, children will be without recourse to the legal protections that they are beginning to enjoy in the juvenile court. The locus of social control may shift, but it may also be without legal oversight.

Complexities of Reform

Lest these cautions be viewed as an exercise in idle speculation, consider just a few issues relative to the young which are inherent in the context of American society but to which little attention has been paid.

[2] David J. Rothman, *The Discovery of the Asylum* (Boston: Little, Brown, 1971), p. 15.

The optimism of the Progressive era did not result merely in
the creation of the juvenile court. The American preoccupation
with children had become widespread. The modern concept of
childhood had become an accomplished fact. The length of child
dependency had increased. A host of developmental theories
were being expounded, elaborated, and reified to explain a biological and social process of growth that would not even have
been thought to exist a few centuries before. Parents were being
overwhelmed by injunctions to take that process into account. A
whole constellation of professional, as well as moralist, child
savers was institutionalized to assist parents—pediatricians, teachers, social workers, and child psychiatrists, as well as judges and
correctional workers. Manufacturers, retailers, and entertainers
organized to appeal to a lucratively subsidized youth market.
New groups of black and brown children, not fully integrated
into the institutionalized developmental process, began to experience many of the problems in our urban ghettos that earlier
groups of urban migrants had already experienced. And a large
collection of social scientists and scholars was subsidized to make
sense of all this. For much of this century, then, the ideological
and institutional structures of society, like the juvenile court, have
been geared to the psychology and biology of child development.

It has only been in the past decade that significant resistance
has arisen to this way of organizing childhood. During the late
1960s college and some minority youth protested their political
and social impotence. The voting age was lowered and younger
people began to engage more heavily in the political process. A
powerful movement was begun to eliminate sexual discrimination
throughout the life cycle. The school-leaving age has been
lowered to sixteen in many states and the power of the school to
inhibit students' freedoms is being challenged. Changing mores
have not only stressed greater sexual freedoms but may signal
important alterations in the institution of marriage, particularly
as ever larger numbers of young women begin to pursue a career.
And a series of court decisions supports the view that children
should be treated as persons in their own right, not only in the
juvenile court but elsewhere. In short, the ideal image of child-

hood is changing and implies greater precociousness than nine-teenth-century child savers would have thought possible.

But these are not the only changes of great significance. A decline in the birth rate, combined with an increase in life ex-pectancy, is creating a societal population that is growing older. For the first time American society, along with some other West-ern societies, is witness to a changing population pyramid that will likely grow increasingly heavy at the top—a phenomenon largely unknown to prior civilizations. For example, the growth in population from 1950 to 1970 was lowest for people under forty-five, 30.5 percent. By contrast, the population of people over sixty-five increased by 63 percent. Even more striking was the growth in the number of people over seventy-five, 97 percent—from 3.9 million in 1950 to 7.6 million in 1970.[3]

Such trends may hasten a decline in our protective stance toward the young. Ever larger numbers of older people will have to be supported by a proportionately smaller and young segment of the population. Resources and attention formerly directed to the young may be turned to the elderly, a possibility that could significantly affect efforts to assist those segments of the youth population who need it most. A decrease in the privileged status of the young, moreover, may bring increased demands for ac-countability, particularly where criminal acts are involved. Mag-nified demands for retribution are not only likely but are already taking place.

The age of childhood has been lowered in some states. The jurisdiction of the juvenile court over older adolescents is being eliminated. And a number of popular treatises are suggesting that the only alternative for controlling young criminals is confinement in prison. In short, there are signs of a counterrevolution which the four D's helped to stimulate—a contingency that was not fore-seen.

Since this is the case, it is important to ask whether sufficient attention has been paid to the implications of the reforms that

[3] U.S. Department of Commerce, *Bureau of Census Reports, 1950–1970* (Washington, D.C.: U.S. Government Printing Office, 1971).

are now being implemented. While these reforms imply significant alterations in our social constructions of both childhood and
delinquency, they are directed more to freeing children from the
jurisdiction of the juvenile court than to making those constructions explicit and to indicating what new institutional devices
are more suitable for them.

If the juvenile court is to be discarded as a backup, child-saving
institution, what other institutions will take its place? To what
extent will they be more capable of addressing the significant
demographic and ideological changes that are underway? If children are to occupy a less subordinate role and are to receive
greater freedoms from the controls of parents, schools, and courts,
at what age are they to be treated as adults, to be employed, to
do as they wish? What institutional changes have been made to
make this possible, particularly for that segment of the juvenile
court's former clientele, who are the least advantaged, the least
educated, the most neglected, and the least capable of individual
autonomy? Mere disagreement with the paternalistic values and
the ambitious goals of the juvenile court will not provide the
necessary answers.

Indeed, in answer to David Rothman's admonition that *other
possible alternatives* should be considered, perhaps we should be
asking whether a more fruitful approach might be the development of *a national youth policy*—a policy which would not only
incorporate a concern with juvenile justice but which would pay
much greater attention to the list of issues that were only touched
upon above. Current levels of youth rebellion, dependency, abuse,
neglect, and crime are not likely to be ameliorated merely by
seeking to eliminate the worst features of the juvenile court.

# Contributors

ROBERT A. BAUER is Director of the Kenyon Public Affairs Forum, Kenyon College. He serves as United States Representative to the Organization for International Economic Relations, Vienna. He is a retired U.S. Foreign Service Officer, and the editor of *The Interaction of Economics and Foreign Policy* and *The United States in World Affairs: Leadership, Partnership, or Disengagement?*

LAMAR T. EMPEY, Professor of Sociology at the University of Southern California, was formerly Chair of the Sociology Department and Director of the Youth Studies Center there. He has published widely in the fields of delinquency and crime and is the author of *American Delinquency: Its Meaning and Construction, The Provo Experiment, Explaining Delinquency,* and *The Silverlake Experiment.* He has been a member of several research review panels and has served as a consultant to various national and presidential commissions.

TRAVIS HIRSCHI is Professor in the School of Criminal Justice at the State University of New York at Albany. He has taught at the University of Washington and the University of California at Davis. He is best known for his theoretical and empirical works on delinquency, most notably *Causes of Delinquency* and *Delinquency Research* (with Hannan C. Selvin). In addition, he is the author of numerous articles and has served on the Research Review Panel for the Center for the Study of Crime and Delinquency, NIMH, and on other national advisory groups.

PAUL LERMAN is Professor of Social Work and Sociology and Chairman of the Doctoral Program in the Graduate School of Social Work at Rutgers University. He is editorial consultant for the *Journal of Criminal Law and Criminology,* editor of *Delinquency and Social Policy,* and the author of *Community Treatment, Social Control and Juvenile Delinquency: Issues in Correctional Policy,* in addition to numerous articles.

JUSTINE WISE POLIER retired from the Family Court Bench in 1973 and became director of the program for Juvenile Justice of the Children's

Defense Fund. She is a member of the Institute of Judicial Administration—American Bar Association Joint Commission on Juvenile Standards, the Chairman of the Policy Committee of the Office of Children's Services of the New York State Office of Court Administration, and a member of the New York City Human Resources Administration Advisory Review Board. Judge Polier was awarded the Hannah G. Solomon Award by the National Council of Jewish Women in 1975 for her efforts to achieve justice for children. She is the author of *Back to What Woodshed?* and *Everyone's Children, Nobody's Child.*

DAVID J. ROTHMAN is Professor of History at Columbia University and Senior Research Associate at the Center for Policy Research, Inc. He received the Albert J. Beveridge Prize in 1971 from the American Historical Association for *The Discovery of the Asylum: Social Order and Disorder in the New Republic.* In addition, he is the author of *The Sources of the American Social Tradition,* "Correcting the Field of Corrections," "Children, Psychiatry, and the State," and "The Promise of American Legal History." Professor Rothman serves on the boards of the Mental Health Law Project and the New York Civil Liberties Union and directs the NIMH Training Program in Social History at Columbia University.

JULIA AND HERMAN SCHWENDINGER have worked as a team in the study of delinquent behavior and delinquent gangs and have written extensively on the nature of delinquency as seen from a Marxian perspective. Formerly on the faculties of the University of California at Berkeley and at the University of Nevada at Las Vegas, they are currently teaching at the State University of New York at New Paltz. Herman Schwendinger is Associate Professor of Sociology and Julia Schwendinger is Adjunct Assistant Professor of Sociology.

JACKSON TOBY is Professor of Sociology and Director of the Institute for Criminological Research at Rutgers University. He has served as consultant to the Ford Foundation, the U.S. Bureau of Prisons, the National Science Foundation, and the Law Enforcement Assistance Administration of the U.S. Department of Justice. His writings include *Delinquency* (with Scrupski and Donahue), "Affluence and Adolescent Crime," "Delinquency Gangs," and "Adolescent Delinquency in Japan," as well as numerous other articles in sociology, juvenile justice, and criminology.